Luck and Circumstance

Luck and Circumstance

A COMING OF AGE
IN HOLLYWOOD, NEW YORK,
AND POINTS BEYOND

Michael Lindsay-Hogg

ALFRED A. KNOPF  NEW YORK 2011

This Is a Borzoi Book
Published by Alfred A. Knopf

Copyright © 2011 by Michael Lindsay-Hogg
All rights reserved. Published in the United States by Alfred A. Knopf,
a division of Random House, Inc., New York, and in Canada by
Random House of Canada Limited, Toronto.
www.aaknopf.com

Library of Congress Cataloging-in-Publication Data

Lindsay-Hogg, Michael.
Luck and circumstance : a coming of age in Hollywood, New York, and points beyond / by
Michael Lindsay-Hogg. — 1st ed.
p. cm.
ISBN 978-0-307-59468-6
1. Lindsay-Hogg, Michael. 2. Television producers and directors — Great Britain —
Biography. 3. Motion picture producers and directors — Great Britain — Biography.
4. Theatrical producers and directors — Great Britain — Biography. I. Title.
PN1992.4.L5355A3 2011
791.4302'32092 — dc22
{B}   2011008656

Jacket art: Author's collection

Jacket design by Carol Devine Carson

Manufactured in the United States of America
First Edition

JMM LAT JM
A L W A Y S

Illustrations

Prologue

As a small boy, even though my empire existed only in my head, there I was Michael, one name, as a King or a Prince of the realm might be known. Not Mike, not a nickname, but Michael. And I had an army.

I would deploy my toy soldiers in spare regiments, not having that many, and sometimes from a purloined matchbook advertising a restaurant my parents had frequented I'd strike a match and, because war has its perils, melt off a lead leg or arm from the little grenadier, once setting alight the field of cotton wool I'd laid down to represent the snow on the Russian steppes. Fortunately, Mary was there to help me put it out.

She gave me a slap on my arm and said, "Michael, I've told you never to play with matches."

So, by what cruel twist of fate had I become Pudge Hoag?

I'd been sent to Choate, the boarding school, when I was thirteen, where my last name, Lindsay-Hogg with the hyphen, proved confusing, in some way irksome to the administration, and so, without notice or discussion, it was shortened to Hogg on school lists, for seating in the dining hall or for sports teams, and since most of the probably well-meaning but dense adults thought to pronounce it properly, hog as in pig, would be rude, I became Hoag. I didn't put up any argument, having more pressing crises to deal with on a daily basis. And because the weight I'd started to gain when I was eight or so showed no sign of going away, one and then another and another of my school fellows sought to find for me an affectionate nickname. Fatso was first, but then they settled on Pudge. Consequently, during my three years there I felt I was living not as myself but more like an enemy agent with an assumed character and fictitious name, which was fine by me because I knew that as soon as I could, I would find another world to live in. It would have to be better, no matter how rigorous its rules and various its weather.

My mother, Geraldine Fitzgerald, was an actress and was rehearsing George Bernard Shaw's *The Doctor's Dilemma* for an off-Broadway production, playing the wife to Roddy McDowall's tubercular artist. It was December 1954, and I was home on vacation and was by then heavily wrapped in the Pudge Hoag shroud. I was fourteen.

I was standing at the window in my room staring out at a flat sky, when my mother appeared in the doorway wearing her nubbly navy winter coat which stopped just at the knees of her trim legs.

"What are you doing today?" she asked.

"I don't know. Nothing much."

"Maybe you'd like to come down and watch rehearsal. I've asked Sidney and he said it would be all right."

"I don't know."

"Just in case."

She put a piece of paper with the address on my table, written in her large-charactered generous handwriting, and went off to work.

After a couple of hours of aimlessness, sitting in a chair, looking out the window again, arranging my hair in its new style (spit curls modeled on Marlon Brando's Napoleon-hair in the movie *Desirée*), I left the apartment.

One subway and a second and I was outside an old building

on Houston Street, at the time a stretch of old buildings in a down-at-heel neighborhood, mostly small stores selling cheap staples with cheap apartments above. But this building had a different role. I took a small elevator up to the first floor, looking at the grimy scissored grille in front of me. The elevator hesitated, then bounced to a stop. I put my hand on the catch and pushed back the stiff old bars. I stepped out.

And my life changed forever.

A slim young man was lying on his front on a wooden bench. One arm was bent and his chin was resting in his hand, and his other hand was on the script he was studying on the floor, a mug of tea beside it.

He turned and looked up at me, took in my age and appearance, and said, "You must be Geraldine's son, Michael."

"Yes, I'm Michael."

"Come with me," he said, getting up, collecting his script and tea. "I'll take you into the theater and we'll find your mother. I'm Roddy McDowall."

He smiled his entrancing smile and we shook hands.

Roddy pushed open a hinged door and we went into the small theater, probably in earlier, pre-television days used by a Yiddish acting troupe. There were some lights focused on the stage and the rest of the theater was in a kind of half light. My mother was at a table onstage, sitting next to another actor, and both were talking to a young man with dark hair and glasses with dark frames who was standing in front of them.

After the conversation, the young man gave them both a hug.

"Find a seat," Roddy said. "We're going to start again."

A man was walking up the aisle and Roddy said in a soft voice, "Phil, this is Michael, Geraldine's son."

"Nice to meet you, Michael."

I shook hands with the actor and moved a few seats off the aisle and sat down.

My mother and the actor beside her, a distinguished-looking

man with crisp gray hair, rose and, scripts in hand, began a scene, occasionally interrupted by the young man with a suggestion or encouragement.

The scene was rehearsed, modified, changed, altered for about half an hour. A powerful feeling was growing in me. What was this place where people seemed friendly to a young stranger, and engaged with seriousness and good humor in a common endeavor?

I felt like I sometimes did in a library or church, where the walls have been indented by feelings, feelings of intent, concentration, wishes, and maybe, sometimes, fear. But the sense in this place was of something good happening. I felt warm and protected and, although sitting alone, somehow included and privileged.

After a while, the rehearsal of this scene and another stopped. My mother found me and brought me to meet the young man with the dark-framed glasses.

"Michael, this is Sidney Lumet."

"Michael," he said, shaking my hand, as if I were an old friend, an equal in some way.

"I'm so glad you could come down here," Sidney Lumet said. "We're going out for a sandwich. Want to come?"

We all walked to a large Jewish deli on Second Avenue where the actors had sandwiches and pickles and tea in glasses as they discussed what they were working on. After, I had to go home and they went back to rehearse into the evening.

For the week or so left of my vacation, I went to the theater every day, and on the weekend, a stage manager being absent, Sidney gave me a dollar a day to be on the book to give an actor a word or a line, if it had been forgotten. I felt I was good at it, letting the actor try to find the thought himself but then, if I sensed it wasn't going to come, I'd slip in the missing word and the actor could go on.

At the Sunday rehearsal, my mother and the actor with crisp

gray hair had a muttered row that grew in volume to shouting and I saw my mother had tears in her eyes.

"Let's break for five minutes," Sidney called.

The crisp-haired actor walked offstage and my mother came to me.

"It was just a disagreement about the scene and I don't want you to be upset to see me cry."

She took a small white handkerchief out of her skirt pocket and dabbed at her eyes.

"I'm not upset," I said.

And I wasn't. I figured that, given the currency of actors was emotion, combining with intelligence, this sort of thing, tears, could occur.

"I'm so glad," my mother said, looking at me as if in a new way, then, "Glad that you're not upset."

Rehearsal was called again. I went back on the book. Sidney gave my mother a kiss and hugged the other actor, who then hugged my mother, and the scene carried on in an amiable way, as though the row had released some underlying tension, which had probably been the point.

And then, a few days later, I, Michael, was back at school and was again Pudge Hoag, but it didn't matter because I knew where I was going.

Luck and Circumstance

One

At first the path seems clear with some light on it but as the slope grows steeper, mist comes around it and then, farther, the top is covered in cloud and I have no idea what I'll find there.

The terrain is memory and it is time to start.

Although we were only there for a year or so, I say I grew up on the beach in Santa Monica, because it's where I was happy or, at least, in hindsight, think that's what I was. We moved there when I was just four. Prior to that my mother, nurse Mary, and I moved around a lot, every six months from one small house in the Hollywood or Beverly Hills to another.

At first, when I was young, my mother told me my father had left us to go back to Ireland to work for the Irish Red Cross. He had been fund-raising for the Red Cross during his time in America.

Edward Lindsay-Hogg, English-born, had become an Irish citizen in the mid-1930s.

He liked living there because I think England frightened him, or his memories were too painful. The grandson of baronet Sir Lindsay Lindsay-Hogg, a tough old man whose family had made money in the China trade, he was the son of an invalid father whose back had been broken in a hunting accident and a nervous clinging mother, and his older brother was vicious, if not a little demented. Brutal years at Eton did not help a temperament already somewhat fragile. Then, when he was seventeen, it was my father who, his mother late returning from being out with the hunt, mounted his horse and went in search of her. He found her body in a stream, her foot still in the stirrup. Her horse hadn't budged from the narrow slatted sideless bridge, from which she'd fallen or been thrown.

I was two when my father left, and I would not see him for three years and then, after that, only every couple of years when my mother would go to Ireland to see her parents and I would have occasional meetings with Edward Lindsay-Hogg. I did not see him at all between the ages of thirteen and eighteen. He never returned to America after he left in early 1943.

Later, my mother changed the story to say the real reason my father left us was because he hadn't wanted to be drafted into the American army. As a resident alien, after Pearl Harbor, he was liable to be called up and thought he wouldn't have been a good soldier and wished to return to neutral Ireland.

I always thought it odd that my father continued to love and understand horses, given the family tragedies which had occurred. And it was horses which had brought him to Ireland. He liked race meetings; as a gentleman jockey over six feet tall, he'd braved the jumps and, after a while, began training. He understood horses and their eccentric natures. Also in his spare time he wrote songs of a slightly sentimental sort, in a 1930s way. In Ireland, he met my mother, home on a visit from England, where she was starting her career as an actress. She did not often come home to see her family, only to spend a little time with her beloved brother, my uncle David, who introduced her to his race-going chum, Eddy Lindsay-Hogg. If asked, and if she hadn't been frightened of saying she was frightened, she would have said she was frightened of her father and would have wished her mother to be more of an intermediary, but her mother, although tender and protective when she was not in bed with mysterious illnesses, was often in bed with mysterious illnesses, and so for weeks or months at a time she would lie in the darkened room at the top of the house, on the floor above the

Edward Lindsay-Hogg, 1941

room in which her husband still slept in what had been their marriage bed.

My mother's father was a lawyer in the firm which bore his father's and uncle's names. Their premises, D. and T. Fitzgerald, are mentioned in James Joyce's *Ulysses* as a place Leopold Bloom passes on his ramble around Dublin on June 16. As a young man, having been sent for advancement to England, my grand-father had been apprenticed to the chambers of the Lord Chancellor and seemed to be on the road to a successful legal career, until one morning he woke up and decided he would never again go above the third floor of a building. He returned to Ireland, henceforth to exist on floors one, two, and three, married and had four children, my mother the second and her favorite brother the eldest. My grandfather was given to depression and violent outbursts and was irrationally fearful of bankruptcy. He instilled a morbid fear about money, or the lack of it, in his two eldest children.

After the time my grandmother took to her narrow bed, the maid who came in daily to do the house would find every morning under my grandfather's bed copies of old weekly newsmagazines, a half-empty bottle of sherry, and a half-full chamber pot.

When they became engaged, my father wrote to an aunt in language which was of the period, but which I find curious, and explained his feelings: "Geraldine is a dear girl and I am very fond of her."

My mother, having had some success in small British Quota Quickies—films made cheaply in order to maintain a quota of jobs in the struggling film industry—decided to try her luck in America. It was 1938 and she was twenty-four. The ship docked in New York and my mother and her husband of three years put themselves up in a small hotel on the East Side. As their money was running out, my mother got an interview for a job at the Mercury Theatre, which was run by John Houseman and Orson Welles, then twenty-two. Houseman and my mother discussed the part of Ellie Dunn, the ingenue, if a Shavian character can be described that simply, in *Heartbreak House*, which Orson Welles would direct and star in. My mother didn't think the interview had gone well, perhaps because Houseman drew it to a conclusion by saying: "Thank you. Let's keep in touch." She rose to leave and at that very moment a door into another room opened and the person described as the "boy genius" came into the room. Orson Welles looked toward my

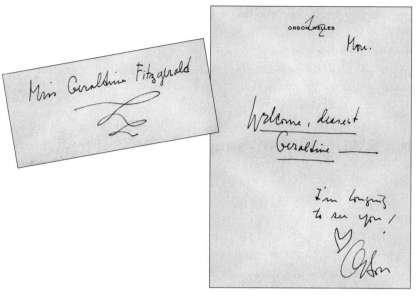

This note accompanied flowers Orson Welles sent to my mother before the first rehearsal of King Lear, *December 1955.*

mother and, on this first sight, said to Houseman, "She's perfect." And then, looking directly at my mother, said, "The part is yours," adding disarmingly, "if you want it, that is."

They calculated her salary based on what my mother and father needed each week for lodging, food, and transportation.

A year after *The Doctor's Dilemma,* I was now fifteen and again home on a holiday from boarding school and my mother was to play Goneril in *King Lear,* starring and directed by Orson Welles. By this time, my mother knew I wanted a career in the theater. She'd asked Orson Welles if I could attend a few rehearsals.

"All of them," he'd said.

I shared a cab with my mother on that early December day in 1955. The rehearsals were in a building on the West Side. We went up in a wheezy elevator and into a large room with white tape marks on the floor. We hung our coats, her old fur and my duffle, on a metal rack.

Orson Welles was at a wooden table in discussion with the stage manager. When he saw us, he rose and came to us.

"Orson, this is Michael."

"I'm so happy to meet you," he said, transferring his cigar to his left hand and holding out his right. I shook his large warm hand.

"Me too," I said.

He was glorious at that time, forty years old, tall, broad, dressed in black, starting to be heavy but not nearly with the weight which must have partly killed him. A big head with glossy dark hair, alert amused brown eyes under the broad forehead, with his enveloping, welcoming seductive voice. But there was something else to him, a kind of emanation of energy and intelligence, curiosity, and originality.

Day after day, I sat there watching the play as it developed, as Orson shaped scenes and marshaled the crowd of soldiers and courtiers. He'd catch my eye often, winking sometimes, sometimes a smile. Or, if one of the actors was not doing a good job, he'd look at me and roll his eyes.

The critic and translator Eric Bentley was also present at some of the rehearsals, and one afternoon we were both asked to leave by the stage manager. We were told Orson was on his way back from lunch and was going to fire one of the actors and didn't want anyone other than the company around. He wanted to get rid of the actor, hire another, and go on working.

The next morning I sat in my room wondering if my paradise was gone forever when my mother, her coat on, came in.

"Let's go," she said.

"Is it okay?"

"Yes, of course. Orson called and said he hadn't meant for you to be told to go. He wants you there all the time. He likes you being there. He said it's important to have someone watching rehearsals who's so interested."

Soon after, the company moved onto the stage at the City Center to rehearse at night. Orson was prowling the unlit orchestra watching the bright action onstage where a stand-in was going through King Lear's moves and reading the lines. As he passed behind the seat I was sitting in, my left arm over the seat beside me, Orson stopped.

I felt a quick aware tension with him behind me, unmoving in the dark.

A moment. Then, as if to clarify his presence, he laid his right hand on my shoulder and squeezed it, kneading it twice, the second pressure stronger than the first, and then he continued on.

I was not used to being touched by male family members. My stepfather had taught me how to shake hands and look the other person in the eye, but he had not been brought up to be a hugger of males, and this was in the middle of the five-year period when I was not to see Edward Lindsay-Hogg at all.

I suppose I longed for a father.

I felt, if it had been my bare shoulder, I wouldn't have ever washed his touch off.

I had to go back to school, and could not be present for the opening. A few days before, Orson had hurt an ankle and was limping and then, after the final preview, my mother told me, Marlene Dietrich had been in Orson's dressing room and he had said to his beautiful Italian new wife, twenty-five-year-old Countess Paola Mori, pointing toward Marlene Dietrich, who was his best friend, "Isn't she the most beautiful woman in the world?" Paola had pushed him, playfully or not, but forcefully enough for him to fall and crack the other ankle. He played the opening night and the rest of the run in a wheelchair and I would not see him for four years.

That next summer, I had my first job in the theater, at the American Shakespeare Festival, in Stratford, Connecticut, which was run by Jack Houseman, who had become one of my mother's greatest friends. "Friends" was not a word to describe the relationship between Orson and Jack. They had broken their partnership bitterly.

"It wasn't so much that he threw a table at me," Jack had told my mother. "But he'd set the tablecloth on fire first."

That summer, 1956, I had one line in *The Taming of the Shrew* and felt I was on my way.

Two

Then I was back in school, this time in New York and, on holidays, going on acting auditions and doing extra work, and had come to the conclusion that the surname I had was not useful for an acting career and found myself putting other choices on a pad. I wanted something simple so as not to find myself saying a name at an audition which the producer's receptionist would question: "What? How do you spell that?"

I'd met a young actor, a few years older, later to be quite successful, when I was an extra on a live TV show, *Playhouse 90* or *Studio One*. I saw him again a few months later, in the front office of a casting director. He remembered me and reintroduced himself.

"Hi, I'm Geoff Horne."

First name, second name, one syllable each.

"Yes, I'm Michael Lindsay-Hogg."

"I remember," he said kindly.

I thought, God, I wish I could say my name was Geoff Horne, easy, direct, and sort of punchy.

He was good in *The Bridge on the River Kwai*.

So I sat in my room putting possible alternative names on a page, testing my penmanship, signing the name as an autograph in case the obligation ever came my way. The first autograph I tried was: Michael Sokoloff.

On Sunday mornings, after my father had left but before our move to the beach, I used to be delivered to the small house behind another, somewhat larger one, on Holloway Drive by my nurse, Mary, where Vladimir Sokoloff and I would read the funny pages together, the comics: Dagwood and Blondie, Jiggs

*With my dear Vladimir Sokoloff in the small garden
behind his house, 1943.*

and Maggie, Prince Valiant, Li'l Abner, and others. We would
sit together on the sofa in his small living room where on week-
days, work being scarce for this actor because of his Russian
accent, he would give modestly priced acting lessons to young
actors and actresses, and his wife, Lisa, would serve tea. As well
as English, he spoke Russian, French, and German and in
Europe had been regarded as a great actor, having studied with
Stanislavsky and worked with Max Reinhardt in Germany. He'd
left Russia during the revolution and came to America when
Hitler took power in Germany.

He would read the words in the bubbles to me and then ask
me to repeat them after him in an attempt to help me learn to
read, something I was not able to do till I was almost nine.
When I was ready for the page to be turned, he had taught me
the Russian *i potom,* which means "and next?"

Mary and I would sometimes stay with Sokoloff and Lisa
when my mother was out of town. He taught me how to knot
a tie.

Then, after we moved to the beach, Sokoloff was called in to
handle a small crisis. There were only women in our household—

my mother and Mary and my mother's assistant, who would also drive my mother to work. Consequently, I was ignorant about adult men, there not being the usual number around because of the war and because I had no father present.

The only adults I occasionally glimpsed naked were women, and this told me that pubic hair was unconnected to a penis, and so I thought that at a certain point, somewhere between childhood and sometime later, when the hair had grown, their penises had fallen off. I asked my mother when this would happen to me. Alarmed at this misconception, she asked Sokoloff if he would have a shower with me so I could see evidence that such a fate was not a condition of male adulthood.

Soaping ourselves together, I looked with curiosity at his penis and asked, "Does General Eisenhower have one too?"

General Eisenhower, the leader of the Allied Forces in the Second World War, was, I suppose, the most quantifiably male person to my four-year-old mind.

"Yes, I think General Eisenhower has one too."

I was relieved. I loved Vladimir Sokoloff very much. He made me feel cherished and protected whenever I was with him.

But maybe his name would make people think I was Russian and, much as I'd have liked that, I didn't think I could pull it off. I tried other names on my pad, including Michael Horne, then others which didn't seem right. Then I wrote: Michael Welles. I tried it as an autograph a few times and found I could do it with an elegant flourish.

I went down to the living room where my mother was nursing an after-dinner drink, a vodka and water. She was alone, my stepfather having gone to bed, to get ready for the next day at his office, where he would, as he said, be "trying to put butter and eggs together."

"What about Michael Welles?" I asked my mother.

"What for?"

"My stage name."

"What's wrong with the name you've got?"

"It's sort of . . . unwieldy, don't you think? And Orson was very nice to me last year."

My mother pursed her lips, which was a sure sign that something did not sit right.

My mother and Orson Welles in Heartbreak House, *1938. She was then twenty-five, he, twenty-three.*

"I'm not sure that's such a good idea."

"Why not?"

She paused, took a sip of her drink, and then said, "Maybe I should have mentioned something to you about it before, but it never came up and I thought it didn't matter." She paused again, another sip, and continued. "The thing is, some people think Orson and I had an affair and that he's your father. It's not true but that's what some people have gotten into their head."

"Oh." Then after a moment, "Why do they think that?"

"At the Mercury we were very close, acting together every night, but he was married and so was I. To your father," she added, unnecessarily. "And then when we were both in Hollywood, and I was pregnant and Eddy was in New York, and Orson and Virginia had split up, I lived with Orson at his house in Beverly Hills. We'd go out for dinner together. And you know how people can put two and two together and make three, well, that's what they did."

"But nothing ever happened between the two of you?" I asked, this all being a revelation to me, to say the least. I was eager for facts and eager to hear the truth from my mother.

"No, not really."

"Not really?"

"Well," here another sip, "one night we were going to elope."

"Elope?" I repeated, the word being an odd one, since they were both married.

"Let me tell you in my own way. One Saturday night, after the show, we were going to elope. He'd hired a car and we were going to New Jersey to a motel, and then we kissed in the back seat of the car and I realized it was the kiss of a brother and not a lover, and so the car turned around and we went back to the city and Orson came up to the room with me, where Eddy was asleep, and Orson patted his foot over the blanket and said, 'Everything's all right, old fellow. Nothing to worry about.' And then he left."

"And my . . . Eddy, did he wake up?"

"Did he wake up?" My mother thought back. "No, I don't think he woke up."

"And, in the car, what did you say to him, to Orson, that you felt it was the kiss of a brother?"

"What did I say? I don't remember. Maybe just that we had to go back."

Then my mother finished her drink and said, "I think it's time for bed. You have school in the morning."

Over the years, of course, I've thought about this first conversation. As a matter of principle, I always believed my mother. She had brought me up that way—to have the belief that she was always truthful. But putting an adult's mind to this information I was given at sixteen, I thought about the word she chose, "elope." Was it a euphemistic way of telling her teenage son that she and Orson were going to spend a weekend together as lovers? Or did it mean that she was going to leave my father and Orson leave his wife Virginia? It's such a strange word to characterize whatever it was that was supposed to happen. Maybe she chose it because it would be just confusing enough to me so she wouldn't have to be exact.

And the kiss? Mightn't it be, or wasn't it, likely that there'd been other signs of affection, at least a kiss, before Orson had hired the car and booked the room in New Jersey?

The kiss of a brother not a lover.

I wasn't an expert on kisses when my mother told me the story, only having kissed one girl a few times the summer before in Stratford. But even from our first kiss, close-mouthed, a peck on the lips, I would never have thought I was kissing my darling sister, Susie. And given that my mother and Orson were in the car and running off to New Jersey, certain assumptions must have been in place and decisions made, and on the basis of this one kiss was my mother not going to take the opportunity to be with the most charismatic man she, and many people, had ever met? I also suspected and later knew from things my mother told me that she had not been innocent when she'd married her husband, Eddy Lindsay-Hogg.

And why, if nothing had happened, did she not say, "Nothing happened" and leave it at that?

And why did my nervous father not wake up, at two or three in the morning—his wife not beside him, the key in the door of their small hotel suite, footsteps, one tread probably being heavy, the presence of two other bodies? Had he taken a sleeping pill?

I am not now, nor was I at sixteen, particularly judgmental of people's behavior. My mother would have known that and maybe that's why she divulged the story in the manner she did, and she probably also knew, all this being so sudden, that I would not know how to challenge her, if I'd wanted to.

From what I came to know of Edward Lindsay-Hogg and his jumpy nature, I know that if my mother had woken up in New Jersey that Sunday morning, she'd have dreaded the call she would have had to make to the hotel room in New York.

For a few days after, at school and in my room, I kept repeating to myself the conversation I'd recently had with my mother, trying to figure out what I thought was strange about it.

I found her again in the evening downstairs with her vodka and water.

"What does Orson say? Do people ask him about it?"

"Oh, Orson's impossible. He likes the idea that people think he has a son, what with three daughters. And the whole intrigue of it, and so he'd probably give his little smile and not say anything, or he'd say . . ." and here my mother put on an affronted bass male voice, as though from a melodrama, "How dare you suggest I'd ever betray my friend, Eddy Lindsay-Hogg. Humph."

I was confused. I'm not exactly sure what I thought, all this so new to me and so, in some way, charged, combustible; maybe it was as though a door had been opened, then shut, then opened again and standing there was Orson giving his little Harry Lime *Third Man* smile.

My mother had been brought up Catholic in Dublin and the woman who'd looked after her and the other three children was the same woman, Mary Gillen, who would become my nurse.

Walking along Fifth Avenue one day when she was pregnant with me, my mother had bumped into Mary, and they'd gone to Longchamps and had a cup of tea. Mary told my mother that she'd been with a family for ten years and had recently been let go, the children now too old for a nurse. On the spot, my mother, knowing she wouldn't be able to look after me full-time, hired Mary to be my nurse, even though as a child she'd been frightened of her Catholic rigor. Terrified by her father and scared by Mary's sternness, my mother didn't tell her that day that she was a lapsed Catholic and didn't believe in God anymore.

Mary had achieved a secure place in my mother's family by saving the life of the youngest child, my uncle Billy. My grandmother became ill after his premature birth, and Mary sat by his little crib and, using a dropper, put minute quantities of milk on his tiny tongue, drop by drop, for three days and three sleepless nights.

In 1943, my mother was rehearsing a play and was on her own in New York. Edward Lindsay-Hogg was in Ireland, and Mary and I were staying with Sokoloff in West Hollywood. My mother had been invited to a cocktail party and, after she'd pushed the doorbell, had said a silent prayer.

Waiting for the door to be opened my mother, even though

With my nurse Mary Gillen and my mother.

she'd abandoned any belief, said this prayer: "Please God, let there be someone in there who'll save my life."

The door opened. My mother went into a group of merrymakers and met the man, Stuart Scheftel, who was to become my stepfather.

My mother told me of this episode fifty years after it had happened.

On that evening, when she was eighty and I twenty-six years younger, I thought: Why did she need someone to save her life? Why did she, not yet thirty, feel so alone or, in some way, afraid that she needed to say an atheist's prayer for a savior? What had happened that she wasn't able to look after herself and, in the bargain, me?

That same evening, when my mother told me of her prayer and meeting my stepfather, she also told me that when she was sixteen, for some invented infraction, her father had attempted to spank her. She'd struggled and, during the struggle, he'd "fiddled" with her. She told her mother, who wasn't in bed at the time, and her mother had rescued her by sending her off to England to stay with friends and, soon after, to become a nanny to their two children.

I found this story upsetting for my mother, but also in some way bemusing to me. I remembered when my mother and I would go to Ireland for me to see my father and she to see her parents, how happy they'd seemed to be, especially my grandfather, laughing till he cried at my mother's jokes.

Time alters all. Or at least puts a cover on things.

Three

It was a year or so after that first conversation with my mother about Orson Welles that the subject came up again, in an unexpected way.

On vacation from Oxford University and back in New York for a few weeks, I'd gone with my parents to a dinner party in the large beautiful apartment owned by the not large but certainly beautiful Gloria Vanderbilt, who was then married to the gifted dynamo, my first employer, Sidney Lumet. A crowded room with all the hotshots of the period. In the taxi home, my stepfather did a funny and accurate imitation of Truman Capote.

After dinner, I had been sitting alone on a sofa, drink in hand, when the fey pretty imp Tammy Grimes, actress and singer, sat beside me. She was then married to Christopher Plummer and was the mother of the sublime baby Amanda. I was grateful that such a well-known young woman would want to talk to me, and found her very attractive, but felt she was out of my league, and not only because she was married.

We talked a bit about this and that. Did I like Oxford? And then, in her beguiling throaty voice, Tammy asked, "Is it true that Orson Welles is your father?"

"Why do you ask that?"

"It's just what I've heard. What people say. And you look like him."

In that I was tall and dark and was struggling with my weight, this last remark was true, and I did not really look like Edward Lindsay-Hogg, who although also tall and dark was lean. He was handsome, but the shape of his face was pointed and angular, whereas mine was full and broad. His nose was aquiline and mine small.

I said to Tammy what I'd been told.

"My mother says I'm not."

I knew with this reply that I was slicing the egg just off-center.

"But what do you think?"

To my current embarrassment, I acknowledge that here I saw an opportunity to make myself, by potential connection to this famous man, maybe more interesting, or, in some way, attractive to this female, and besides, my mother's story had not quite found itself settled in my mind.

So I said, as insouciantly as I could manage, "I don't know," and shrugged my shoulders casually, as if it didn't really much matter to me.

Tammy gave me what I'd call a knowing look, smiled her little cat's smile, and, to my regret, went on to talk of something else.

Whatever the truth, and I really was not sure: the way Orson had treated me, his touch, the queerness of my mother's story, her explanation of Orson's attitude, I knew I had a little extra social currency in my pocket, to be doled out carefully, and only on special occasions.

Age eighteen, around the time of my conversation with Tammy Grimes.

I was four by the time we moved to the beach and was old enough to enjoy it. Being in one place for a year or so meant that there would be a sort of continuity to my life and I could make friends and keep them for a while.

We lived in a small house right on the beach, not far from the Santa Monica pier. We had a front yard which was sand and a five-foot-high wooden seawall, with steps on one side onto our section of sand and steps on the other down to the sand of the public beach.

Next to us lived Virginia Welles, Orson's ex-wife, and their daughter Christopher, called Chrissie. Virginia was remarried to Charlie Lederer, the sought-after screenwriter, but he was away with the Air Corps and only back when on leave. Orson was now married to Rita Hayworth.

Chrissie was a little older than I and took on an almost sisterly role during my time at the beach.

We were sitting at a table early one evening eating our supper, and she told me that chewing with my mouth open was an unattractive habit, and she illustrated, mouth open, then closed, and I understood her point.

She told me scary stories. We sat on the sand, and she frightened me with fictions about my father being in battle and blown up and maimed. Even though I knew he was in Ireland, wherever that was, she made me anxious.

Something happening to a father might have been on her mind. I remember she had a birthday party and kept saying Orson would soon be there, but he never showed up.

On the other side of us, in a larger house, lived the family of Richard Berlin, the president of the Hearst Corporation. Two of his little girls, Richie and Brigid, would each later be inextricably linked to Andy Warhol and his set in New York. Brigid became, if not the first, then one of the earliest plaster casters. This involved a procedure in which the erect penis of a rock star would be wrapped in a papier-mâché substance, and this object, when finished, could be used as a mantelpiece ornament.

A couple of houses down from Virginia and Chrissie were Linda and Gyl Roland, the daughters of Constance Bennett and Gilbert Roland.

I was in and out of love with all of these girls during my time in Santa Monica.

And then, in a house a bit away from the Rolands, was Johnny Register, the only other little boy on the beach. We were friends and probably realized two boys and five girls was not a proportion we might ever find again. John Register became a very good and successful painter in California, until a cancer and its subsequent treatment left his head disfigured and he died, after a valiant fight, too young.

And then farther up on the Berlins' side was the house, later to become a beach club, where William Randolph Hearst and Marion Davies spent weekends.

One day I was adventuring along the beach wearing my little wool bathing suit and carrying my favorite toy, a foot-high hollow tin replica of Li'l Abner, the cartoon character.

Since I felt I owned the beach, I had no hesitation climbing stairs I had not been on before. I went up onto the platform of a white boarded seawall and down the other side to see a large swimming pool with many fabric-covered chaise longues around it and beyond, the biggest house I'd ever seen on the beach. There didn't seem to be anyone around, and so I lay down at the edge of the pool near the diving board and put Li'l Abner into the water to see if he could swim. While I held him and moved his arms, he could, but when I let go, he couldn't manage and sank to the bottom of the pool.

I was perplexed because I could not swim and didn't know what I should do. I stood up and paced back and forth on the pool lip looking at my little toy under the water. And then out of the house came a woman who was friendly right away. She was wearing white slacks and a fine white blouse, and although somewhat puffy in the face you could see some prettiness still. She went to a little cabana and brought out a long pole with a net at the end, put it deep into the pool, and lifted out Li'l Abner and gave him back to me.

"Thank you," I said, shaking water off, not wanting him to rust.

"Where do you live?"

I pointed to my right down the beach.

She asked my name and I told her.

"You're Geraldine Fitzgerald's son, aren't you? She and my nephew, Charlie Lederer, are great friends. We've just started lunch. Would you like to come in and have something?"

I thought to go inside the immense house would be interesting so I followed her.

She went through several rooms, me padding, barefoot, behind.

We stopped at a large doorway.

The dining room I looked into was dark. At the end of a long, long highly shined dark wood table sat a tall man silhouetted against a large window some ten feet behind him, the light of the midday sun diffused by cream-colored linen curtains.

"Michael," Marion Davies said, looking toward the dark figure at the end of the table, "this is Mr. Hearst," and then to Mr. Hearst she said, "Michael is Geraldine Fitzgerald's son."

After a momentary silence, Mr. Hearst said, "Come and sit down, Michael."

I walked the length of the table, feeling a little chill, wearing only my bathing suit.

Mr. Hearst held out his hand and I shook it. He was a substantial man with a head proportionately smaller than the thick neck and shoulders on which it sat. He was wearing a soft wool jacket with the large collar of his silk shirt lying over the lapels.

Marion Davies went to the sideboard and, from a large crystal bowl, spooned some fresh fruit into a small crystal bowl, put the bowl onto a plate, picked up a spoon, and set them on the table opposite her place, so that we were flanking Mr. Hearst, with fifteen feet of highly polished empty table between us and the doorway.

It wasn't that I was uneasy as I lifted my heavy silver spoon, but a room this large was unfamiliar to me, that and it being so cool inside and the sun so hot outside and large Mr. Hearst at the head of the table, and the darkness behind him except for the shaded window made me feel that everything was strangely muted and, somehow, gray.

Mr. Hearst asked to look at Li'l Abner and I handed it to him. He turned it in his hands and said that it was one of his.

"How do you mean?" I asked.

"Well, I have some newspapers and we run the cartoon."

I told him about loving comics and about Sokoloff, who I called Lok, reading them to me.

"You don't read yet?" he asked mildly without criticism.

"No, not yet. Soon I hope."

"Maybe that's why you like comics."

"Because I don't read?"

"Yes. They tell their story in pictures as much as in words, with a different emphasis from panel to panel."

He gave the metal figure back to me and as I held it, I felt I treasured it even more, it being a tangible connection to the wonderful complex world of "emphasis" and pictures and the richness of comics.

Mr. Hearst turned to Miss Davies and they continued their conversation from before my toy had been rescued.

Then Miss Davies said, "Michael, if you've finished your fruit cup maybe you should get home. We've kept you too long and your mother will be wondering where you are."

"Mary," I said.

She looked quizzically at me.

"Mary will be wondering where I am. My mother is at Warner Brothers."

"Well, Mary then."

I got up to go. Mr. Hearst gave me a little wave.

"And," Miss Davies said, "we're not here that much anymore so if you want to swim in the pool when we're away, you and Mary come over."

"Thank you," I said and left the big dark room, Li'l Abner under my arm.

When I got back to our house, a two-minute walk on my sturdy little legs, I asked Mary what "emphasis" meant.

"Where'd you get that word?" she asked, always on the look-out for corrupting influences.

"From Mr. Hearst up the beach."

I knew something had impressed her but didn't think it was the new word in my vocabulary, but perhaps the fact that it had been given me by Mr. Hearst who owned comics.

"Emphasis?" she considered. "It means what's important one way or the other. That's what it means."

I preferred paddling in the ocean to a pool and so Mary and I never took Miss Davies up on her offer.

The reason I needed a nurse (in England, I suppose, Mary would have been called a nanny) was that my mother was seldom at home.

She was the sole breadwinner for the family, not only support-ing us in California but also sending money back to Ireland to my father and, sometimes, her brother. She was an actress under contract to Warner Bros., a particularly grisly place for this sort of indentureship, playing the friend in A pictures, at least once to a real friend, Bette Davis, in *Dark Victory,* and then in B pic-tures playing the lead female. I don't know how much she earned, but it was stretched pretty thin because as well as me

*With my dog Freckles, a Christmas gift
from my mother, Santa Monica, 1944.*

and Mary there was Mary-Ellen Quinn, who'd handle the mail and do whatever extra driving was needed, my mother never having tried to master that skill. When she was working, with the early start and late finish over in Burbank, I'd only see my mother on weekends, or when she was on unpaid suspension from the studio for refusing a picture.

She told me later, remarried and in New York, that she'd hated Hollywood. Although off to a good start, receiving an Oscar nomination for her first American picture, *Wuthering Heights,* she said she'd never learned to play the game and always felt weak (and probably frightened [about money as much as other things]).

And also, it probably didn't help that her two best friends, Bette Davis and Olivia de Havilland, were more successful, not only in their careers but also at fighting the studios. Olivia actually won suit against one of those oppressors—Warner Bros.—saying her contract amounted to a form of servitude. But when my mother tried to fight, with her smaller quiver of arrows, she'd be suspended and then, money being tight, would be forced to do the picture she hadn't wanted to do, or a worse one. And in her recreation time, she was in a raffish set of drinkers and renegades—Bogart, Sam Spiegel, John Huston—and this didn't help her reputation with the sanctimonious whoring hucksters who were her bosses. My mother had a quick temper.

She threw her drink in the face of a successful director, Lewis Milestone, who'd made a lame joke, suggesting, because my mother's very young agent, Gloria Safier, often stayed with us, that they were lesbians. I loved Gloria very much and as I got older the fact that she was a woman who liked women made her more interesting to me, since I liked women too.

With my mother on the beach in Santa Monica,
on one of the rare days she wasn't at Warner Bros.

Women friends of my mother did sometimes stay with us. I remember one early evening at the beach when I was in the little kitchen, which had an eating nook with a shiny leatherette banquette, using a knock at the back door as an excuse to escape the beets that Mary had decided were good for me. I opened the inner door to see, on the other side of the wire mosquito screen, a lean lanky figure. He smiled a disarmingly modest smile, like a gambler holding four aces.

"Is Livvy in?" John Huston asked.

He would sometimes call on Olivia de Havilland when she stayed with us. Olivia de Havilland was always nice to me and showed great patience playing games under the instruction of a four-year-old.

My mother later said that she didn't think John Huston had treated her friend kindly, which was why, my mother said, she'd turned down the female lead in *The Maltese Falcon* when he'd offered it to her. To me, this seemed like a misjudged hubristic act of solidarity, given the amount of romantic goings-on at this time, with people treating each other no better or worse than in any other society where talent and beauty meet.

Many years later, I read in an account of the making of *The Maltese Falcon* that the studio hadn't wanted my mother for the part, and I wondered why she'd told me a different version. But then she often told me different versions.

Mary-Ellen Quinn had a boyfriend in the navy. Pete Raskovitch had close-cut curly hair, a ready smile, and the build of a fullback. The only way I was allowed to go into the ocean out of my depth was if Pete put me on his shoulders or in his arms. We'd run from the beach and hit the water with a splash. He seemed to me the epitome of a man: brave, friendly, strong, competent, decent. I felt safe with him, on his shoulders or when he'd hold me as I practiced swimming.

There were few adult men around on a regular basis.

But near the pier, a small army camp had been set up where young soldiers would be billeted before shipping out for the war, to places like Guam and Iwo Jima. These plucky and nervous young men were kind to Johnny Register and me, the boys on the beach, and would sometimes let us hold their revolvers, the rifles being too heavy and cumbersome, and allow us to finger the bullets.

Marion Davies's nephew, Charlie Lederer, was an attractive prematurely bald man whose gentle manner did not prevent him from being wickedly funny and one of Hollywood's most elaborate practical jokers.

A story my mother told me about Charlie appealed to her sense of humor as much as to mine.

Captain Lederer was in India, serving in an intelligence unit. He met a European lady he thought attractive enough to ask out for dinner. The dinner went well but, as the wine was drunk, the lady began to make vaguely anti-Semitic references. Somewhat perturbed, Charlie nevertheless accompanied her back to her lavish apartment; a key feature in the living room was a small inlaid cabinet sitting on spindly legs with a dainty and valuable collection of porcelain inside, cups, saucers, swains, forest animals.

They each had a whiskey, and Charlie found any ardor he might have felt cooling to freezing as the woman's conversation continued to disparage Jews and blame them for the world's woes, which at the time were many.

"Do you actually know any Jews?" Charlie asked mildly.

"I'm sure I must know a few but not if I could help it."

Charlie took a sip of his drink and asked, "Has a Jew ever done anything bad to you?"

"No," the woman replied, perhaps wondering what had happened to the kisses she might have been looking forward to and why the conversation was taking this turn.

"So you don't have anything personal against the Jews?" he asked.

"That's not the point but no. Not that I can think of."

Charlie went over to the filigreed wooden cabinet, holding her little treasures. He tipped it over, smashing all of the valuable objects.

"Well now you do," Charlie said and walked out the door.

He gave me my first taste of beer when I was five. I was in my bathing suit standing on the beach skimming stones toward the water. Chrissie was running at shore's edge and, unluckily, ran in the line of fire and my stone clipped her on the ankle.

"That hurt me," she shouted. "You did that on purpose. I'm going to tell my mother and she'll tell Mary and you'll be in trouble."

She ran up the beach to her house and I ran to mine. Virginia telling Mary was not something I wanted because of Mary's almost Old Testament view of retribution.

I went up to my room and hid behind the door.

Shortly, Mary called up from the kitchen, "Michael, come down right now. Mr. Lederer is here. He wants to talk to you."

"No, I won't."

I was crying behind the door.

"You'd better if you know what's good for you."

I made my shaky way down the stairs and went into the kitchen.

Charlie was there dressed in casual clothes and holding a bottle of beer. He wasn't a big drinker but the day was hot.

"Mary, let me talk to Michael."

Mary, respectful of someone of employer standing, left the

room with evident reluctance, disappearing behind the kitchen's swing door.

Charlie looked at me trembling in front of him.

In a quiet tone, he began, "You didn't mean to hurt her?"

"No, of course I didn't."

"That's what I thought," Charlie said. "Although maybe it's not a good idea to throw stones if someone might get in the way."

"I know," I said, starting to recover my composure. I knew he wasn't going to hurt me.

"If you could say you were sorry to Chrissie, that might be good."

"I will."

He moved to a shelf which held a variety of drinking glasses and took down a shot-sized one. He carefully poured some of his beer into the small glass, leaving a little foamy head on top, and handed it to me.

"Here's to you," he said, holding out his bottle, to toast.

We clinked.

"Drink up." He took a swallow and I did also, liking the sparkling taste.

"Don't you worry about anything," he said. "Tell Mary you and I settled it together."

"Thank you."

He left and went back to Virginia and Chrissie next door and I, alone in the kitchen, finished my beer.

Thirty or so years later, Charlie Lederer died as a result of addiction to heroin.

My mother had an affair with the great photographer Robert Capa. The images from the wars he covered are unforgettable.

She was to tell me about Capa when I was much older and said, although she loved him, he was too unreliable for her.

My mother and me taken by
Robert Capa, 1942.

"He'd say he'd see you on Friday, but then he wouldn't show up and you wouldn't see him for two months. After a while, I couldn't take the uncertainty."

She paused and then said, with an ironic laugh, "And he was having an affair with Ingrid Bergman at the same time."

In an old album I found after Edward Lindsay-Hogg's death, I saw some photographs of my mother and me in a pool, taken by Capa. Guessing at my age I'd say I was about two when the pictures were taken, not long before my father left. In the album, under the photographs, in my father's elegant thin handwriting, are the oddly innocent words, "Photographs taken by Robert Capa."

Whether the affair had already begun or did not start till after my father left, I don't know, but no photographer, before or after, made my mother look more beautiful or alluring.

Warner Bros. was a cruel place for her.
I can only imagine how, when she had an interview with Jack Warner to request better parts, the kind Ingrid Bergman had, his reply must have stung like a blow across the face with a ruler.

Jack Warner had said, "How dare you mention your name and Ingrid Bergman's in the same sentence."

I saw in the newspaper one day in 1954 that Capa had been killed in Indochina, stepping on a land mine.

I went into my parents' bedroom. At that time, my mother sometimes tried to sleep again after breakfast, so I entered quietly, the door being ajar. She was lying on her side, her eyes open. I told her what I had read, calling Capa "that nice man who sometimes came to see us when we were in California."

"I know," she said, maybe having read *The New York Times* before me, or maybe my stepfather had told her.

And then she said, "Would you mind leaving me alone for a while. I just want to go to sleep for a while."

I left her room so she could sleep.

It was some months after this that she told me about their affair.

Recently I was in a bookstore, the most enticing of places, and leafing through something or other found I was beside a shelf on which there was a biography of Robert Capa. I looked in the index to find if my mother was there. She was. I looked up Ingrid Bergman and read that she and Capa had not met until 1945, when the war was over, in Paris, and that's when the two had begun their romance. But who knows? Maybe they had met

*Robert Capa, photographed
by my mother, 1942.*

in Hollywood in the earlier part of that decade and carried on in secret. Or maybe not.

When I was sixteen or seventeen, Henry Miller would sometimes be in New York from his home in California and he would come for dinner with the wife to whom he was currently married.

My mother described him as an old friend from her Hollywood days. I'd read the *Tropics* and had been whirlwinded by his energetic headlong prose and, of course, loved that he wrote about sex, about which I could not get enough information.

His manner was totally unaffected, and he seemed to take a friendly curious interest in me, and he, thin and sinewy, standing casually, hands in khaki pockets, Brooklyn accent, would talk to me. He didn't care about school, the subject other adults took refuge in, except to say life was the school. He'd ask me what I wanted to do and how I'd go about it, and I felt that, with him, the conversation could go anywhere with nothing to censor it.

My mother talked about him after he left.

"Isn't he wonderful? He stands there like a teenager leaning on one leg, the other hip cocked. We should all be like that when we're his age."

"I really liked him. How old is he?"

"Mid-sixties, probably."

"Where do you know him from?"

"You must have met him when you were a little boy. In California. Maybe you didn't. Maybe you were asleep. I'm glad you've met him now. He's just an old friend."

On one of their visits, I hadn't been there and was sorry I'd missed the chance to talk to him. Mrs. Miller had written my mother a chatty thank-you note and ended it with, "And how is Michael? Does he still look like Orson Welles?"

Orson Welles, age eighteen, 1933.

My mother always told me when anyone mentioned me or said something nice about me, and she showed me this letter, perhaps because she thought it would be good for my confidence, which like most teenagers was an up-and-down thing—being told I looked like a famous man.

Four

In my mid-teens when I was going to school in New York I'd sometimes have tea with my mother on my return.

I loved being with my mother, having tea and cinnamon toast, and our conversational net would hold many subjects and ideas.

She told me what Stravinsky had said to Sokoloff, friends and fellow Russians, when they both were living in California during the war. And that was, that all art attempted to create order, seeking to make something different and coherent out of the difficult confusing mess that life can sometimes be.

And no matter how violent or disturbing the subject, Stravinsky had said, there was a deep need to find order with each art's particular means—painting with color and line, writing with character and words, acting with emotion. With music, no matter how complex or unfamiliar, there is a statement, elaboration, conclusion—form and order out of sound.

"Like," my mother said, "the psyche is always looking for order."

She paused and had a sip of tea. I'd never heard her use that word, "psyche," before but I was glad she did, because I knew that I was seeking that, that order. I knew it was something to be desired.

And then she said, "Although the psyche doesn't always find it."

On another afternoon of tea and, this time, English muffins, we had a conversation that made me question not what my mother said, but why she said it.

We were talking about Moorefield, the house in County Kildare, which she'd bought with her first movie earnings. I've seen watercolors and it was a substantial small house from the mid-seventeenth century and had a cannonball lodged in the dining room wall from some trouble going on at the time. It was in this house she'd said where I might have been conceived.

She'd taken a sip of tea and then added, matter-of-factly, affectionately, "You were an accident."

"Oh yes?"

"When I told your father, he was very surprised. He didn't know what to say at first."

"Oh. Why not?"

*My mother—pregnant—and Edward
Lindsay-Hogg returning to America
from Ireland, 1939.*

"We weren't expecting me to be pregnant."

"Why not?"

"We just weren't. That doesn't mean we weren't thrilled that you'd be born. It's just that it was a surprise."

I didn't mind being an accident. I assumed a lot of people were. And I didn't mind her telling me. I just took it as an interesting fact for me to put in the "interesting facts" section of my brain. I've never forgotten this little chat but, as I got older, I wondered why she told me, given the paternal conversation which she knew might someday come.

My father went back to live at Moorefield when he returned to Ireland and stayed there till the house had to be torn down because of damage from previously unnoticed woodworm.

One of the things I find in writing about people who are dead is that, after a short or long time, no matter how close the relationship was, they become like characters in fiction; in that, since they are no longer able to explain motives or clarify obfuscations or tell the truth, however simple or complicated, the author must do it for them and use imagination to decipher the information and decode the memories. But with this comes a daunting responsibility—to not come to easy and tidy conclusions about someone's life and to not avoid new evidence which runs counter to what seemed clear earlier. And to remember that people can change; what someone was at twenty-five or thirty might bear no resemblance to the person at fifty or sixty, they having weathered fate and circumstance, exalted by the good, buffeted by the bad; and the part that luck plays, how it can be cruel or grand, or just have gone somewhere else.

Although we knew each other for fifty years, I never felt totally at ease with my stepfather. I think there was some mismatch in our personalities. I am sad about this because, as I look back to my youth and, indeed my whole life, I see that he always attempted to be on my side, was responsible in his advice, according to his lights, and wished the best for me. And when I was in my late forties and he asked me to come to his office so we could be alone and talk, I am sorry I didn't know how really to reply when he asked me, "What went wrong between us? I love you but don't know if you love me."

"I do," I said, and I did in my guarded way.

"Was it my fault?"

If he had a fault, it probably was that he'd married my mother, supplanting my little self who would occasionally sleep in her bed with full-time possession of it. And this with no preparation or warning. When we first went to stay with him, just near the end of World War II, I was sent off to bed to sleep in a room with Mary and the next morning when I went to see my mother, found them in bed together. Natural for them but not, at that age, for me, especially since there'd been no man sleeping in our house with my mother since my father left. My stepfather was the larger male with, I think, a powerful connection with my mother, and both of us were unused to having to deal with another masculine person in daily domestic proximity, with me only having had females in my life till that point, and being smaller.

Nor was he at ease with ambiguity, whereas I had grown up with it, not ever being sure how the sand was shifting to do with my mother's presence or absence and my desire for her to be constant in my life. Her work took her away, press junkets, a play in New York (though Mary and I did go for a few weeks during the months she was there). Even when she was at home, she wasn't; long days away at the studio and, whatever her private life was after my father left, some of the nights as well.

My stepfather, Stuart Scheftel, was a grandson of Isidor Straus, who owned Macy's with his brother Nathan. It was only his mother's cold which prevented them, he in his infancy, from joining her parents on the *Titanic*. Mrs. Straus is famous in the tragic *Titanic* lore for saying, when offered a place on a lifeboat with the women and children, "I've been with my husband for forty years and I'm not going to leave him now."

Stuart Scheftel's father died when my stepfather was five, leaving him and an older brother in the care of a somewhat irresponsible, flighty, and anxious young widow who, soon after the death of her husband, gambled away a small fortune at the card tables, thereafter to be supported by her brothers, until her second long marriage to a bluff gregarious stockbroker.

My stepfather spent his late teens in France and England. Before he went to Oxford, he was the first American to win the British Boys' Golf Championship and then, at Oxford, through friendships he'd made and his skill at golf, he was taken up by a glamorous social set, playing in foursomes which included the Prince of Wales (later to be, briefly, King Edward VIII) and the Duke of York (later to be King George VI). Because he was the youngest in the group, people would hail his arrival with, "Here comes the Boy." (This became his nickname. His brother Herbert was known as Buzzie.)

He was darkly handsome and devotedly heterosexual so it would have been surprising to him when, a few years later, sharing a late taxi after some nightclubbing in Paris, another English royal duke made a clumsy pass at him which was rebuffed.

I can imagine Boy saying, "Sir"—the way you address a royal duke, even if his hand is high up on your trousered thigh—"I'd prefer you not do that."

Two days later, a gold cigarette case with a sapphire on the clasp, and a friendly inscription inside, arrived from Cartier and accompanying it was an envelope, heavy paper with a royal embossment on the back. The letter inside, also on heavy paper with a coronet at the top, apologized for "disagreeable and unasked for behavior" and wishing for forgiveness and for the friendship to be untarnished.

Stuart Scheftel had raised enough money to start a magazine called Young America. *In 1940, Prime Minister Winston Churchill, who was not young and only half American, was an early interviewee.*

The next evening, Boy went out for dinner and when he came back, he could tell that the security of his apartment had been breached; things were not quite as he'd left them. He looked around to see what might have been stolen. Valuable pieces were in place, including the cigarette case. The only item which had been removed was the royal letter.

When he returned to America, wishing to become a journalist (which he did), one of his letters of recommendation was written by the Prince of Wales.

Good-looking, athletic (the way he'd drive a ball off the tee was grace combining with motion), and seemingly confident in all circles, surprisingly (by the time I met him anyway), my stepfather was not an easy man. There was a fundamental tension in his nature which caused an unsettling volatility in his behavior and great, often manifested, anxiety. Anxiety was our household's weather. As a small boy, I remember going off to school in the morning with a sense that if I got back in one piece that evening, it would have to do with luck more than anything else.

The anxiety could have come from his mother, or from an early bout with rheumatic fever that left him always somewhat delicate, or from feeling constantly on guard against the anti-Semitism he'd first encountered as a small boy. Maybe it was because the sensitive, courageous, inquisitive nature that was his always had to fight to burst through the cold earth of family and social expectation. Or maybe it came from the fact that he, who as a young man had lived in a glittering group of the well-to-do, had lost most of his money in his late twenties as a result of bad stockbroker advice, but thought it necessary to live as if he were still rich when he was, in fact, broke for most of his life.

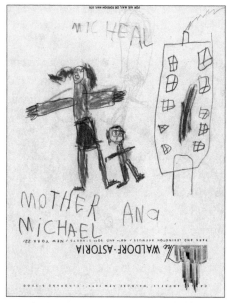

My mother, Boy, Mary, and I were
at the Waldorf-Astoria for two weeks
before moving to an apartment on
East 86th Street.

With their marriage, when I was six, my mother and Boy and Mary and I started our life in New York and I was enrolled in the same day school which he had attended. I couldn't read and soon became quite fat and the object of the ever available sadism of young boys and, the times being what they were, often the teachers too.

Although I loved Mary Gillen and knew she loved me (she had to, as far as I was concerned, because she was the one constant in my life), she was not easy, either.

She had been born fifteen years before the end of the nineteenth century in the north of Ireland and her education had been under strict Catholic discipline, the strap having as much to do with schooling as the ABCs.

I always felt protected by Mary against all others, although maybe I should have had the occasional intermediary between her and me.

I remember one night when I was about seven and she was tucking me in bed, after my milk and gingersnaps. She'd turned out the light and then said, "Don't worry, you'll be all right."

"All right about what?" I asked, terror starting to bubble. "Who won't be all right?"

She pushed my hair off my forehead and said, "You'll go to Heaven but your mother and father will go to Hell."

"To Hell? Why?"

"Because they're divorced. Now, say your prayers."

And then the worst night of my early youth. I was eight. The evening had started well. I'd gone to a boy's birthday party, the whole class invited, and they'd served my favorite dish, chicken à la king.

On the way home, Mary and I stopped at a corner store and I'd gotten a double Red Ryder comic book, two episodes for 15 cents.

In bed, I looked at the comic, interpreting the story through the pictures, their emphasis, and with no homework for the next day went to sleep easily, not as anxious as usual about going to school.

At first the raised angry voices were at a distance, and I included them in a dream, but they grew ever closer, to arrive in Mary's room next door to mine. I woke up to hear the three adults shouting, closet doors slamming, suitcases pulled from a top shelf.

As things were becoming seriously unstable, my mother blew into my room, turned on the overhead light, and gabbled something.

"What, what did you say?" I called, blinking, not understanding and frightened.

"Mary's decided to leave us."

"What are you saying?"

"Mary's decided to leave us and we've agreed. Don't worry, I'll look after you."

"How can you look after me?" I shouted.

What an impossibility that would be, and what was this "us"? What were they to do with it, my mother and stepfather? Me. Me. It was me. What could I do, how would I survive if the only person who'd been with me day and night, nursing me through illness at Sokoloff's when my mother was away, who'd wiped me after I'd been to the bathroom, who washed me in the tub, who fed me, made me say my prayers, who tucked me in bed at night, if the only person who'd been with me always since I was born, would leave "us"?

My mother stood, indecisive, blasted by my fury.

"No, no, she can't," I started to cry and quickly became hysterical, in the way that only a child can who thinks he's about to be abandoned.

Nothing could stop my crazy tears. My mother took a step toward me. My flailing arms turned her away.

In a panic, not knowing how to deal with her son, my mother

went back into the other room and shut the door. The one male and two female voices were muffled. Miserable as I was, I strained to hear as the voices grew quieter, as if negotiating.

Then after several minutes my mother came back and said, "Mary's decided to stay. Try to go to sleep. Everything will be all right."

I can't remember if she came to kiss me.

She turned out the light, and I lay there, safe again but realizing that my safety was not as certain as I'd believed it to be a few hours earlier.

When I was a teenager, my mother told me what had happened; they'd fired Mary because they didn't like the Catholicism she was imposing on me, the rosary, Sunday masses, the nightly prayers.

"And remember," my mother'd said, "I'm an atheist. I don't believe in God. I had too much of that when I was young."

When Mary had been her nurse.

Many years later, when I was in my thirties, I brought up this evening again to my mother and said how it had knocked me off balance.

My mother didn't speak for a moment and then told me a different version.

"I thought I had to do something. I was afraid she was hitting you too much."

I remember sitting on a school bus returning from a baseball game, leaning my head against the window, thinking to myself, as of a mathematical certainty, "I'll be happy when I'm sixteen." It was my eighth year and sixteen was my whole life over again.

I don't know why I chose sixteen. Perhaps I felt I'd be sort of grown up by then and free of the constant humiliation of childhood and its deceptions.

And when I finally was sixteen, on a particular day in June, two things happened: I left boarding school, never to return, and went to work at the Shakespeare Festival. Two such glorious events on the same day gave me a sense of happiness and liberation I've never forgotten.

I realize I've been going back and forward in time, but it is memory I'm dealing with, and that's the way it works, as when looking in the dictionary, one word will lead to another, by proximity or by reference: oligarch, oleaginous, unctuous.

And sometimes the memory will be there in clear focus, sometimes not.

Imagine you're a dog and your owner throws a stick for you to catch. If you're alert and quick enough, you'll grab it on the fly; if not, and it's gone beyond you and is lost in the grass, you look, sniff, turn in confused circles till you find it and bring the stick back to your owner with your indented teeth marks on it and your own fresh glistening saliva.

Five

During the years of my early teens till I was eighteen, I never saw Edward Lindsay-Hogg. He would write to me probably twice a year and I'd reply. Occasionally, not by design, we would speak on the phone. He'd ring, usually late at night his time, from Ireland or, later, Italy or Spain. Boy would usually answer and hand the phone to my mother, with a look partly of sympathy and partly exasperation. Sympathy because he knew my father had never gotten over my mother, and exasperation because he knew how the call would go. There would be the thin desperate voice from three thousand miles away and my mother would listen and then say sadly that she was sorry or what my father was suggesting was impossible and that he needed to calm down. I could tell these calls put my mother in a state of great agitation. Then, sometimes but not always, depending on my father's state, of emotion or inebriation, she'd ask, "Do you want to speak to Michael? He's here."

This was a good ploy on my mother's part, I suppose. Knowing I was in the room, Eddy couldn't say no and then he would have to attempt to recover his composure and it would be up to me to hang up. We'd speak briefly. He'd ask how I was, how was school, then he'd tell me he loved me. I'd mutter, "Me too," but I didn't know how I felt about him or how I was supposed to feel about him, in relation to Boy, who had taken on all the responsibilities of a father. And then we'd say good-bye, I would hang up, and that would be that. For several months anyway.

One of the reasons for my mother's extreme agitation was because of her feelings of guilt, above and beyond the norm in a broken marriage. I know this because of something she'd told me in my teens. And that was: after my father left America in early 1943 till she and I went to Ireland at the end of the war in

Stuart Scheftel as a GI, August 1944.

1945, she never told him the jig was up, that she'd met Boy Scheftel and wanted to marry him. She'd write Eddy with the usual endearments, and so he had no idea what was going to hit him. I asked her why she'd done this and she said it seemed unfair that my father was stuck in Ireland by wartime travel restrictions, not to mention the danger of crossing the Atlantic, and so he couldn't come back and put up a fight.

I remember thinking this was an odd way of looking at things. Why would she want him to put up a fight, if she'd fallen in love with someone else? And what was the state of their marriage when he'd left America for the duration of the war, and forever, as it turned out? Probably she couldn't bear to write the letter. Maybe her own anxious nature was not up to imagining how he'd deal with it, he being a man of fragile temperament. Or maybe she could imagine the noose in the attic all too well.

Because of my stepfather's rheumatic heart he couldn't be drafted into the army in World War II. So he enlisted. Because he spoke perfect French, he was assigned to the French section of a psychological warfare unit, making broadcasts from London, arranging for propaganda drops into France. He was in London for much of the bombing. He went into Normandy ten days or so after D-Day. During this time he wrote many longing and loving letters to my mother, asking her to write more often, "to make a G.I. happy," and hoping for a brighter day and asking after me. So it would be with great relief when the war in Europe was over that he was able to rent a little house on Long Island in the summer of 1945, where my mother and Mary and I went to stay. I'd only met him a couple of times and this was the first occasion I'd be under his roof. Our first night there was the night my mother and Boy slept in the same bed.

The next day, with a long pointed stick I murdered a number of frogs who were sitting idly, at first, on the cool damp floor of the dark garage, their blood and green wrinkled still bodies satisfying something inside me. Then I went in for the lunch that Mary had made and threw up on the mashed potatoes. I didn't say what I'd done, and Mary was afraid I had been exposed to polio, and I was put to bed for a few days.

After some weeks on Long Island, it was time for my mother and me and Mary to leave for Ireland to see my father, who was expecting us back with him now that the European war was over.

We left from Idlewild Airport in a pontooned seaplane with forty or so passengers. I was excited as the wash sprayed the windows on takeoff and, later, sat on the floor playing with my blocks, and asking my mother and Mary, "How close to Heaven are we?"

Perhaps closer than anyone wanted, because the plane lost an engine over Newfoundland and wasn't able to get to Gander, the usual refueling stop. We had to make an emergency landing on a lake in a little place called Botwood that had a small army base. We stayed there for three days because we arrived on V-J Day, the end of the war with Japan. World War II was over and the crew in Gander went on a bender and couldn't fly the spare parts over to us.

My mother and I were billeted in a small two-bed Quonset hut; Mary in another.

I looked forward to using our proximity to sleep in my mother's bed and have her hold me. But each night, I could stay less and less time with her because each night she was hotter than the night before. By the time we got back on the plane she was clammy and feverish.

The plane landed at Shannon and my jubilant father met his returned family. We took the train to Dublin, where, since Moorefield had fallen down, my father had been staying with my mother's parents. On the journey, my mother hardly spoke. I suppose my father connected this to her not being well.

I met my only living grandparents for the first time at their house in Dublin and my mother collapsed at the front door.

Her life was saved, something I'm not sure she wanted, because her doctor brother Billy, whose life Mary had saved years before with the little milk dropper, got his hands on some penicillin, which was the only thing for my mother's pneumonia.

As she started to recover, she told Mary to take me up to the north of Ireland to stay with Mary's sister and her husband. My mother knew what she was going to do and didn't want me there. I can, with a chill, imagine the scene in her family's house where my father had been living, the urbane son-in-law used to having breakfast with his affectionate in-laws; my mother in bed, pale, and my father being told of her plans for a divorce and marriage to an American. His relief that we were reunited, all that he'd looked forward to, smashed like an egg thrown against a rock.

The small cottage in Ballycastle was damp and gaslit. At night in the front room, I'd be in my pajamas in the bed which had been put there for me and Mary. Having been instructed to repeat after her, I watched as Mary knelt alongside her sister and farmer husband to say their lengthy prayers, silhouetted as they were in the dark stone-floored room by the fire in the grate behind them, the flames fingering higher, harsh and crackling.

After six weeks there, with my breakfast milk warm from the cow, which was not to my California-raised taste, Mary and I returned to Dublin and the deed had been done. I did not see my father again on that trip.

My mother, Mary, and I flew back to New York in a small plane which encountered what the pilot said was the worst Atlantic sea and air storm he'd ever been in. For the many hours the plane careened and slammed left and right and passengers and air stewardesses vomited into paper bags, I was in a cot bed in the back, having said my prayers, safe in Mary's arms.

B oy Scheftel had been at Oxford and since my mid-teens had been encouraging me to try for it.

I was not easy in those years, heavy, shy, somewhat solitary but eager for adventure, somewhat subversive, trying to figure out who I was, if I was anyone at all. And unenthusiastic, to say the least, about school, so Oxford seemed an impossibility.

I'd left Choate, then went to a school in New York.

In my second, winter, term at Trinity School, my stepfather said if I passed my physics exam, an unlikely prospect, I could perform at the Phoenix Theatre in a remounting of *The Taming of the Shrew* from the summer before in Stratford, in which I had my one line. The twenty-year-old girl for whom I felt a (mostly) unrequited love was also to be in the production. Consequently, I did pass the exam, just.

A week later, I presented a note from my stepfather, requesting I be released from a pointless afternoon study hall to attend the dress rehearsal, to the headmaster, an unsympathetic fellow who reacted true to his nature.

"If you go, you don't come back."

I called Boy who said, "I made you a promise and I won't go back on that. I'll speak to him."

I left the school at lunchtime to go to the theater, wondering if perhaps I was stepping into an uncertain future.

At the supper break, my mother arrived at the stage door, her face pinched by the cold and worry.

"They're going to expel you if you don't drop out of the play. What do you say?"

I was wearing my school blazer with its emblem and motto sewn on the breast pocket.

"This, this is what I say." And I ripped off the patch.

I went back to Trinity the next day to collect a few things from my locker to find myself surrounded by a mob of previously indifferent boys who questioned me about what had happened, then exclaiming how lucky I was to be escaping, and, as I left carrying my satchel, they started to cheer and applaud, only to be quickly swooped upon by anxious flapping teachers.

As I passed the headmaster, standing by the front door, he said, "You're making a big mistake, but I suppose I should say good luck. You're going to need it."

The day was crisp and bright as I walked home from the West Side, feeling an almost violent sense of freedom and possibility. And a few days later I found myself at a much more congenial place.

The Tutoring School, in the East 50s, was run by an unsmiling lady with a short haircut who wore brogues. The arrangement was you'd go for five hours a day and have separate lessons alone with English, Latin, and mathematics teachers and then leave—no sports, no other activities, no connection with other students—just right as far as I was concerned. And with this intensive instruction, I got into Christ Church, Oxford.

But before that, I was going to see my father, who was living in Majorca.

"And you'll love the food over there," my stepfather said. "You like food."

I did not like my unwished-for and, I thought, undeserved corpulence.

"Yes."

"And you haven't seen your father for . . ." the mild question hung. My mother wasn't sure.

"Five or six years, I think."

I knew but didn't want it to seem important, for their sake.

"I envy you," my stepfather said. "Your age, no responsibilities, going to Europe for the first time. Here's to you." A glass was raised by both of them.

"Thanks." I lifted mine in reply.

"He'll be so glad to see you again."

"I wonder what the new wife is like," said my stepfather.

"I'm sure he'll be happy with her," said my mother.

The plane took eleven hours from New York to Lisbon and then another few to Barcelona.

My mother refused to step onto a plane for many years after our return from Dublin in 1945, and I had become frightened of flying, ever since a couple of years earlier when a plane I'd been in had dropped a mile of height just after the voice from the dim loudspeaker told us we were over the Rockies. I'd been looking furtively in my seat at the pictures in *Playboy,* the new magazine, and as the plane lurched and jumped I'd lost my erection.

In the Lisbon airport café, I had a cup of coffee. The workers about to start their morning shift were eating bread and garlic and drinking small glasses of white alcohol. I was thrilled to be in a new world, especially since it was the Old one.

The smaller plane landed in Majorca. After I'd had my passport souvenired with a Spanish stamp, I was approached by a Spaniard, stout, mustached, and damp from the heat.

"I'm to help you with your things," he said. "Your father

asked me to guide you through Customs." He smiled and offered to take the carton of Marlboros I'd purchased cheaply at the Barcelona airport, leaving me to carry my duffel bag, books, and magazines.

In the hall inside, carrying my bags, the Spaniard having disappeared along with my cigarettes, I saw my father for the first time in five years. We faced each other for a minute, then hugged. I found myself kissing the lapel of the taller man's light gray jacket. I was introduced to my new stepmother, Kathleen, a pretty woman in her late forties, who'd spent a lot of time in the sun. I was indecisive for a moment whether to just smile, shake hands, or kiss this stranger. I sensed I was the stronger and gave her a kiss, as a sign of acceptance.

A car drove us to the other part of the island along thin roads guarded by trees unfamiliar to me with open land to either side. We sat in the back, wedged together, talking, each of us wishing to make a good impression. The other two said what a valuable and trusted friend the airport Spaniard was.

We arrived at the town. As we drove past a small square, I fell in love with a beautiful girl of perhaps my own age or a little younger, maybe sixteen, slim and graceful in her shapeless dress, with short dark hair and eyes that seemed to be longing for something. She looked toward me in the back of the black car, and I felt I could be with her forever.

The car arrived at the bottom of a wide stone staircase. There were houses on either side, my father's rented one about halfway up the 365 steps, the number of days in the year having some religious penitent significance.

The window of my room looked out on a small garden. I touched the weathered shutters as though all the centuries of European history were in them.

My stepmother had made a dinner of Spanish sausage and rice, and several bottles of red wine were opened and praised by my father as good, the first, a Marqués de Murrieta, being the best and most expensive, the others good for their price. After coffee, my father looked at my stepmother and nodded. She said she felt tired and was going to bed early. My father and I were left alone. I suppose I'd been looking forward to this for a long time. My memories of him were fond.

When I was seven, we were going to the cinema one day and were waiting on O'Connell Street for the light to change. As we started to cross, he reached down and took my hand, holding it with a gentle pressure. No other male adult had done that. I'd never forgotten it.

And when I was nine, he'd met me off the bus my mother had put me on and we'd gone to his large dark flat in Mount Street and he'd made me an omelet for lunch and then we drank tea and had a nice talk. He was sympathetic and kind and curious about what was going on in my life.

There was another, less happy, memory from earlier in this period. He'd come to collect me from where my mother was staying with her parents. We'd gone for a walk, my little legs struggling to keep up with his long stride. We'd sat on a bench and he started to cry.

"Why are you crying, Daddy?"

He patted his eyes and wiped his nose with his handkerchief and said, "Ask your mother."

But that was a long time ago.

Sitting opposite each other, my father poured us each a glass from a new bottle of good-for-its-price wine.

I was almost eighteen, he almost forty-eight. Conversation traveled easily from one subject to another. He seemed interested in what school had been like, my beginnings in the theater, what I felt about soon going to university in England. He said he hoped to move back to Ireland where there'd always be a room for me. We drank more wine.

Then as though to put to rest some doubt, he said, "You

know, even though I've remarried, it doesn't mean I don't still love your mother."

"No, I'm sure it doesn't. I'm sure she still loves you too."

"I know she does and if she hadn't met that man, that man," he repeated, "everything wouldn't have turned out the way it did." He poured himself another glass of wine.

I had a boil on my right ear and started to play with it, edging and pushing it, as unobtrusively as possible, hoping that, after several disagreeable weeks, I could get it to burst. I felt it a slight disfigurement and wished it gone before I saw again the girl in the shapeless dress from the square. I stopped to accept another glass of wine.

"That damned war, if it hadn't been for that, none of this would ever have happened." He paused and then asked, "Do you like Shaw?"

Unsure of this change of subject, I said, "Uh."

"The greatest playwright of the past hundred years. I think of him as the Master." He said this last word with an emphasis meant to convey both perspicacity and reverence. My father had written a play once, I remembered, which had been performed in Dublin.

"Yes, he's very good."

My hand returned to the boil.

"*Saint Joan, Major Barbara, Pygmalion,*" he listed the plays.

"Oscar Wilde is good too," I said. "Sometimes. I think." This was the first opinion I had ventured. I wanted to show I knew something about plays and playwrights. He seemed to.

"Overrated. A few good lines, I'll grant you that, but terribly overrated. I don't know what anyone would see in him compared to Shaw. The Master I call him," he repeated. "Think of the plays: *Saint Joan, Major Barbara, Pygmalion.*"

He poured himself another glass of wine, emptying the bottle and putting it alongside the two we'd finished since my stepmother had gone to bed. He rose to open another bottle.

Standing by the table, pulling the cork, tall, he looked thin in his light gray suit, with something frail in his thinness. My father returned to his chair and poured us each another glass.

A silence fell. My father stared down at the floor as I worked on the boil. Then my father said, "Don't misunderstand me."

"No, you're right. I think Shaw is better than Wilde," I said, lying.

"I'm very happy to be married again. She's very good to me."

"I'm sure she is. She seems very nice."

"If it weren't for him I'd never have done it."

"I'm sure you'll be happy together. She seems very nice," I said to him. "Don't think about the past."

"If it hadn't been for him . . ." He paused, took a swallow of wine, then continued, "I wouldn't have written my play. That's why I call him the Master."

"Oh. That's a good reason," I said.

We knocked back the wine and as quickly the glasses were refilled.

"He's sort of . . . dry though," I said. "Don't you think, sometimes. I mean, brilliant certainly but not very . . . sexy." This was a word much in use in my group in New York. "But brilliant of course."

"I'm not sure what you mean. No, of course not 'sexy.'" He said the word as though it tasted bad in his mouth but then continued agreeably so as not to distance the unfamiliar person opposite. "But the intellect, the construction. Everything in its proper place, nothing left to chance. A toast to the Master." He emptied his glass and poured another.

Something was happening with the boil, something exciting, pus seemed to be concentrating itself toward the head.

"That man," he said.

"Which one?" I asked.

I was confused somewhat by the wine, distracted by my boil, but trying to keep on top of my father's Dodgem car style of late night conversation: steer into a subject, go sideways into another, and then bump into the first one again.

"If it hadn't been for him, nothing would have changed."

Finally, it happened; an extra bit of pressure from the nail released whatever had been inside. I took a handkerchief from my pocket to tidy up the ear. At first I brought the handkerchief to my nose, as a sort of decoy, and then to my ear, as though a quite normal progression. But the man opposite wasn't noticing. He was staring at the glass he was holding in his lap.

"A toast to the Master." He raised his glass, emptied it, and poured another.

There was some blood on the handkerchief. I pressed it back to my ear, knowing I'd feel conspicuous if there'd been more people in the room. But there was only my father. I felt drunk and tired, wanting to go to bed but relieved because the boil was gone, at last.

A few days later I saw the girl again in the same square. I walked fast to try to get near her but was unable to before she disappeared down a narrow street into a doorway. I never saw her again.

Six

I had been at Oxford for a year and had failed my exams, which was not a surprise since I had spent most of my time away from Oxford in London, where, having sought out and been accepted by a raffish set of roués, gamblers, idlers, procurers, pranksters, criminals, call girls, strippers, artists, and drunks—to my mind the perfect society for an eighteen-year-old—I felt at home.

I had hardly any money and so my time in nightclubs, at chemin de fer tables, and cigar stores and tie shops meant I had accumulated a certain amount of debt, with the consequent bounced checks, which was burdensome in a slightly different way than it is today.

In the halcyon days before credit cards, you could come and go in a hotel and run up a tab or order a handmade suit, say, and ask for the bill to be sent to the hotel and then, suit on back, return to Oxford and then you'd need the mental resources to invent a variety of preposterous excuses as to why you couldn't pay the hotel or the tailor and the emotional fortitude to handle the threats of litigation and then, when up against the financial wall, send a small portion of the money, receive a polite letter acknowledging receipt, and start all over again.

But, as is often the way, good times and excess can be followed by the lemon juice of dreariness. As a result of failing my exams, I was rusticated, which sounds like a form of torture but is only an old university custom which meant I wasn't allowed within three miles of the city of Oxford until the next round of exams the following spring, which was why in December of that year, 1959, I found myself, broke, staying with my mother and little sister, Susie (her father was Stuart Scheftel), in a house in a suburb of Dublin. Why my mother was there I don't know, and why for most of our time there my stepfather was in New York, I also don't know.

We had just sat down to dinner one evening, my grandfather and grandmother also present, and his favorite dish, mutton with onion sauce, being served, when the telephone rang. I answered it.

"Michael, it's Hilton."

(Hilton Edwards with Micheál Mac Liammóir founded the Gate in the 1920s, the first experimental theater in Ireland. They produced mainly European plays as opposed to the Irish fare at the Abbey. Orson Welles had worked there as a sixteen-year-old and a couple of years later, my mother. Orson, Hilton, and Micheál had formed an enduring friendship. I had been Hilton's assistant on a play the previous summer.)

"What I'm calling about, dear boy, is what are you doing for the next few months?"

"Nothing much," I answered and didn't add "except for living in the Dublin suburbs with my mother and sister, driving an old car drunk at night and not opening any letters from creditors."

He continued, his voice a robust mixture of theatrical projection, years of cigar and pipe smoking, and general well-being. "That's wonderful. We're starting with *Chimes at Midnight* and then doing *Twelfth Night*. We're rehearsing in London, then going on a short tour, and want you to have a few small parts and to be my assistant. Probably more fun than being with your darling mother and sister in the suburbs of Dublin."

"Yes, of course, sure, I'd love to. Who's 'we'?"

"Oh, didn't I say? Orson and I."

We began rehearsing in the cold early winter of 1960 in a large room on the second floor of a building in Russell Square, near the British Museum. We had a read-through of

Chimes at Midnight—a version of *Henry IV, 1* and *2*, that Orson had adapted. He was to play Falstaff, Shakespeare's great witty, fat genius, undone by his fleshly desires and broken by Prince Hal's pragmatic ruthlessness.

We finished the reading and Orson said he had a luncheon appointment and that we should carry on without him, guessing, I suppose, that his midday meal would be long and copious. He said he was seeing a potential investor for the production who might put up the money for the costumes.

Hilton started work with the actors with his usual command of staging, if not, always, of character motivation.

"Just do what I'm asking and figure out why in your spare time."

His skill was delineation and the stage picture. He was also a master of lighting.

The next morning, I happened to get in the lift just as it was closing, to find myself alone with Orson. He was smoking a large cigar, filling the small cubicle with its delicious fragrance, and had a box of Henry Clays under his arm. There was also a scent of eau de cologne, with a brooding sweetness to it.

("Caron," my mother said later when I asked what it could have been.)

He smiled and asked, "Would you like a cigar?" and offered me one from the box, with its Havana stamps and verifications.

"Thank you. I would."

He was fuller-figured than he had been four years earlier, really quite heavy. He was wearing a black outfit of loose cut and a white shirt with a dark bow tie folded under the collar. And, although he signaled a benign awareness of our previous time together, he seemed distracted somehow. I put it down to his concern about money for the costumes.

Every day, at the beginning of rehearsal, he'd give me a large cigar, so that I, earning £6 a week as an assistant and actor, was the poorest big cigar smoker in London. His gifts did not go unnoticed by the other small-part actors and so I found myself gravitating to some of the featured actors, Patrick Bedford, who was Hilton's boyfriend, and Keith Baxter, who was playing Prince Hal, being my main two friends.

The rehearsals were taking the usual slow course when, after a week or so, Orson approached Hilton at the desk from which he conducted the day's work.

"I've got a terrible toothache," Orson said.

"My dear boy, you must see a dentist."

"Yes, I think I should."

And so Orson went to see his dentist. Who was in Rome.

Which was the last we saw of him until we all met at the train station in London to travel to the coast to get on the boat which would take the company to Belfast, where we were to open two nights later. We all felt that, perhaps, we weren't as ready as we should have been, no matter how much Hilton had been drilling us, what with our star not having been around for the last few weeks.

On the train and then the boat, in Orson's cabin were his wife, Paola, and their young daughter, Beatrice, and her nanny and Mrs. Rodgers, Orson's assistant, who was coaching him on his lines for Falstaff which he didn't yet seem to have a handle on.

We arrived in Belfast in the early evening and all, except Hilton and I, went to their, according to station, various hotels and bed-and-breakfasts.

Part of my job as assistant was to walk the lights for Hilton so that as he was refining the lighting plot, I, knowing the blocking, would stand in the various positions which needed definition. I loved working late at night in the theater and, except for a taxi crash on the way to my boardinghouse on a rain-slicked underlit road of that unfortunate city, when I got in my bed at 3 A.M., I considered I'd had a good day.

We were due to reconvene for a run-through that morning at ten, which came quickly.

By this time, I was wearing my shirts with a bow tie tucked under my collar, an affectation that was not unnoticed by my fellow small-part actors.

The company was assembled in the Mezzanine Bar when Orson arrived sometime after ten. He greeted everyone jovially, gave me a cigar, had a cup of coffee, told a few jokes, and then gave us a pep talk, saying that he knew we were all, all of us, going to open the following night (with the implication that of the burdens to be lifted, his was by far the heaviest, and so who were we to worry?) and though we, the company, might feel under-rehearsed (we'd never had a full run-through), everything would be all right. He knew that. Then he told us a story from the last days of the Mercury Theatre which, though it was meant to hearten us, ended with a description of what had happened when the mechanics of a stage lift had failed and the lift had crashed, injuring several actors. But the show had gone on, more or less, and so we weren't in such bad shape. We didn't have any contraptions like that and so nothing could go wrong. We'd just have to roll up our sleeves and get to work.

We would not leave the theater for more than twenty-four hours.

Back in London, while Orson was away, having his tooth fixed in Rome, Hilton had blocked a scene in which Falstaff would walk upstage and I was directed to enter, running from the wings with my sword pointed. This was the scene in which Falstaff pretends to be killed in battle.

After the first rehearsal, Hilton took his pipe out of his mouth, looked at me, and shouted.

"Aiyee!"

"Aiyee?" I repeated, questioning, the word being unfamiliar.

"Yes, yes, dear boy. *Aiyee!* Shout it as you rush on with your sword, to show you're a serious assailant, capable of killing."

I took the cigar out of my mouth that Hilton had offered me earlier and, running from behind the white tape mark on the rehearsal floor with my arm outstretched (no props yet), I shouted, "Aiyee!"

The timid gentleman who'd been hired a few days before as Orson's stand-in threw his hands up, as if to show he'd been frightened, and ran off toward another white tape mark.

"That's the way," Hilton said.

We came to this moment about three in the morning, and everyone was tired, having been onstage without any real break since Orson's little pep talk seventeen hours earlier.

Orson was smoking his cigar and staring into the small copy of the text which was always with him. He was dressed in the Falstaff costume, belly protuberant, his and Falstaff's, and had turned from downstage and was walking upstage, concentrating on learning his lines from the little book. My cue came and I rushed on, steel sword out.

"Aiyee!" I shouted.

I missed Orson by not very much and exited stage left, having done my job,

"Hold it!"

Orson's heavy voice boomed out and I wondered if it could be in any way to do with me, my acting.

He began, "I don't care if none of the music cues are working. I don't care if the stage manager is *sitting in the house,* when he should be backstage, working on the *music cues.* I don't care if some people are tired. This is the *theater*! That's what happens."

The boom grew louder as he said, "But, when at three o'clock in the morning, in Belfast in the north of Ireland, Michael Lindsay-Hogg tries to kill me, I quit."

And Orson walked off the stage. The rehearsal stopped.

What had happened, to *us,* since that morning in the bar when he'd given me a cigar before the pep talk, to make him tip this bucket of embarrassment on me? I found myself alone, fixed,

in the wing I'd "Aiyee'd" into, the other small-part actors snig-
gering, I felt, as they went to hang out in the dressing rooms for
who knew how long in this night which showed no signs of ending: so much for those big cigars and bow ties under his collar.

Micheál Mac Liammóir, the cofounder with Hilton Edwards
of the Gate Theatre, was a flamboyant actor, artist, designer,
memoirist, fluent in six languages, including Irish. Iago to
Orson's movie Othello, friend to Orson since his short stint at
the Gate in the early 1930s, and one of the very few un-
ashamedly homosexual men I'd met, which, at that time, we
must remember, took a reservoir of courage or an almost inso-
lent degree of nonchalance. (In England, consenting males
found together were still being imprisoned.)

He and Hilton, both in late middle age, were still known
around Dublin as "the Boys" and made an endearing, if mismatched couple, although they had both found other, younger,
companions. Hilton, stout, bald, energetic, huffing and puffing,
large frame spectacles on a sizeable nose, tobacco ash on his
lapels, looked like an avuncular bank manager; Micheál was
elaborately dressed, corseted, a daily application of pancake
makeup, a little mascara, and a jet black toupee, which, as an
evening wore on, would sometimes adjust itself to a more rakish
angle so from a distance you might think he was wearing a beret.
He was in Belfast that night because there had been a plan, to be
unrealized, for him to replace the old actor who was playing
King Henry IV. As this actor sat on the wooden throne, under
his wig and crown, his hearing aid was transmitting intermit-
tent bursts from a local radio station. But, for Micheál, if he were
asked to take over any part, it would be the young Prince Hal or
nothing, which, for many reasons, was an impossibility.

"Dear boy," Micheál began, having searched and found me
backstage where I was still rooted. He put his arm through mine
and walked us back and forth across the stage talking the while
in a conspiratorial phlegmy whisper which could probably be
heard in the tenth row.

"He's such a monster sometimes. Oh, I could tell you some stories. But that's for another, happier time. What occurred had nothing to do with you or anything you did. At times, when we're depressed or tired, or hungry"—he stressed this last word—"we lash out and it's usually at someone we care about. You might say he needed an ally to help him release his fear. Yes, fear; he knows he's not really ready and he knows also that you're resilient and wise and talented and that you'd see it for what it was. Imagine how crushed another young actor might have felt to get that thrown at him."

We stopped our perambulation and stood, looking out at the empty house, the others having gone for quick naps; there wasn't really anything to eat, it was three in the morning, the dry sandwiches from hours ago were finished. I was much relieved by Micheál's sweetness. Even if it was snake oil, I was glad of its balm.

Then, in an effort I suspect to make me feel sympathetic to Orson (he didn't really need to), he decided to include me in some of the production worries. His voice dropped to a lower note, something intimate and hushed, like that of a brothel keeper acknowledging a familiar perversity. "There are money problems. He designed some wonderful costumes, and then no one would pay for them. Don't tell me you haven't noticed that what you and the others are wearing are somewhat, shall we say, Sherwood Foresty? They're all rented from the television series *Robin Hood.* Perhaps you'd recognize the source more easily if everyone had a quiver and arrows on their back. I'd have thought the little green peaked caps would have given it away to someone with such a good eye, as you have. How's your mother by the way?"

"Good, I think, the last time I spoke to her."

"I must see her when I'm back in Dublin. We *will* have a lot to talk about. Now go and get yourself a cup of cold coffee and don't worry about any of this. He didn't mean it."

"Thank you. You've been a great help."

I walked back into the wings, poured myself a mug of cold acrid coffee from the uncharged machine, and waited.

About twenty minutes later there was a commotion from near Orson's dressing room, powerful voices raised, doors banging. I was on the other side of the stage and so just had a sense of something disagreeable going on. I found out later that Orson had thrown Micheál out of his dressing room, accusing him of *betrayal*, saying he never wanted to see him again because he wouldn't take over the part of the old King, and had slammed the door in his face.

Rehearsal was called again at 4:15 and Orson appeared, in seeming good humor, having fortified himself with a roast chicken and red wine which had arrived from his hotel shortly before 3 A.M.

I had another character to play, and after we'd re-rehearsed the battle scene, without incident, I went up to the dressing room and experimented with a pale makeup which made my face rather blank, and just before my entrance had pushed my hair forward, hoping it would make me look a bit dim, which I thought might suit the character. It was now sometime after five.

As I entered, Orson had started to say a line, but when he saw me the words turned into a chuckle, a chortle, and then his tired eyes creased and he laughed as though he were more entertained by my makeup and appearance than by anything ever before in his life. The other actors laughed also and I felt my place regained. I was loved again.

Children were at school, housewives on their second pot of tea, and men in their office, or at the docks, when we left the theater, red eyes blinking at the pewter sky. And so the first time we ever performed the play in sequence and its proper running time was on opening night. The curtain was delayed a while because Orson had arrived at the theater before the half-hour call and fired the nice actress playing Lady Percy, who was already putting on her makeup, and the understudy had to have the Maid Marian dress altered, and Hilton in his dinner jacket had to go on for the understudy who had been playing the (female) Prologue. The tears of the ex–Lady Percy could be heard as she packed up her makeup box.

The production got quite good reviews for its Belfast launch, and I was praised, with some others, for giving solid support.

Once we were up and running, except for the matinee days, I'd get up around one in the afternoon and meander down to the tea shop located on the floor above a place which sold corsets and have what my mother always called the best meal in the world, a full Irish breakfast with eggs and rashers and tomatoes and fried bread and soda bread, then thick white toast with marmalade, and many cups of milky tea. After, I'd walk the half hour to the theater where I'd read or somehow pass the time till I started to put on my makeup and then my little green peaked cap.

And after the show, some of the other actors and I would nip across the street to the Opera Pub and get a drink or two in before the 10:30 closing. I liked talking to some of the regulars with their hard, bitter accents, their nicotine-stained fingers the color of old mustard. Then it would be back to the boarding-house where the landlady would have laid out a plate of cold ham and salad. There'd be a bottle of a sort of watery mayonnaise and a pot of tea covered by a cozy.

After two weeks, we went to Dublin, to the large Gaiety The-atre, to carry on with *Chimes* and, in theory, to start rehearsing *Twelfth Night* in preparation for our short European tour.

In *Chimes at Midnight,* at the end of Act I, my first character had a couple of lines, and feeling them to be important, I wanted to give them their value. I'd get to the end of my first line, let it sink in with the audience, and then crank up and deliver my sec-ond line. At one of the last performances in Belfast, Orson had jumped in with Falstaff's line before I'd finished speaking. I assumed this was a mistake.

But in Dublin on the first night, again Orson interrupted me, and I gave him what I hoped he'd perceive as a dark look.

The next night nothing happened, so I felt my brown-eyed warning had done its job.

But on the following night, I hadn't even finished my first line when in he came again, headlong as a stallion, running right through my second line as well. I knew I would have to speak to him about this. I went to his dressing room when the curtain came down.

"Um, Orson, I don't know if you've noticed, but sometimes you seem to be jumping in before I've finished my lines."

He'd already started to relight his cigar, left in the ashtray before the first act. The match flamed, and he looked up from under his brow as he concentrated on this important business.

"Yes. I have noticed. You're right, I do. I've been meaning to ask you a question about those lines."

He puffed a few puffs, shook out the match, went on, "You know, you take a long pause between the end of your first line and the beginning of your second one. So what I've been meaning to ask you"—he looked at me as though my opinion might be of value—"is would you like us to take the Intermission before, after, or during your line?"

"Oh," I said. "You think I should tighten that pause?"

"I would."

"It's too long?"

"A bit."

"Oh. Okay."

And I realized that as a young actor I still had a lot to learn.

Then, a few days later, I had another question to ask, this time of Hilton. I needed to go to England for three days to retake my Oxford exams for which I'd been studying in much the same way as Orson had been learning his part when he'd been in Rome. But I was afraid I'd be missed and let down the production.

"Oh, don't worry, dear boy," Hilton said. "We'll put the

understudy on. If there is one. I'm not sure. Otherwise we can
give your lines to one of the other actors or perhaps cut them for
a few days."

So, no problem there, which I was glad about because not
only could I take my exams at Oxford but also spend a little
time with the girl I'd met in London while we'd been there
rehearsing.

"Also, Hilton, I was wondering what part I'll have when we
start *Twelfth Night*."

"I'm afraid there's a glitch there," Hilton said, taking a draw
on his pipe, sending out a cloud of Kapp and Peterson's No. 1
mix.

Could it be I wouldn't have a part, that Hilton and Orson
hadn't liked my acting? But it was worse.

"The fact is the money's fallen through, not that it ever was
there in the first place. A shame. We had bookings in Paris and
Brussels and Rome. But there you are. See you when you're back
from England, dear boy."

I had not at that time been to Paris or Brussels or Rome and
was mightily disappointed, but at least it wasn't anything to do
with my acting.

I took the exams in Oxford and was in London that evening.

Sandy was a stripper, two years older than I, a beguiling combination of the young French sex-bomb Brigitte Bardot and
Bugs Bunny, pretty, with a full mouth and long teeth with a
gap between. Sometimes she wore her blond hair down and
sometimes in a modified beehive, the fashion for young women
at the time. She said she was English but had a French accent
and later told me she'd run away from her family in France. I'd
met her in January in a strip club where I knew the owner, and
we got on right away, perhaps because we were both so young,
she, twenty-one and I, nineteen. Asleep on a Sunday morning in
a little place where I was staying, we were almost asphyxiated

together because of a carbon monoxide leak from a gas heater. We felt sleepier and sleepier till I blearily thought the sleep was unnatural and had thrown open a window. She was funny and oddly innocent, with a modesty about her body when she wasn't onstage. She seemed to be friends with many of the people she'd pass on the streets of nighttime Soho. I liked her very much.

She would work in two or three different clubs, starting in early evening and going back and forth between them. A club would be a dark room, sometimes on the second floor above a firetrap staircase, sometimes a basement. A small bar would have versions of whiskey, gin, brandy, and beer, and there'd be three or four stools in front of it. In the rest of the room was a haphazard arrangement of a few tables and mismatched chairs and a small platform on which the girl or woman would strip down to panties and pasties. Some were older than Sandy and did not have her lithe body, and I wondered what would happen to them when they were washed up. There was a lamp lashed to a pole which shined an unforgiving white light on the women—click on, when the act was about to start, click off, when it was over. The barman did this job knowing it wasn't likely he'd be serving drinks during the performance. The customers who'd been sitting at the tables would scoot their chairs without lifting their bottoms right up to the edge of the platform when the light would come on and then seemed stranded there when the light went off, as though returning to their table was a more difficult task than leaving it.

As she took off her clothes, Sandy was careful not to look directly at any of the nearby men, but she would sometimes catch my eye and smile. I would wait till she finished her last show around 2 A.M., then go back to her small room, also in Soho.

I telephoned the stage manager in Dublin trying to get an extra day in London with Sandy and gave some excuse about the planes being full.

"Oh, don't worry. There's no need to hurry," he said amiably.

"What do you mean?"

"You'll see when you get back."

I took the extra day, and then the night accompanying Sandy from Wardour Street to Dean Street and then to Meard Street, carrying her little bag of cosmetics, comb, panties and tassels, and tampons, just in case.

We wrote. I received a letter from her which told me her father had found out where she was, and she had moved to Düsseldorf and was working in a club where she'd be till four or five in the morning, and in between her stripping she was expected to sit and drink with the customers, which she didn't like. She finished by asking how I was and was I happy? I wrote back asking her to be careful, but I never heard from her again.

I arrived back in Dublin late the next afternoon and was at the theater for Half Hour to find the dressing rooms deserted. I went out in the street to see an audience coming in as was normal, and I went into the theater. At 8:05, the curtain rose on a bare stage with a lectern in the center. Orson entered to applause, wearing an enveloping black suit, with bow tie tucked under his white silk collar. He explained that someone in the company was ill (who?) and so he was there to entertain them himself. Then, with a self-deprecating little laugh, he offered them their money back if this plan wasn't satisfactory. Then he talked, told stories, and read beautifully from Isak Dinesen, one of his favorite authors.

I never knew what happened in the few days I was away. Maybe Orson got bored by the play, or maybe the business wasn't what had been expected, or maybe he thought he'd get twice the audience, some for the play, some for the solo act, which he probably enjoyed more and he could get to dinner earlier, no costume and makeup to take off, and a running time he could expand or contract, according to how it was going or how hungry he was. I think we did *Chimes at Midnight* a few more times, but I don't really remember; anyway it didn't seem to matter. It wasn't going anywhere. No other production. No tour.

Several evenings each week of our month in Dublin, after whichever show, Orson would ask Keith Baxter and me to join him and Paola for dinner upstairs at his favorite restaurant, Bernardo's, which served Italian food, good for Dublin, and kept the kitchen open late for us. Orson and Keith would talk about Orson's plans for a movie of *Chimes at Midnight* with Keith, of course, to repeat his triumphant Prince Hal. Paola seemed charmed by Keith, as we all were. A tall, strapping, very handsome man, part Welsh boyo and part wicked raconteur, whose career had first prospered under the benign or otherwise influence of the iron-fisted suede-gloved impresario Binkie Beaumont.

Orson asked me what I wanted to do.

"Act," I said.

A look of perturbation crossed his face. "Anything else?"

"Or direct."

"Direct. Yes, that might be better. Film, theater?"

"Both. In fact I thought I'd like to do a stage version of *The Trial,* the Kafka," I explained unnecessarily to him. "I had this idea of the set being made of paper bags and when they arrest Josef K. in bed at the beginning, they break through the paper bag walls."

"That could be good."

I felt the emotional sun shining on me.

"And then what?" he asked. "It's a good start, the flimsiness of things, but then what?"

I had been so taken with my first idea that I hadn't gone much further, except I wanted Hilton to play the judge.

"I'm not sure yet."

"Well, keep working on it. *The Trial* is an important book. I should reread it."

I never did *The Trial* but he did a baroque film version two years later with Tony Perkins as Josef K.

He finished his main dish and looked down balefully as though the plate, now empty, had somehow deceived him. After a moment he said to me, "It's always a good idea to start where things are fresh and you can make your own way quickly without interference."

I knew about the freedom he'd had when he made *Citizen Kane*, and how it never happened again.

"Mongolia," he said.

"Mongolia?" I questioned.

"Yes," Orson said emphatically. "I hear they're starting up their own studio there. It's a fascinating place."

"You've been there?" I asked.

"Sure, when I was your age."

I wondered if he were pulling my leg. I didn't want to be caught out, but why would he tease me, knowing I was so eager.

"Look into it," he said sympathetically and turned to Keith and asked, "Why would I give him advice if I didn't think it might be useful?"

"You wouldn't, Orson," Keith said and looked at me and raised his eyebrows as if to say, "Your guess is as good as mine."

I took a sip of wine to give myself time to consider this idea of going to Mongolia, when Orson asked if I'd liked Oxford and was I going back.

I replied to the first question, "Some of it," then the second, "Probably not. I want to work."

"I never went to university," he said, "but I'd have liked Oxford, I think."

"Yes?"

"Yes, the handmade shirts and shoes and the naughtiness."

He winked and laughed, as though he knew how I'd spent most of my time.

And then, as we finished that bottle and he ordered another, delivered by the waiters who seemed quite content to be serving this man at this late hour, he'd talk, soliciting our opinions too, about this, that, and everything, and his knowledge, wit, insight, originality of view and opinion, compassion, depth of experience, heady highs, and frustrating harsh lows left one never wanting to be away from him, not to be out of his company. Then dinner would be over and he and Paola would go back to the Shelbourne Hotel and it would be as though something desirable and sustaining had been taken away and you'd feel a little deflated.

Near the end of the Dublin time, as we were smoking our cigars after dinner, he told me he was going to direct Ionesco's *Rhinoceros* in London with Laurence Olivier and would I like to assist him on it.

"I'd love to."

"If it works out, that'll be marvelous," my mother said when I told her.

"What do you mean 'if it works out'?" I asked, suddenly angry.

I could tell my anger upset her and she said, "I don't mean anything except what I said. It's just that things don't always work out the way we want."

"I know that. But he asked me himself. I'm not inventing it."

"I know you're not," my mother said. "I'm sure it will then. Work out."

I left the room, to punish her for dampening my enthusiasm but with the worry that her wariness must have come from somewhere.

My mother gave two little parties in our house in the suburbs for Orson during his month in Dublin. One was after the show, with food and drinks, a dozen or so people, including her aunt, the actress Shelah Richards, for whom Sean O'Casey had written his young women's parts, and Eddy Lindsay-Hogg and Kathleen. Orson and Eddy chatted amiably, Orson laughing exuberantly at Eddy's jokes. I joined and came to mention that a few years earlier I'd worked as a prompter on an off-Broadway production for the talented (unstoppable) Sidney Lumet. I pronounced the *t*, Lume*t*.

Orson said, "Surely not, it must be French. Lu-may."

"I don't think he's French," I said. "And anyway, it's Lum*et*," I said as if to vouch for someone who'd been kind to me.

"Well, it should be Lu-may," he said with conviction.

(Sidney had already directed the faultless *12 Angry Men* and was on his way to over fifty years of achievement. I was surprised there was something that Orson didn't know, but I put it down to the fact that he hadn't been in America for a few years and wasn't up on the younger directors.)

After the food, Eddy took one of Orson's cigars, lighting it and puffing contentedly. On this evening, Eddy Lindsay-Hogg was careful with the drink and seemed somewhat shy, the lower dog to the larger, but also alert, not wanting to spoil old memories.

So attached did I feel to one of these men that I was somewhat distant to the other, but hoped my father wouldn't notice.

And then on the night before Orson left for London, when we were done at the Gaiety, there was a small cocktail party. I was waiting for the bell to ring so I could greet him myself.

I was aware of how massive he seemed in the doorway, shoulders, bulk, and dark clothes filling the frame. He seemed somewhat unsteady as though he'd been drinking, his eyes little currents in pink jelly. He joined our party, Keith, Hilton, a few others. (He and Micheál Mac Liammóir had not yet made up.) We all drank and told stories and made jokes about our recent time together.

I went upstairs to get something to show to the others, a photo I think. On my way down, I saw Orson standing alone in the hall, as if marooned, as though unsure, a little turn this way, a little turn that. From above, his large dark head on his large dark suit squashed together.

I called from the landing, "Orson? Anything I can get for you? Are you okay?"

"I'm fine," he said without looking at me. "Come down. We'll go on with the party."

I went down the stairs and crossed into the living room. He didn't follow and only rejoined the group several minutes later.

By now, the party had run its course and it was time for everyone to leave.

At the door, Orson kissed my mother on the cheek, then turned to me and said, "I'll call you from London in a few days and tell you when to come over for *Rhinoceros.*"

He left, leaning heavily on the outdoor stair railing, and got into the waiting sedan with difficulty, as though how to put his large self into the small back seat was something of a puzzle.

The next morning I was in my mother's room while she had tea and toast in bed.

"I think last night went well," she said. "I hope Orson had a good time. You'll be off to London soon, I suppose."

"Looks like it," I said with a mildly triumphant smile to remind us both of our previous conversation on the matter.

"Yes, Mrs. Kane," my mother said, turning toward the door. Mrs. Kane was our nice lugubrious housekeeper. Citizeness Kane.

"Mrs. Scheftel?" Mrs. Kane hesitated before she went on.

"Yes, Mrs. Kane?"

"In the basement this morning there was a large pool of liquid."

"Oh. One of the pipes broken, do you think?" my mother asked.

"I've cleaned it up."

"Thank you. Do you think we need a plumber?"

"I don't think so. Not a plumber."

She paused as though she had an idea of what it was we needed, if not a plumber.

"It was . . . pee, I think."

Mrs. Kane did not say this in a censorious way, just with the weary voice of a woman who'd cleaned up after many an Irish party.

I didn't see or hear from Orson for three years. The production of *Rhinoceros* was an unhappy one with Laurence Olivier apparently dismissing Orson before it opened.

Seven

A few weeks later, my mother, her sister Pam, who was also my darling gentle godmother, and I had dinner at home, and after went into the living room with another bottle of wine and my mother continued in the same vein she'd started in the other room—stories of her younger days in London and Hollywood. (She was now forty-six.)

When my mother first started working in English films, age twenty or so, she lived on a houseboat on the Thames near Chiswick. Her boat mates were two impoverished young actors who had only one good pair of socks between them. On the boat they'd gone barefoot or worn thick wool socks under gum boots, so if one of them went on an audition he'd wear the socks, but if they both had to go, they'd flip a coin, and one would wear the socks, and the other would paint his ankles and whatever part of his foot that would show above his one pair of shoes with black shoe polish.

Although it had a few pretty houses inhabited by some of the left-wing intelligentsia, I imagine Chiswick in the early 1930s to have been a doleful place, not much money around, with working-class resentment banging against lower-middle-class gentility.

Around this time my mother caught the unwelcome attention of Patrick Hamilton, who later would write the plays *Gas Light* and *Rope* about obsession and murder, which George Cukor and Alfred Hitchcock made into movies.

The nights, my mother remembered, were the worst times, cold and drizzly, as she'd get off a late bus and start the ten-minute walk toward the boat, the streetlamps just ocher lozenges in the murk, and Patrick Hamilton would follow her, going from doorway to side of building to corner to doorway,

*My mother, age twenty-one, at the start
of her career in British films.*

footsteps in the fog, not letting her out of his sight till she ran
up the gangway, hoping one or both of her actor friends would
be onboard. She felt Patrick Hamilton might harm her or even
go so far as to kill her. She feared for her life. (This was not in my
mother's imagination. Patrick Hamilton's obsession with her is
confirmed in chilling detail in the biography by Nigel Jones,
Through a Glass Darkly. In Hamilton's novel, *Hangover Square,* a
character based on my mother is murdered.)

Somewhere around this time she found a lover. She didn't tell us who it was or if he had been her first, but he was unstable and one night threw her down a flight of stairs. He remained on the landing above and watched as she reached for the banister and pulled herself to her feet and limped out of the mean little abode.

Pam may have known of some of this before but I did not. My mother talked till well past midnight. I hadn't spent such a strangely intimate night with my mother ever before and was avid to know as much about her as I could, no matter how troubling.

She talked about her time in Hollywood. About how much she liked Humphrey Bogart.

She said she'd sit in the Warner Bros. commissary with him and Ingrid Bergman while they bitched about the movie they were shooting together, *Casablanca,* saying they didn't think much would happen with it. Bogart had acted, with a shaky Irish accent, with my mother in *Dark Victory,* also with Ronald Reagan, whom Bette Davis referred to, perhaps because of how she judged his acting talent, as "Poor Ronnie Reagan."

In 1949, we went to Los Angeles for Christmas to stay with Charlie Lederer, and for Boy to play golf, and my mother took me, wearing my first suit, gray, with long pants, just the two of us, to lunch at Romanoff's, the hot restaurant of the 1940s, owned by self-styled "Prince" Michael Romanoff, a short, suave, punctiliously well-mannered man with a slim mustache on top of a fleshy upper lip. As my mother and I were leaving we passed a table from which a man's voice called, "Geraldine."

Humphrey Bogart wore a tweed jacket and bow tie and had in front of him a glass of scotch with ice. We joined him and his agent. His manner was shy and modest, and he was very sweet to my mother. And to me, asking what I wanted to do. I didn't know, so I said, "I used to want to be the Lone Ranger. But now I'm not so sure."

"That's okay," he said, as if indecision was to be expected in someone of my age.

"Anyway, there already is a Lone Ranger and Clayton Moore would probably be pretty worried if he heard you were after his job." He winked at me so as to include me in his tease.

"I love baseball," I said.

"I did too when I was young. Maybe you could be a ballplayer."

"My hitting's not so good."

"Don't give up," he said and smiled his singular smile with its signature twitch.

My mother said that when they acted together he told her he thought he'd never really have a big career; he was almost forty and was afraid he'd missed the boat. And then came *The Maltese Falcon.*

She told Pam and me of her friendship in the early 1940s with Charlie Chaplin, saying in conversation he was not so interest-

Front row, left, age eleven, on the baseball team. I got two hits in four years.

ing, but when he wished to describe someone, rather than using words, he'd act out the person with his or her quirks and you'd feel you knew that person.

And then she told us that after a reporter had interviewed her for her upcoming cover story for *Life* magazine, as the reporter was putting away his notebook, he said, "You know Charlie Chaplin was in love with you." My mother said she didn't know, and the reporter told her that Chaplin had hired a private detective to follow my father to see if he could catch him in any indiscretions.

That evening in Ireland, my mother looked at her sister and me, and said, "I didn't believe it. There was never any sense of that between us. But the funny thing is, when Charlie and Oona had their first child, a girl, they named her Geraldine."

And then a story about my godfather, Gene Markey, boulevardier, ex-husband of Hedy Lamarr, and how my mother didn't

My mother on the cover of Life *magazine, 1944. She'd recently had a success playing Mrs. Wilson in a movie about the twenty-eighth President.*

speak to him for a year after he had, by previous conspiratorial plan, left her alone in a hotel suite with Walter Wanger, a famous pouncer. With all that was going on in my mother's life at the time, she said, she didn't need to be dodging and feinting around a desk with a powerful producer. Her gripe with Gene Markey seemed to be that since Walter Wanger left unsatisfied, it might have some adverse effect on her career. It was hard to be a woman on her own in Hollywood, she said.

More wine, and my mother mentioned some other names including one of the Hakim brothers. Raymond and Robert Hakim were producers and I remember feeling the name Raymond Hakim carried with it an exotic air, part carpet salesman, part adventurer, and found myself idly wondering if Michael Hakim would be a good stage name for me but dismissed the idea quickly as being wine-driven.

I was in London a few days later and had been asked to lunch by my stepfather, who was on his way from New York to Ireland to spend some time with my mother and sister.

He was staying at the Ritz Hotel, and so that's where we had lunch, sitting at a favored table on the left in the grand dining room where the large windows, heavily swagged curtains flanking, looked on to Green Park. He told me he'd stayed there sometimes during the war when the dining room windows had been heavily fortified with sandbags and that upstairs he and some pals would be playing poker when the warning sirens sounded. Knowing there wasn't time to leave the hotel and get into the safety of the Underground, they'd continue playing, hoping for distraction in three-of-a-kind or two aces, but as the bombs fell, they'd sometimes get under the table or a desk if the explosions, shaking, shattering glass, and presentiment of mayhem were too frightening, is the word, I suppose.

We ordered and after some desultory conversation, he asked, "How is your mother?"

"She's fine."

"And Susie?"

"Fine too. Probably needing a tooth fairy soon."

He smiled. He loved his only natural child. I was not jealous, we all did.

To continue the conversation, I said, "Ma and Pam and I had a good time a few evenings ago."

"Yes?"

"Yes. Ma was telling us stories of her time in Hollywood."

Our smoked salmon arrived. We squeezed lemon, had a piece of brown bread.

"Much wine?"

"A few bottles. Well, there were the three of us," I said, an explanation of how things worked in Ireland.

He was only a moderate drinker. In the fifty years I knew him, I only saw him intoxicated twice. I could not say that of my mother.

"What was she talking about?"

"Oh, some of the adventures she had when she was living in Hollywood, when we were living there," I clarified, "like Gene Markey trying to set her up with Walter Wanger."

"She's told me about that. What a shit," he said, referring to Gene Markey. Boy was very proprietorial about my mother. He swallowed a bite of his pink smoked fish.

"Anything else?" he asked. He put his knife and fork down.

I wished to be thought sophisticated but it was my innocence which made me answer his question. Innocent, in that I had not considered that my mother would have talked of anything which was not for adult family consumption. I had not thought her revelations were to do with drink; they were more to do with entertaining her sister and me. And she'd have been too proud to ever say to me: "Don't tell your stepfather."

"She told us of a walk-out she'd had with someone called Raymond Hakim, a producer."

I chose the word "walk-out" because I'd heard it used when I was younger to describe an affair which had not meant anything and had had no consequences, and thought it did justice to the way my mother told it.

"How dare you?"

His hand slammed down on the table, agitating the water in the glasses.

"How dare you suggest that your mother would ever, *ever* have anything to do with someone like Raymond Hakim?"

I realized I had stepped on what I thought was grown-up turf, but it was really a dangerous construct of grass, branches, twigs, and leaves which covered a pit into which I was now tumbling and I didn't know how to rescue myself, or him. But I tried.

"I'm sorry. I must have misunderstood. It was late. The wine. It was nothing. She didn't mean it like that, I'm sure. I'm sorry."

The lunch was ruined. He and I never referred to it again. We were both sorry a second course was coming. I couldn't wait for the lunch to be over. Nor, I'm sure, could he.

When I next saw my mother, she showed no sign of resentment that anything I might have told my stepfather had caused any trouble for her. Perhaps they didn't speak of Raymond Hakim.

A few months later we were all in New York and I was studying with a tutor for one last go at my Oxford exams.

One evening, my mother and stepfather and I went to a cocktail party that the actress and singer Paula Laurence gave for Virginia Welles Lederer, now Mrs. Pringle. Paula Laurence had known my mother and Virginia during the days of the Mercury and was the godmother of my Santa Monica playmate Chrissie Welles. In the cab on our way there, my mother said she didn't really want to go, that she didn't really like Paula Laurence.

In the crowded smoky room Virginia was friendly to me, and although somewhat chubby now, you could still see a touch of her foxy prettiness and I was happy to see Chrissie again, like me, in her early twenties. We talked and hoped we could meet before she had to go somewhere. We exchanged telephone numbers. When we got back to our apartment, after dinner, I said I hoped Chrissie and I would meet and that I liked Virginia from our days at the beach.

My mother had fixed herself a drink and said, to my remark, "Well you can like her. I don't. She's a pathological liar."

My stepfather was reading the *New York Post,* a different, more serious, paper then than now, and dropped the page slightly to look over to my mother, to see if she'd elaborate.

"How do you know?" I asked.

"Charlie told me that on their wedding night, Virginia had told him that I'd said to her that he was a homosexual."

"Did you?"

"Of course not," my mother said sharply, as if mine was a question which had not needed to be asked. "He was my friend. Why would I say that? He was cold to me for a few years until he explained what had happened. I told him it was nonsense and we both agreed Virginia was a liar. A pathological liar."

My stepfather had returned to his paper, as though this was a familiar story.

Years later, I thought what was this wedding night, as in the coming together of two young virgins? But maybe my mother meant it as on the day, the occasion of their wedding, joined together, but my mother had said "wedding night," so there was the image of the two of them, Charlie and Virginia, starting to get ready for bed, ribbons and tin cans tied to their car outside; Charlie sitting down to take off his shoes, Virginia, her hands behind her neck, to unzip her dress.

"Geraldine says you're a homosexual."
Is that how it went?

Early the next evening, when I came back to the apartment, my stepfather told me Chrissie Welles had called.

"Oh. I'll call her back."

"She's going out tonight, she said, and leaving tomorrow morning for Chicago."

"That's too bad."

"When I answered the phone, she said, 'Hello, it's Chrissie. Can I speak to my brother?' "

Then he rolled his eyes as if to express: "The things people say."

I gestured with my own eye roll: "Beats me."

But I was thinking where did this come from, why did Chrissie ask for her brother, was it what she thought or was it information from her mother, Virginia, now playing the part of "The Liar."

Eight

The first great male friend of my teenage years was Peter Bogdanovich. We'd met at the Shakespeare Festival in Stratford, Connecticut, as apprentices in 1956 and were both going to school in New York. We'd spend hours on the phone each night talking about books, plays and movies, and girls, instead of doing our homework. He let me know that he was more sexually experienced than I, sometimes, he said, booking a room at a large mid-range hotel, the Biltmore, say, where he'd take his quite young girlfriend for trysts. He said he was often anxious in case that figure from noir and pulp, the hotel detective, might put his eye to the keyhole and arrest them for teenage fornication. I admired his effrontery and, also, was always entertained by his gift for imitation, spot-on mimicry of Jerry Lewis and Dean Martin and other stars of the period.

In 1961, after *Chimes at Midnight* and Oxford (failed again), Peter and I and Ivor David Balding (a wonderful name I thought, although I comma'd it in my brain, as Ivor David, balding) got together at the Phoenicia Playhouse in the Hudson River Valley for a summer stock season, Peter and I directing with David having raised the money. And Peter and I had both fallen in love with Polly Platt.

Polly had arrived in New York from Carnegie Mellon as a very talented bright young widow. Her husband had been killed in an accident. She was small, delicate, tough-minded, funny, and pretty in an off-center way, and we'd hired her as our costume designer for the summer season. Being a young widow at that time had an alluring savor in that she was legitimately sexually experienced. To my serious dismay, it was Peter she fell in love with, and a few years later they were married and went to Hollywood for Peter to begin his, initially, successful film directing career. I did not like the way I'd found out about their affair, and so things changed between us.

In that hot summer at the Phoenicia Playhouse, a theater in a field, I directed three plays and acted in two. And in the hotel bar where the actors gathered after the show, only sometimes joined by Peter and Polly, I'd put coins in the jukebox, for Gary U.S. Bonds' "Quarter to Three" and Floyd Cramer's "Last Date." This instrumental had the slow triste feel of prom night's final smooch number, with the sense of what would be lost when the lights came up and the couples have to separate their keen pressing bodies. And I knew that I was destined, in my mind anyway, to know and understand women, and with that in view, on a self-invented diet, featuring melons and celery, I lost thirty pounds of detested weight.

After Phoenicia, a production I'd done there of Saroyan's *The Cave Dwellers* starring my mother and using my sister in a silent part opened off-Broadway and closed a week later.

I went to Ireland to work as a floor manager at Telefís Éireann, the national station preparing to go on the air. I had an ambition to be a TV director and worked hard there to learn from the bottom up how things worked. For the first several months, I stayed with my father and Kathleen in their small flat in Dublin. A certain amount of booze fueled our good times together, and sometimes when I'd go to bed to get an early start at the station, they'd stay up drinking long after in the room above mine, which often led to my father expressing himself by shouting and the two of them fighting. One morning on my way to work, I looked into the living room to see, lined up by the little electric heater, five empty wine bottles, mementos of how my father and Kathleen had spent the night before.

My stepfather, mother, and sister came to Ireland for the summer of 1962. I was still working at Telefís Éireann and was by then sharing a basement flat in Fitzwilliam Place with an Australian director and his girlfriend.

My stepfather went to England for a few days on business and was stung by a bee and returned to Ireland and then felt not quite well. His doctor said maybe it was his gallbladder and put him in hospital for the night. The next afternoon, my mother, sister, and I were having an ad hoc lunch with my mother's aunt, the O'Casey actress. The phone rang. Answering, Aunt Shelah passed it to my mother, who listened, then asked the question, as flatly as possible because my sister was there, "You think his heart is involved?"

Shelah and my mother went to St. Vincent's Hospital in Leeson Street and Susie and I went to the rented house in Wicklow, which was near my stepfather's favorite golf course.

My mother had gotten into Shelah's three-wheeled bubble car. We were all anxious driving with Shelah because her concentration often seemed to be on other things and the vehicle had all the safety potential of a balloon. I knew from my mother's question to the doctor and the controlled agitation of her manner, and her charge to me, "Look after Susie. I'll call the house when I know anything," that she was frantic, the more so because she was trying to act as though she wasn't.

Susie and I arrived at the pretty pink eighteenth-century house, with its small blooming garden outside. I was used to not being with my mother or stepfather, not having seen them for a year or two at a time. Susie was not. In fact, she was unusually attached to being with her mother and father as a result of being schooled at home for four years, because my mother had thought that would protect her from the vicissitudes of a child's life.

Susie tried to reestablish things by playing with a doll. Although she was nearly beyond doll age, she had gone upstairs and come down with the one that usually traveled with her, just in case she needed some memory of her earlier childhood. She sat in her little blue jean overalls at the bottom of the staircase and spoke to the doll, arranged the hair, fussed with the clothes.

I needed to talk to someone and knew she was intelligent but she was only eleven. I dreaded the idea of the phone ringing in case it would be what Citizeness Kane, the housekeeper of the pee, would call, referring to the death of an ancient relative, the "mortal news."

Looking at her doll, Susie asked, "Is everything all right?"

I found myself lying to this child, hoping that my lies would not be exposed, so that my love for her would not be tainted. And I had no information except for our mother's wild eyes.

"Everything's all right. There's nothing to worry about at all. Your father's just in hospital for a while to be looked after. Ma will be back soon."

"So everything's okay?" Susie asked, her brown eyes checking mine, her fingers leaving the doll's hair for a moment.

"Yes, okay. Are you hungry?" I asked, looking for an escape; to go into the kitchen to fix her some bread and honey was an idea.

"No. Not hungry." She went back to straightening her doll's dress.

"Are you all right then, just sitting there?"

"I'm all right."

She sat at the bottom of the stairs, her shiny dark head bent to her plastic playmate, I standing near her, not wanting to infect her already uneasy psyche with my own uneasiness.

"Well, I'll just go into the living room and read for a while. Just give me a shout, if you're not okay."

"I'm okay."

I went into the other room and flipped, with no concentration, through whatever magazines were left lying around the rented house, last year's *Punch, Horse & Hound.* A white Bakelite telephone was at my elbow, its cord coiled like a snake to its plug at the baseboard.

An hour must have passed in this unfocused way. I heard Susie go upstairs to her room. I got up.

"You okay?" I called.

"I'm okay."

"Are you hungry?"

"No. Not hungry," she answered from above.

The front door opened and in burst my mother and Shelah from the dark outside. Night had fallen and I hadn't turned on any new lights. They seemed possessed by outside forces. I was exultant at older adults being there, the people who'd take care of everything.

"He's had a heart attack," my mother said, "but Dr. Mayne says it's not a bad one."

She went upstairs to Susie and put her to bed, then Shelah and my mother and I had a late makeshift supper with a couple of bottles of wine.

"So, it's all right?" I asked.

I saw my mother and Shelah exchange a look.

"Yes, he said it wasn't a bad one but," my mother stopped, then continued, "that we ought to contact the rest of his family, in case they should come over."

I looked at her.

"Just in case, he said." The desperate look had come back into my mother's eyes.

She was exhausted and went up to bed, Aunt Shelah to stay in a spare room. My mother asked me to call Buzzie, my stepfather's brother, who was in San Francisco, to tell him what the doctor had said.

I reached my uncle, who was not an easy man. Small, with limited empathy, ramrod straight in his well-tailored suits, he'd been known even after the war as "the little colonel," and was exact in a crisis.

"Call Dr. Levy, his heart doctor," he instructed. "He's in Paris. Here's the number of his hotel." I could sense him thumbing through his address book. "I'll fly over tomorrow."

I went upstairs to my mother's room. She was not asleep.

I told her I'd be on the phone a while longer.

"Buzzie said to tell Dr. Levy in Paris to come here tomorrow."

"I'll try to sleep," my mother said. "Thank you for looking after Susie."

I went to the door and she turned out her bedside light.

Her voice came from the dark. "They said they'll only call from the hospital if something bad happens. So let's hope the phone doesn't ring tonight."

I went downstairs to the small library where one of the house's other phones was.

In those days there was no easy dialing. You had to go through an operator.

I dialed the operator and requested a number in Paris and said it was a personal call for Dr. Levy.

"What's your number?" the female operator asked.

"Wicklow 46."

"I'll ring you back when I've reached Dr. Levy."

"That won't work," I said.

"What won't?" she asked.

"What's your name?" I asked to ingratiate myself, with a purpose.

"Sinéad. What's yours?" (Sinéad is Irish for Jane.)

"My name is Michael."

"So, Michael, what's the problem?"

"I'd like to stay on the line while you try the call."

"It could take a while, Michael, and it's not what we do, to ask you to stay on the line."

"Sinéad. The thing is, we've had an illness in the family, a serious illness, and everyone is asleep. I'm the only one awake to try this call. And if the telephone were to ring, it would wake everyone up and they'd think it was bad news, be frightened."

"I understand. You just stay on the line then. I'll try to get it through as fast as I can. What was the illness?"

"My stepfather. He's had a heart attack. And I want Dr. Levy to come over to see him."

"Hang on the line, then. I'll try to get it through as fast as I can."

I hung on, waiting to be put through to Dr. Levy at his hotel in Paris.

Then Sinéad was on again.

"The hotel says Dr. Levy is at a dinner party."

"Oh."

"But they've given me a forwarding number for Dr. Levy. Do you want me to try that number?"

"Yes, please, Sinéad."

"Hold on a bit longer then. Are you all right?"

"I am, thank you."

"Heart attacks are terrible things."

"They are."

"My uncle had one last year. He was my father's brother."

"I'm sorry."

"He wasn't in good health anyway. He died."

"I'm sorry."

"May he rest in peace," Sinéad said.

"Yes, may he."

"I'll try Dr. Levy now for you. Hold on a bit longer."

The phone went into its still place again. I waited. There was a pad in front of me and I did some little drawings. I turned over the page and did some more.

Then, "Michael, here's Paris for you."

"Good. Hello. Dr. Levy?"

"Yes, this is Dr. Levy." There was party noise behind him.

I explained who I was, what the issue was, and that Buzzie wanted him to come over. I felt this last piece of information would do the trick.

"I'm on vacation."

"Buzzie's coming over, from San Francisco," I said to contrast the difference and distance from San Francisco and Paris.

There was a pause, then Dr. Levy said, "Can you arrange the flights for me, a first-class hotel for the night and a car from and back to the airport?"

"I can do that."

We hung up. It was after midnight. I sat there, spent, but unable to move, and went back to drawing on the little pad when my mother entered the room.

"I can't sleep. I thought I'd make some tea."

"I'll do it for you."

"No, I'll do it."

She went into the kitchen and came back some minutes later with a pot of tea and two mugs. We sat by the fire that Shelah had lit to give comfort to the house.

"Is Susie asleep?" I asked.

"Yes. Sound asleep."

My mother and I sat there together and, for the first time in my life, I felt that I was her protector, probably the role I'd always wanted to play. And I could fulfill it. I think I always knew that, underneath her beauty, intelligence, and wit, there was something that was somehow unsteady, not to be exposed, not unstable but fragile, with a fear inside her which only, I felt that night, I could recognize, I, her son. No one else knew of it, her carapace too artfully constructed and burnished.

We talked a little of her afternoon in the hospital, of her feeling unsure how to deal with the doctors and nurses and their description of what kind of heart attack it was and the prognosis. Then we changed the subject. She asked me how my work was at the TV station, did I like my flatmates in Fitzwilliam Place.

The tea was finished and we sat in silence for a while, looking at each other with a deep connection. Our eyes told each other what a density of feeling we had, son to mother, mother to son, what a winding path we'd been on from California to New York to this little house in Ireland. I thought we've always been thus, in it together, she and I.

It was almost two when the telephone rang.

She jumped at the bell and a look of dread came over her face.

I rose and went to the telephone.

I put my hand to the receiver, fearful, but with a strange exhilaration, a dreadful excitement, excitement and dread brewed together.

It rang again. I picked it up.

"Yes?"

A familiar voice.

"Michael, it's Sinéad. I was just wondering if you'd got Dr. Levy to come over and if everything is all right."

Rage and a sense of absurdity coexisted.

I turned to my mother and said, "It's okay," and then to Sinéad, "Yes, thank you, Sinéad, everything's all right," and back to my mother, "It's just the operator wanting to know if everything is all right."

"Thank God, everything is all right," my mother said.

I replaced the receiver. My mother sat for a minute or so before she stood up.

"I'll try to sleep," she said. "Thank you for everything today. And tonight. I love you."

"I love you too."

I kissed her and she went upstairs. I stayed in the little library for half an hour or more, so conflicted was I.

Visited by his brother and attended for a day by Dr. Levy, my stepfather recovered, and a month or so later I had a nervous crackup which lasted more than a year.

Nine

At that time in Ireland, psychiatric treatment was not available. The Catholic Church ruled the country with an iron foot in a steel boot and equated psychiatry with Freud and Freud with sex and sex with anarchy. Books were banned and condoms confiscated at the airport.

I was referred to someone who was known to dispense pills for troubled minds. He worked at a hospital for the marginally insane built in the eighteenth century.

I sat on a wooden pew outside his office. You could distinguish the patients from the doctors with your eyes closed. The heavily sedated residents shuffled listlessly in their slippers while the doctors' leather shoes rat-tat-tatted on the old smoothed stone floor.

Dr. Ryan was in his forties, a stocky man, muscle more than fat, who asked what was wrong with me.

"I'm afraid of dying."

"We all have to die," he said, so I'd know how things stood.

"I know that but I mean immediately, soon, tomorrow or perhaps right now."

"That's a possibility for all of us, if that's the way you want to look at things."

"Unfortunately, that's how I do look at things."

Dr. Ryan stared at me a moment, as at a knot in the carpet, then asked, "Do you have any symptoms?"

"My heart beats fast a lot of the time," I answered.

"Have you seen a doctor?"

"He says it's just palpitations."

"That can be quite normal. Anything else?"

There was.

"I'm afraid to cross the street. I'll wait for the light to turn green, then not be sure whether I should go, and then it's red again and then green, and still I won't be able to cross."

"How long will you be there, waiting to cross?"

"Five or ten minutes."

"Are you often late then?"

"Late for what?"

"Your appointments."

"I don't really have appointments."

"Why not?"

"I work at Telefís Éireann five days a week. I just turn up and then have a day or so off."

"And that's when you're on the street corner, waiting to cross?"

"Sometimes. But on my days off, I sleep a lot, when I get to sleep that is."

"You don't get to sleep?"

"I sleep when I go to sleep but I'm afraid to go to sleep."

"Why's that?"

"In case I die."

"You're afraid of death, then?"

"That's what I said."

Dr. Ryan and I had formed a perfect conversational circle.

He did not want to start again so he opened his desk drawer and took out several bottles of pills. He put on his glasses to look at the labels.

"I think I've got something for you."

This began Dr. Ryan's pill treatment for my anxiety.

The first pills he gave me were to be taken half an hour before bedtime.

Two weeks later I was back in Dr. Ryan's office.

"I'm afraid these pills aren't really working."

"Why not?" he asked uneasily, as if his competence was connected to the pill.

"They make me faint."

"Faint?"

"Instead of just going to sleep, I feel dizzy, then disoriented, then unconscious."

"But at least you're asleep, which is what you want, isn't it?" he said, as if explaining why I should be satisfied with the pill.

"I don't know if it is sleep exactly. I faint, then I come to after a few hours and lie awake again."

"It works for others."

"Maybe they like fainting."

"Why would they like that?"

"Maybe they don't tell you."

"Tell me what?"

"That they like fainting."

"Why would they like that?"

I could see that we were en route to another conversational roundabout but, although curious to see how perfect we could make it, I had a greater interest in dealing with the sleep problem.

I put the half empty bottle of blue pills on his desk, like playing a chess piece. He pulled it to his side of the board and replaced it with another, shiny pinks inside.

"This should do the trick."

Back in his office a few weeks later, I said, "I'm sorry to be a bother to you but these pills aren't really working."

"Why not?"

"They don't really have any effect on my going to sleep, but in the daytime I feel like a zombie, as though part of my brain has been removed."

"I've heard that. Some people like the effect."

"Why would they like that?"

"They feel calmer."

"I don't feel calmer. I just feel absent."

"And you don't like that?"

"It's like being dead."

"And you don't like the feeling?"

I paused for a moment to consider how far Dr. Ryan and I had come over these few weeks.

Then I asked, "Do you take pills?"

"No. Squash," he said with emphasis.

I took it that "squash" was meant as a kind of trump, the victory word of the non-neurotic over the pill taker. I looked at him.

He gestured a racquet stroke with a quick flick of his wrist.

"Do you play sports?" he asked.

"I used to play baseball."

"Not much of that here."

We sat looking at each other for a moment. Dr. Ryan indicated it was my move.

"Do you have anything else?"

He looked at me as though he didn't want us to meet again. He reached into his drawer.

"These are new. They'll be the answer."

The pills did help me to go to sleep but had strange side effects. When I drank red wine or ate cheese, my face would turn puce and I'd feel some constriction in my head, as though a vise had been placed around it and slowly tightened.

I took them for a year or so and then I was briefly in England and went to see a doctor for something or other. The doctor asked if I was on any medication. I named the pill.

The doctor pulled back and looked at me.

"Those pills have been withdrawn from the market. They've been found to give people strokes, especially if mixed with red wine or cheese. They could kill you."

Around that time, I met Lucy Davies, who'd be my first wife, dark-haired, blue-eyed, tall with a natural elegance of body and spirit and a deep sense of empathy; she was by my side as I struggled to pull myself out of the hole.

Going to pick her up at the airport on her return from a few days in England, on a thunderous harsh night, lightning aimed at her little Viscount airplane, I suddenly understood, as if the lightning had struck me, as if what had been buried had erupted and was again exposed, the deep murderous instinct inside me and what a dire thing I'd wished for that night of the Dr. Levy phone call—for the death of the man who only wished the best for me—in order to claim my mother, and, understanding, I saw and, shortly, was released from my vicious incapacitating sickness.

Ten

I was better and after a few more months at Telefís Éireann I went, with some money saved, to London for a week.

I asked a girl out to lunch. She was a year or two older, someone I'd known and liked in New York. She had recently married a longtime boyfriend but was happy enough to join me and catch up on our friendship.

We went to Le Caprice, a high-end restaurant which had a glamorous show business clientele. We sat down on the banquette and a few tables to our left, at a facing angle, was Orson having lunch with Henry Sherek, a successful London theatrical producer, who was a very fat man due, I'd heard, to a wartime stomach wound as much as an inclination to heavy eating. Together, they took up a large section of seating, Orson having gotten considerably heavier in the three years since I'd seen him. He nodded to me as if to say, "I'll stop on my way out," which he did.

I introduced him to my companion and he asked what I was doing.

"Irish television, working as a floor manager."

"Still in Ireland, huh?"

He said it as though he took it that I'd not left since *Chimes at Midnight,* and there was, I felt, a soupçon of criticism that I hadn't yet chosen to swim in deeper waters. I didn't think this was the time to fill him in on my résumé, he seeming anxious to leave.

He said his good-byes and he and Henry Sherek made their girthful exit from the restaurant.

Debbie said to me, "Isn't he your father? He didn't seem particularly friendly."

"Where did you hear that?" I said to her question.

"Oh, just what people used to say in New York."

"I don't see him very often. But you have a famous father." Her father was a very good popular novelist.

"Yes, but we're very close."

What I'd done was not directly answer her question, but by changing the subject to her well-known father, I let the New York rumor lie there, the possibility of a connection, for my own benefit (in case she ever got divorced), to this large man who, on this occasion, had not been particularly warm. Perhaps he hadn't liked his beef daube. Or maybe Henry Sherek would not invest in a production he wanted to do. Or maybe it was something else.

B ut I was making plans to swim in deeper waters and, within eighteen months, driven by ambition, cushioned by innocent optimism, having learned guile and been blessed with luck, I was at the age of twenty-four directing the premier English TV rock 'n' roll show, *Ready Steady Go!*, where the regular bands were the Rolling Stones, the Animals, The Who, and the Kinks, joined by Dusty Springfield, the Everly Brothers, the Supremes, Roy Orbison, James Brown, the Byrds, Otis Redding, a young American who'd been busking in the streets of London, Paul Simon, and all the others.

I was having quite a lot of success directing *RSG!*, partly because I was close in age to the musicians, partly because I loved rock 'n' roll since I'd first heard "Sh-Boom" on Radio Luxembourg in Ireland when I was thirteen and then "Heartbreak Hotel" when I was fifteen at boarding school, and also because I'd come up with vivid and dramatic ways of shooting the bands, which they liked.

As a result of the notice I'd attracted, I was asked to direct an episode of a private-eye drama, *The Informer*, where I met Jean Marsh, who became a central person in my life from then till now. We would rehearse in a large room for two weeks and then

We turned a whole RSG! *over to James Brown. After he reviewed the playback, he shook my hand and said, "You've got soul."*

go into the studio for two days of rehearsals with cameras and then we'd shoot it. At 9:30 in the morning, I was in the studio waiting to begin the first day with cameras half an hour later, and I was excited and nervous, when I got a message to go to see the prune-faced woman who was in charge of assigning directors. Although producers could ask for me, I was under contract to the company and could be told to direct a program about canaries if they so decided.

I sat warily opposite her. My youth and flair and the extra attention I'd brought to *RSG!* did not make me popular with everyone. There was an older generation which scorned all that my age group represented.

She looked at a memo in front of her and did not speak to me right away. Then, "We've had a request from NEMS."

NEMS was Brian Epstein's company. He was the manager of The Beatles.

"Oh, what for?"

"I'll come to that. You've only been here a short while and you've been moving along very quickly and been doing well, in a way. But we don't want you to get above yourself."

"I wouldn't want that either," I said evenly, knowing a knife might be hidden in her remark.

"It's to direct a video with The Beatles."

I don't know if my heart stopped or just skipped several beats.

"That sounds interesting."

"We don't think we should release you. You're under contract to us and it'll take several days apparently. After all, we're paying your wages."

"Maybe I could reimburse you, the company."

"That's not the point."

She scowled at me as though I didn't understand that the purpose of this interview was to inflict some suffering on me.

But I did understand and wondered how to deal with this opportunity which was about to be quashed, when she said, "But, as it's a request from Mr. Epstein himself," she said, as if swallowing bile, "the company has decided that in view of his influence in the world of Light Entertainment (which is what they called anything to do with music) that we'll give you a leave of absence. Reluctantly."

"That's very nice of you," I said, mealy, through clenched teeth.

She looked at the small watch on her wrist.

"You'd better be off now. You don't want to be late for camera rehearsal."

"No, I wouldn't want that. Thank you."

I rose and went to the door.

"And you'll be off salary for the days you're away."

I left the office, thrilled to have been asked to direct The Beatles, and on my way to direct my first TV drama. Could life be any better?

As I approached the control room a few minutes before ten, a Tannoy announcement said: "Telephone for Michael Lindsay-Hogg. Please pick up the nearest telephone."

I did and was connected to an operator.

"A call for Michael Lindsay-Hogg?"

"Yes, hold on. We have a call for you."

"Hello," a woman's voice said, "Michael, it's Mrs. Rodgers, Mr. Welles's secretary."

I remembered her from the prompting sessions on the way to Belfast six years before and said hello and asked how she was.

"I'm calling for Mr. Welles. He wanted to know if you could join him and Marlene Dietrich for dinner at Le Caprice tonight at eight."

"Oh, Mrs. Rodgers, I'd love to. But I'm rehearsing till ten tonight and we're in Wembley and I probably wouldn't be there till eleven. Is that too late?"

"I'm afraid it would be. Miss Dietrich has an early flight to Paris in the morning. I know Mr. Welles will be disappointed."

"Me too. I'm disappointed but please thank him for me. I know he'll understand that I can't. I'm rehearsing."

"I'm sure he will. Perhaps another time."

She hung up and I stood there, feeling heartbroken about not being able to make the dinner but in another way overwhelmed by riches.

I never met Marlene Dietrich and would not hear from Orson for another four years.

The Beatles were the most famous people the world had ever known.

This is not hyperbole. They were deserving and in 1966 the mechanism was in place: the methods of communication for the world to be told about them, although more than there were a hundred years before, were many fewer than we have today, so, oddly, fame could be more fully enshrined. And fame to that degree was perpetuated because it was good for the purveyors who convinced the buyers it was good for them and, the belief was, for the famous also. Newspapers, magazines, radio, and television were much more controlled and less maverick than what exists today, when fame can be sudden, perhaps undeserved, sometimes unwelcome, and come and gone in the blink of an eye, or the click of a mouse.

Great fame is rare but when it appears it takes the form of an inevitable social necessity and no one deserved it more than John, Paul, George, and Ringo.

Not only were The Beatles wonderful but they had helped to lift up the great wounded beast that was America after the assassination of President John F. Kennedy. The president had been killed in November 1963 and The Beatles came on *The Ed Sullivan Show* for the first time in February 1964 and the stunned grieving citizens were given an elixir they had not thought to taste again so quickly.

As the Gods of Mythology had their particular domain, so The Beatles were the Gods of Joy. Joy in music, joy in singing, in laughter and jokes, joy in fame, in having such a great connection with each other and with us, joy in being alive.

So it would have been unimaginable then, and is ghastly now, to consider that of those who came from Liverpool, principally Brian Epstein, Peter Brown, Mal Evans, Neil Aspinall, John, Paul, George, and Ringo, that by the end of 1980 three would be dead and another would not reach the age of sixty.

I was a week or so into my twenty-sixth year when I arrived at Abbey Road in the early evening. A uniformed commissionaire rose from behind his desk. He led me down a corridor. We passed a door, with a blinking red light above, and he nodded solemnly. In that studio, behind that door, was where The Beatles were creating joy.

I was shown into a large room where there was a sofa, a couple of heavy chairs, a leather hassock, and a dining table with a white tablecloth, laid with silver, china, and crystal for six.

I chose the sofa and had an attack of nerves. I was worried if my voice would hold up. A few years earlier I'd been interviewed by the great theater director Tyrone Guthrie for a stage manager's job. Tyrone Guthrie had the look and bearing of a Grenadier guardsman, as all of his six feet, six inches rose to greet me as I walked onto the stage where his worktable had been set. I was struck by his good manners, in contrast to some of the producers who were lolling nearby, one of them belching into his tuna sandwich. I'd run from the subway, anxious not to be late, and, then, out of nerves, couldn't get my breath back and hence couldn't speak. Tyrone Guthrie poured me a glass of water from his carafe, looked at me sympathetically, and talked about the play till he judged I could talk and then asked me about myself. It was a lesson to me in how to behave to even the most junior in the theatrical family.

A nxious, I sat on the sofa for about twenty minutes and then the door opened and a tall, husky, shaggy man wearing glasses smiled and said, "They won't be long."

This was Mal Evans, who was one of the original few who'd come from Liverpool and was now their head roadie and because of his size an impediment should anyone try to get too close. (His heft masked a friendly, gentle, and humble nature, and so it was a shock to learn that he'd been shot and killed in 1975 in Los Angeles by the police. They'd gone to his apartment to check on a dispute. Mal was holding a rifle that he refused to put down.)

He smiled again and closed the door and I sat back to wait and get more nervous when, almost immediately, the door opened again and in came six people, Mal, and Neil Aspinall, who had the hard shiny face of someone who could be an unwelcome foe. He'd started by driving their van in Liverpool, Beatles and instruments crammed in the back. He went on to run their company, Apple Corps, for almost forty years.

And the four of them who looked like the four of them. Their faces had become so famous that it was like being in a room with iconic characters, as from the comics, say—Mickey and Donald, Archie and Jughead.

I had gotten to my feet as they'd all entered, out of politeness I like to think. They took random places around the table as prawn cocktails were served by a maid, with white, rosé, and red wine on offer and Coca-Cola with or without scotch. Everyone started to eat, pour drinks, and continue to talk about whatever they'd been talking about when they'd come in. I stood there wondering what was going to happen next.

Paul was beside Neil, facing my way, and was the first to speak to me.

"Michael, right? Come over and give us your ideas."

Those with their backs to me did not turn around.

I did not think he meant for me, as I gave my ideas, to stand while they sat. But the problem was there was nowhere to sit at the table. The chairs were all taken. The sofa and armchairs were too big to move. So it was to be the hassock. I looked at the hassock. The hassock looked at me, dark leather and fat. I gauged it was too large in circumference and bulk to lift. I put my foot at its base and applied pressure, hoping to seem, until I tested its weight, that I wasn't doing anything other than just standing there. It did not budge.

Paul and Neil had gone back to eating. The others were talking, backs to me, unconcerned.

I'd have to shove this malignant object, and so I leaned down and initiated a pushing-like activity, ungracefully angled, ass out. The hassock started to move but not as though willing, with the carpet being no friend, fibrous and resistant. It was harder than I'd thought.

Maybe wondering what had become of me, in relation to his invitation to "come over," Paul lifted his eyes from his prawn cocktail and took in the sight in front of him.

"Are you all right?" he asked.

Sensing something was going on, the others, Mal, John,

George, and Ringo at the head of the table, previously obscured, turned in their chairs toward me.

"I'm fine," I grunted, in a manner which I hoped conveyed no sense of strain.

Mal started to rise to give me a hand.

"No, don't get up!" I heard myself shout. "It's no problem."

With a final muscle-tensing effort, I maneuvered the hassock the last half dozen feet and slammed it into a space between Mal and George.

"There, I've done it."

Those at the table, including the four most famous people in the world, had stopped eating and were staring at me.

I stood back and smiled as though what had just occurred had been, for me anyway, a pleasant, familiar experience.

I started to sit down and it was at this point that I realized a hassock's original purpose was to rest weary legs after a long day and consequently it was lower in height than a regular chair and so I'd be sitting somewhat lower than the four most famous people in the world.

My chin was at table level as I wiped the sweat off my forehead, looked up at The Beatles, and said, "I really like the record."

What they saw was some white tablecloth and a disembodied, flushed, moist head which had just spoken to them.

I waited for the discussion to begin.

There was silence until George, courteous by nature, asked, in a slightly concerned voice, "Would you like some water?"

"Sure, that'd be great."

Mal poured me a glass of water.

There was another silence as I drank the water until, leaned over the table a bit, John turned to me, eyes only somewhat curious behind round specs, and asked, "Which side do you like best?"

Side A, "Paperback Writer," featured McCartney, Side B, "Rain," Lennon. I knew that. I thought it right to start this relationship by giving my honest opinion to John, who himself seemed to wish to be seen as honest and therefore to require honesty.

"They're both so different," and I paused, looking for the most honest way to sum up my opinion. "I like them both."

John turned away as Paul said it was good to like them both. Ringo gave a little snort. I couldn't actually tell by his tone if Paul meant it the way he said it or if he was teasing me in a codified way for the others, but I had a sense he thought we should get things going.

I began to give them my ideas but they weren't an easy audience.

I'd worked with the Rolling Stones on *Ready Steady Go!* and found with all of them, and Mick Jagger in particular, a fairly even exchange. Maybe, I thought, that whereas the Rolling Stones came from near London, the sophisticated metropolis, The Beatles were from Liverpool, a tough blue-collar port city in the North of England, and that might be an important distinction. With Mick Jagger, I'd suggest, he'd question, I'd clarify, and he'd agree, usually.

But with The Beatles that evening, I found an idea was something to be mauled, like a piece of meat thrown into an animal cage. They'd paw it, chuck parts of it from one to the other, chew on it a bit, spit it out, and then toss the remnant to me, on the other side of the bars.

And I understood, as I was watching, that as Ringo once said, "Only the four of us will ever know what it was like," that their bond, at that time, was still closer than any stranger could intrude on and, in some way, they were testing, to see if I were of their mettle.

And as I understood, I found I wasn't as disturbed by their method, and things got easier.

By then, their lamb with mint sauce was finished and George asked, "Have you ever seen *Citizen Kane*?"

"I have, yes."

"Rosebud," he said, as if exchanging a password.

"Rosebud, yes."

"Brian said to look at it. I saw it last night. We should do a video like that."

"That would be great," I said, eager for an ally, although not exactly sure how a "Rosebud" video would go.

A few minutes earlier, I'd suggested for "Paperback Writer" a story video about someone working in a newspaper office who in his spare time was trying to write a paperback novel.

They thought there might be something in this and that we'd talk more. They finished their trifle pudding and went back into the studio to create more joy, and I went for a long walk.

A few days later, I was called by Vyvienne Moynihan, a NEMS giver of information, and was told that Mr. Epstein did not want anything "unusual, just a video of the boys performing."

Me on the left. The day we shot "Rain," 1966.

"Paperback Writer" was done in a studio in several takes, interrupted by them disappearing for half an hour at a time to try on clothes for their upcoming tour. And on the next day, a filmed version of "Rain," on location on the grounds of Chiswick House.

It was a gray warm day as I sat on the grass having a paper plate lunch beside Ringo. I looked up, curious, also wishing to make conversation, and said to him, "What kind of tree do you think that is? A yew?"

"No, I think it's a me."

"That's what I said," batting the joke back.

Brian Epstein was delivered by chauffeured car to watch us shoot. He and they joshed in what seemed to me a slightly stilted way, but maybe it was for the crew and other onlookers. He and I stood under a tree as I talked to him about my ideas for story videos.

Brian Epstein was a well-dressed, young-looking, aloof or, maybe, insecure man whose connection to "the boys" was devotional and ferocious.

In a friendly-seeming way, he waved me off.

"Maybe next time," he said.

A couple of years later, I did my next videos with The Beatles, "Revolution" and "Hey Jude." They were performance videos too, because that was what we thought best. Brian Epstein had died the year before.

We shot "Revolution" and "Hey Jude" on an afternoon which went into evening.

As I was walking toward the studio to shoot the first, John was going the same way and we fell into step. He wasn't looking his best that day, pasty and his hair was lank and bedraggled. A late night, maybe. I asked him if he wanted any makeup.

"No," he said. "Why?"

"I was just thinking maybe it would make you look, uh, healthier."

"I don't need to look healthier."

"Why not?"

"Because I'm John Lennon."

We pushed the door open together and walked into the studio.

The point is what he meant. I don't think he meant it the way it sounded: "I'm John Lennon and I'm too important to have makeup." Rather it was something more clear-eyed, and making a distinction between a musician and, say, a movie star: "I'm not an actor pretending to be someone else. I'm just me. And if I'm not looking that hot today, so be it."

After the first take of "Revolution," we looked at a playback and John said the only thing that mattered to him was that he have a close-up for the line "But if you go carrying pictures of Chairman Mao, you ain't gonna make it with anyone anyhow" because he considered it the key line of the song. After a few more takes, purposely rough, we were done with "Revolution." And then we started on "Hey Jude."

Paul and I had met a few days before to consider how we would do the songs and we discussed the "problem" of "Hey Jude," which was the four-minute final chorus. We agreed that just being on The Beatles wasn't enough and so Paul and I came up with the idea to have a cross section of people to join in with The Beatles, a mixed-race collection of not only the usual young fans but also housewives and people of middle age, including a village postman.

We did "Hey Jude" in six takes and between each take, while the cameramen were getting notes and repositioning and the video reels were being reloaded, The Beatles jammed for the audience, old hits, some Tamla Motown. This was the first time they'd played in public for any kind of audience since they'd stopped touring in 1966. And they found themselves enjoying it, more or less, reluctant at the beginning, just to keep the audience from getting restive, and then with more vigor and delight as the evening went on.

Like The Beatles, the Rolling Stones had become fed up with appearing live on television with the attendant hassles and security issues. I had once been in the car with them after a *Ready Steady Go!* when some of the unruly desperate fans had managed not only to open the door of a bulky Daimler but to almost pull it off its hinges. And like The Beatles, the Rolling Stones were powerful enough to dictate to the television stations and say they'd produce their own videos. In 1968, I did the Rolling Stones' first videos, which were then called promos—"Jumpin' Jack Flash" and "Child of the Moon."

Then Mick asked me to come up with an idea for a television special which would allow the Rolling Stones to headline the show with other bands they admired.

I was getting worried because after a couple of weeks sitting in their office in Maddox Street I was drawing a blank. There was a yellow legal pad in front of me, and I was doodling on it, stick figures and circles. Circles, circles, circus, and then, bam, it was a title that came into my head and all was clear.

I dialed Mick's number, and as I waited for him to pick up, I was aware of how much I liked my collaboration with him, he with the face of a Botticelli cosh boy; his intelligence was quick, his imagination and cultural appetite wide-ranging; he was funny and knew where every penny went.

When he answered I said, "I'm going to say seven words to you, tell me what you think."

Right away he got "The Rolling Stones Rock and Roll Circus" and then started to ask for and suggest specifics. We decided it should have the look of a tatty European traveling circus, with clowns, trapeze acts, fire eaters and would be the place where a collection of rock 'n' roll bands would play.

The idea that Mick proposed next was a good one. It was to try to get Brigitte Bardot to be our ringmaster/mistress.

We said what a nice sight it would be to see her in silk top hat and shiny red tailcoat, her shapely legs in black tights, fondling a whip.

"At least we'll get the masochists to watch," Mick joked.

It was a couple of evenings later that our cameraman, my friend Tony Richmond (who went on to shoot many wonderful movies, including Nic Roeg's *Don't Look Now*), and I boarded the night train to Paris. (I had decided not to fly for a while.) Tony was two years younger than I, and was also doing well. His suits were handmade and that night he was wearing an eye-catching large maroon Borsalino.

"The night train to Paris," just the words, revives yet another world which has vanished—steam clouding out from under the wheels of the giant black and gray locomotive, men in soft hats and hard Crombie overcoats, leather luggage, women whose slim legs would have the sheen of silk stockings, a seam up the back, and the old station clock affixed high on the wall, its maker's name under the center point, its black metal spider fingers, the short one on ten, the longer coming to twelve.

Tony and I sat in the club car ordering the "Chef's Popular All-Day Special," bacon and eggs and chips.

It was to be a quick trip.

First there was to be an afternoon meeting with an enterprising French company which was encouraging us to use their new experimental cameras for the show. Then Brigitte Bardot and back on the train that night, because there was a lot to do in London.

With our eggs and bacon, we drank red wine and lots of cognac.

At eight o'clock the following morning, we were in the lobby of the Scribe Hotel in Paris, where we'd booked rooms for the day, to sleep and freshen up.

They weren't ready and I had a nasty hangover.

"Unless you want me to throw up right there," I said to the desk clerk, pointing to a particularly glistening piece of marble floor, "you'll need to find us a room."

Just at that moment, an ex-girlfriend of Tony's walked through the lobby. She was in Paris for a modeling job. She gave us the key to her room and Tony and I slept for a few hours and then played pinball in a bar till it was time for our first meeting.

It was late that November afternoon when Tony and I went to the office of the camera company.

We knew that the cameras had not been used often because of certain technical issues, but they could be just what I wanted.

Although they shot on film they could be mounted on television dollies and so could be maneuvered quickly, and an added piece of equipment would feed the images onto the control room monitors, and so I could call the angle changes from camera to camera as the live performances went on, which I thought imperative when shooting rock 'n' roll. The bands would be on their toes and I had to be on mine also.

The office was small, and outside the only window the sky was darkening and the streetlamps were coming on. There was just room enough for two desks and a few chairs.

Tony and I sat opposite Mr. Foulet, who owned the company. He was thin and balding, with an optimistic comb-over.

Another man was sitting, his back to us, at the second desk, intently looking at technical drawings and making notes. Mr. Foulet did not introduce us. We did not know his function but he was to become a memorable participator in our meeting.

Since Tony's French and mine, at the time, were not up to speed, Mr. Foulet began in English. "All the camera will have led of ten minutes, reals led, load, excuse me, in regards to that, so, every ten minutes you'll need real change."

"What's he saying, Tony?" I asked.

"I think he's talking about camera reels," Tony said. "It means you have to stagger the camera loads. You'll lose one camera every ten minutes. I think that's what he means."

Mr. Foulet nodded in approval at Tony's explanation.

Then he said, "Sometimes also it happen, they break down, but do you know, so do your car sometimes."

He smiled as though he'd made a comparison which would be helpful to everyone.

The man with his back to us farted.

Mr. Foulet scowled at him over our heads, took out a pack of Gauloises, lit one hurriedly, and puffed quickly, blowing smoke into the small room.

I looked at Tony. He looked away. Communication between us might lead we knew not where.

Wishing to get our meeting back on track, I asked Mr. Foulet how often did the cameras break down.

Another odor was in the room, testing its pungent self against Mr. Foulet's urgent smoking.

"Not to worry there," Mr. Foulet said. "Because"—he stopped and blew a welcome draft of Gauloises our way—"because with each camera there will be one French technician."

The man with his back to us farted for a second time. I wondered what he'd had for lunch.

"Pascal," Mr. Foulet whispered sharply. "S'il vous plaît!"

Nothing from Pascal, which was a relief.

Mr. Foulet took a few quick puffs on his cigarette and, without inhaling, blew smoke.

He was fighting a losing battle.

Mr. Foulet looked at us, his eyes watery, the room dense with humanity and his own corrective smoking. But I wondered if, in his look, he was asking for sympathy, questioning how his ambition to be a suave successful businessman, with all his hair, in a large cool office had been misinterpreted by the Deity of Business, who'd sent him baldness, a small room, and Pascal, instead.

But he soldiered on, talking about the technicians who'd accompany the cameras. "And they will all bring their screwdrivers to do the trick."

Tony and I, on the spot, decided to laugh, no other choice, but to take Mr. Foulet's remark as a joke, a reason to laugh, because we had to, and did so heartily. We looked at each other and laughed more, slapping our legs till our eyes were watery too. We recovered and looked again at Mr. Foulet.

He stared at us, as though disappointed and puzzled by the different senses of humor which existed between one country and another.

(In England, a few weeks later, I was to learn it was not a joke.)

As we walked down the stairs after our meeting, both of us in high good humor, I asked Tony, "Who do you think that guy was? What does he do?"

"I don't know what his job is," said Tony. "But I do know something Pascal does really well."

And then it was on to Brigitte Bardot.

Her apartment was in the swank 16th Arrondissement. The door was opened by her agent, Olga Horstig-Primuz, whom I'd met before. She led us into the library. The room was elegantly furnished with long curtains drawn against the night.

In a chair was Patrick Bauchau, a handsome actor, with a louche, slightly eccentric reputation. Tony and I sat on a sofa.

Patrick Bauchau took a bottle of champagne off the ice from a silver bucket and poured Tony and me a glass, and then turned to his right to refill Brigitte Bardot's glass.

Brigitte Bardot was sitting on the floor near me, in front of the fireplace which warmed the room.

She was one of the prettiest women I've ever seen. She was wearing faded blue jeans over slender legs, short soft caramel-colored suede boots, a fringed suede jacket, and around her brow and honey-colored hair was a headband with glass beads—a sort of French version of American frontier wear.

She was thirty-four and her face was even more provocative in the flesh than in the movies.

Her manner was sweet but with a sophistication to it also. She was intelligent and friendly and spoke sufficient accented English. Her teeth were perfect and her smile bright and she knew it could dazzle. She was a natural flirt, I felt; it was instinctive, and not feigned. When our eyes connected she would hold the look.

Mick had given me a handwritten letter in French to give to her. I handed it to Brigitte Bardot, feeling like an emissary from a Prince to a Princess. "Chère Brigitte," it began.

She took it from me and read it, then folded it and put it on the floor beside her. She laughed a little laugh.

"Mick is naughty, no," she said to me. "Do you know him well?"

"Yes," I said. "Pretty well."

She asked me what the show might be like and we started to talk.

Tony was on the sofa beside me, and Patrick Bauchau, from across the room, thought to engage him in conversation and leaned forward.

He'd misheard Tony's name on introduction.

"Listen, Tiny, you know what Descartes said?"

"What was that, Patrick?"

Brigitte Bardot asked me if there'd be any other girls on the show.

" 'Je pense, donc je suis.' "

"Ah-ha." Tony nodded seriously, as if comprehending.

"Probably Marianne Faithfull," I said.
"I love her, she's so beautiful," Brigitte Bardot said.

" 'I think therefore I am,' Descartes said. You know what I think, Tiny?"
"What's that, Patrick?"

"Could you get an elephant for me to ride in on, Michael?"
"Sure, Brigitte, I could get an elephant for you."

"With me, Tiny, it's I . . ." Patrick Bauchau made a discreet upward thrust with his right arm, bringing it into contact with his left, ". . . therefore I am. What do you think, Tiny?"

"Maybe," Brigitte Bardot said, "you could get someone to throw knives at me."

"That's certainly a way to look at things, Patrick."
Tony gave a little laugh. He was no stranger to the delights of female company. But Tony's voice was getting thin. I knew he had not yet really recovered from our previous meeting, the infection of hysteria, nor had I.

"I don't know if we could get you insured for that, Brigitte," I said.
"But with trick photography, we could do the knives?" Brigitte Bardot asked. "Or maybe I could swallow a sword," she said, pronouncing the w.

She leaned her head back and comically mimed it with a trembly hand as she took the invisible blade into her mouth and down into her gullet. She looked at me and laughed.

Tony was staring at Patrick Bauchau's socks.

"Patrick," Tony asked, "why are you wearing one blue sock and one red one?"

"I woke up this morning, and I thought who says I have to match my socks? It makes me look at life in a different way. You should try it, Tiny."

Fortunately, it was at this moment that Olga Horstig-Primuz came to the unknowing rescue and told us that Brigitte had a contract with an American TV company to do a special and she didn't know if she could get them to release her for the Rolling Stones, but she'd try.

Our business had drawn to a close.

Brigitte Bardot said to Tony and me, "Patrick and I are going out for dinner. Why don't you join us? We'll have fun."

I shook my head.

"I'm afraid we have to take the train back to London this evening, so, much as we'd like to, we can't."

Tony looked at me as though someone he'd previously regarded as somewhat intelligent had lost his mind.

Patrick Bauchau said, looking at me, "Come on, you fellows, you and Tiny can take an early morning flight. Believe me, we'll have some fun."

"I'm not really flying at the moment," I said.

So we left, with Brigitte Bardot giving us both a soft double kiss on our cheeks.

And took the train that night back to London, with Tony, a man of usually unfailing good temper, sulking.

Unfortunately, Olga Horstig-Primuz wasn't able to swing it for Brigitte Bardot to be on our show.

The Rolling Stones, each of whom was enthusiastic, and I decided who we wanted on the show and then Mick would find their numbers in the little black phone book he carried in a back pocket and make the calls himself. The first went to Pete Townshend and so The Who were in.

Mick and I wanted a new group and after hearing a lot of demos, narrowed it down to two and chose Jethro Tull and rejected a band we thought too guitar-heavy, the newly formed Led Zeppelin.

Steve Winwood was going to gather some musicians he wanted to play with, to make a one-time-only super-group, but he dropped out just two days before the show. Mick and I needed someone who might be willing to put a band together, overnight really, to join our merry troop. We thought John Lennon might have the temperament for this challenge and so Mick dialed the number.

"Sure," John said. "I'll call Eric [Clapton]. We've already been playing together. Can you get us a bass player?"

Keith Richards said he'd love to play bass for John and so we were on, with Mitch Mitchell of the Jimi Hendrix Experience on drums.

On the evening before our only day of rehearsal, I had a worried phone call from Jo Bergman, who ran the Rolling Stones office, to tell me that Taj Mahal and his band, who were to be on the show and who had already arrived in England, had been denied work permits and were to be deported.

Knowing that the work permits were not in order, we'd asked Taj and his band to come in wearing suits and to say they were tourists. But they'd arrived in jeans and leather, with floral shirts, carrying guitar cases, with feathers stuck in the hatbands of their sombreros, and had, unsurprisingly, been identified as musicians on their way to a gig.

I went to Mick's house in Chelsea that night around ten. He had a wariness about the authorities, having been sentenced, with Keith, to prison the previous year following a dodgy drug bust. They'd been released but Mick had been very unsettled by the experience. We agreed it was too bad Taj wouldn't be able to play and started to think who we would get to replace him on the morrow.

Then Keith Richards arrived and we filled him in.

"You two are such pussies," Keith said, glaring at us.

"But they're not allowed to work in England," I said. "No work permits."

"So what?" Keith said, gimlet-eyed, exhibiting an unbuckling tenacity I'd not seen before, but perhaps Mick had. He went on. "Shoot them tomorrow on the rehearsal day and no one will be the wiser. I'm disgusted with the way you two are looking at this. Taj will be on the show or you can go fuck yourselves."

As I took part in, and witnessed, this conversation, I realized it was really a struggle between Keith and Mick, and saw the complexity that existed in a relationship that had started in grade school. On this occasion, it was as though a rabid dog had gone on the attack against a wily agile cat who, I was sure, would always find a safe perch to land on.

The next day, we did film Taj and his band, but in tighter shots than I'd wanted, so as not to expose the sparse audience behind them.

John and Yoko Ono and John's young son, Julian, came out that day for the only rehearsal we'd have. They sat looking as some of the circus acts were being auditioned. Afterward, Yoko took me aside and said that if we used the boxing kangaroos, John wouldn't appear. I'm not sure if she'd talked to John about this but, needless to say, the kangaroos hopped back to their holding pen and were not seen again.

I got home after rehearsal around midnight. Jean Marsh and I were staying in Parliament Hill near Hampstead Heath. As she and I were having the late supper she'd prepared, the phone rang. I answered it reluctantly, not wanting my meal and relaxation interrupted. The caller was Brian Jones, who had an apartment nearby. He had been a central part of the Rolling Stones since the beginning and thought it was his band until Mick and Keith had felt it necessary to shoulder him aside.

He was crying.

"I'm not coming tomorrow. I can't go through it anymore."

I couldn't tell if he was drunk, but he was slurring his words a little.

"What do you mean? You have to," I said, wondering how many more crises our little boat would have to weather.

"You don't know how they're treating me, how mean they are to me. I hate the Rolling Stones."

"But you're part of them. What would they be without you?"

"They don't deserve me."

Brian's nature had become somewhat self-pitying since I'd first met him three years before. Debauchery had taken a, alas, predictable toll. And on his golden beauty too; at only twenty-six, he was on his way to becoming the portrait in the attic.

Jean brought my plate and a glass of wine to the phone as Brian and I continued to talk. After twenty minutes or so, I convinced him to be there the next day.

I hung up feeling sad, but not surprised, that the world in which he was living had become too extreme for someone whose character was not strong.

The following day we started to shoot, but the cameras that Tony and I had imported from France did keep breaking down. In the afternoon as yet another French engineer went on the attack with his screwdriver, I wandered backstage.

I looked into one of the utilitarian dressing rooms to find some of the musicians—Mick, Keith, John, Pete Townshend, Eric Clapton, and others—drinking tea or coffee and whiling away the time improvising, playing, and singing old R&B, doo-wop, Tamla Motown, with Keith Moon playing spoons on a table.

I think if any image of those years of rock 'n' roll, the mid- to late 1960s, captured for me the connection of those young men, this was it. (Marianne Faithfull is a beautiful presence in *RSRNRC* and of course there were other women but the culture was mainly male.) Rivals but intimate friends in this still (just) innocent time, these men only in their twenties had created or

John and Mick. I'm wondering when the camera will be fixed.
(Photograph by Ethan Russell. Copyright © Ethan Russell.
All rights reserved.)

"Yer Blues." Eric Clapton, Mitch Mitchell on drums, John Lennon,
and Keith Richards on bass. (Photograph by Ethan Russell.
Copyright © Ethan Russell. All rights reserved.)

were part of the English bands which were exploding and sending their shards of brilliance all over the world and into the history of the century.

The ferment they caused reminds me of another group of,
mainly, men who a hundred or so years earlier, coming from all
parts of the country, had gathered in Paris, as these musicians
had in London, and although knowledgeable of what had gone
before were determined to take things in a new, sometimes, at
first anyway, scorned and ridiculed, direction. Their names were
Monet, Manet, Seurat, van Gogh.

At about 10 P.M., John and his band did "Yer Blues." During
the song, in the control room, I was puzzled by a black bag
which had been placed at the foot of the stage. Song over, the
bag wriggled and, like a dark butterfly, Yoko Ono emerged

wearing black, her long hair flowing, and she did an extended mesmerizing ululation backed by John's band and an exasperated imported violinist who thought this was supposed to be his spot.

Ian Stewart started to set up the Rolling Stones' stage at one o'clock and so it was not until after 2 A.M. that the band was ready to go on. The afternoon jam session seemed a long time ago and they'd been there since noon when we shot the entrance into the Big Top. They were tired and irritable and, in one or two cases, a little unsteady. But think of it this way—if a group of singing nuns had been sitting around for fourteen hours, with only their guitars for company, imbibing nothing stronger than tea, they too might be in a fractious mood.

"You Can't Always Get What You Want" went okay after many takes, then some of the *Beggars Banquet* album, take after ragged take. And then it was 5 A.M. and time for "Sympathy for the Devil," the one we'd all looked forward to when we were fresher and clearer earlier in the day/night. We did a take which was a shambles, for Mick, for them, for me, for the cameramen who'd had their heads in the viewfinder for seventeen hours.

We had a short break. Mick and I discussed stopping and coming back the following evening, but it proved too expensive. He asked if I and my guys could do another take.

"We can if you can," I answered.

Pissed off and tired, Mick went to talk to his troops, "a little touch of Harry in the night," and then when the music started again, he forced himself into a performance, teasing, dismissive, jaded, electric, the likes of which I'd never seen before. Then the song over, the half-naked twenty-five-year-old boy stood up and his sharpshooter's mind relaxed and his marathoner's body drooped. He looked at the others, grinned, and yawned. One more song, "Salt of the Earth," and we were done, everyone now giddy with tiredness, Brian Jones smiling along with the others. It was the last time he played with the Rolling Stones and seven months later he was dead.

We finished the Rolling Stones' thrilling set after dawn had broken on that December morning.

In November of 1968, as I was preparing *The Rolling Stones Rock and Roll Circus,* I got a call from Paul McCartney asking me to come to Apple, The Beatles' office building in Savile Row. I walked over from the nearby Rolling Stones' office and went up a flight of stairs to the floor-through space which served as office, living, dining, and conference room. They were all there, and Mal and Neil Aspinall.

Paul said they'd been happy with our recent videos and knew I was busy working for their friendly rivals, the Rolling Stones, but, if I could fit it in, The Beatles wanted to do a television special, partly as a result of their experience playing to the hundred or so people who sang along on *Hey Jude.*

We'd meet every week or ten days during November and December. After a while it became clear that though Paul was the driver of the bus, one or two of the others might get off at the next stop. The harmony which had existed when they'd first started, and during the heady days of their striding onto the world stage and through *Sgt. Pepper* and their time after the Maharishi, had gradually been fraying as they spent more time on their own. Touring often holds rock 'n' roll bands together.

A few afternoons after we'd finished shooting the *RSRNRC,* I was at Apple with The Beatles for our last meeting before we were to begin work on the TV special at the beginning of January 1969.

There was a slight sense of project fatigue in the room (this was before we'd even begun). But Paul pushed on. He had the idea that I should shoot documentary footage as they rehearsed, to use as a half hour teaser to be shown the week before the TV special and, as for that, well, we'd figure out what we wanted to do as time went on, because we hadn't figured it out yet, what it would be or where it would be shot.

As the meeting was drawing to a weary close, John, not this day with Yoko, who hadn't seemed particularly connected with what was going on, said he wanted to play us a tape he and Yoko had made. He got up and put a cassette into the tape machine and stood beside it, looking at us as we listened.

The soft murmuring voices did not at first signal their purpose. It was a man and a woman but hard to hear, the microphone having been at a distance. I wondered if the lack of clarity was the point. Were we even meant to understand what was going on, was it a kind of artwork where we would not be able to put the voices into a context, and was context important? I felt perhaps this was something John and Yoko were examining. But then, after a few minutes, the context became clear. John and Yoko were making love, with endearments, giggles, heavy breathing, both real and satirical, and the occasional more direct sounds of pleasure reaching for a climax, all recorded by the faraway microphone. But there was something innocent about it too, as though they were engaged in a sweet serious game.

John clicked the off button and turned again to look toward the table, his eyebrows quizzical above his round glasses, seemingly genuinely curious about what reaction his little tape would elicit.

However often they'd shared small rooms in Hamburg, whatever they knew of each other's love and sex lives, this tape seemed to have stopped the other three cold. Perhaps it touched a nerve of residual Northern reticence.

After a palpable silence, Paul said, "Well, that's an interesting one."

The others muttered something and the meeting was over.

It occurred to me as I was walking down the stairs that what we'd heard could have been an expression of 1960s freedom and openness but was it more likely that it was as if a gauntlet had been thrown down? "You need to understand that this is where she and I are now. I don't want to hold your hand anymore."

As I went toward my Christmas with Jean Marsh, I wondered

if working with The Beatles on their TV special would be a happy experience. After all, how lucky could I be, first the Rolling Stones and then The Beatles?

Like one of those soldiers who doesn't know the war is over and emerges from a jungle hiding place, blinking, into a new world, *The Rolling Stones Rock and Roll Circus* was, for a variety of reasons, not seen by the public until twenty-eight years after we made it. It premiered at the 1996 New York Film Festival, where it was a great hit.

Eleven

On January 2, 1969, The Beatles arrived more or less as scheduled at the large chilly sound stage at Twickenham Film Studios and began, in a listless manner, to see if they could create joy again.

As the days progressed, The Beatles were acting as anything but a single entity. Paul would usually be on time and the others usually within an hour or two of the call time, John always with Yoko, so for the first time there were five people sitting within the creative circle. But "call time" is a movie term, and though they'd all acted in movies, they weren't actors. They were musicians and the idea of being filmed as they were doing something intimate, and subject to change, was unfamiliar to them and, maybe, unpleasant. On some days, one of them wouldn't show up and the ones who were present would just rehearse bits and pieces and then go home.

But there were good days when they got stuck into making a song work. But things had changed so much since their early collaborative days. They weren't writing songs together anymore, as Lennon and McCartney had done as teenagers sitting in the parlor of Paul's house in Liverpool or in a hotel room on the road. Now one of them would write a song and then come in and demo it for the others, go through the chords, and the songwriter would really regard the others as sidemen, instructed to play their parts.

And there was no idea that any of us could agree on, to do with the TV special. Ringo wanted to do it at the Cavern, the little club in Liverpool where Brian Epstein had first seen them. John and Yoko didn't really care where we did it but did seem up for some sort of adventure, or maybe they just wanted to get out of the cold barn at Twickenham. George didn't seem to want to do it at all. Paul was the one who kept pushing for us to make a plan. His character is resolute, and I think in his heart Paul felt if he couldn't get them to agree as a group to do something as a group that they might fall apart, and, because of his nature, that was the last thing he wanted.

I had heard of an amphitheater on the coast of Tunisia and had the notion that The Beatles would start at dawn plugging in their amps and setting up the drum kit in this place where the stone had been beveled by the sand of centuries. Then they'd start to play, and, song by song, the music would float across the land, and, like traveling to an enlarged Noah's Ark, not by twos but by fours and then scores, people would come to the music, and what better music could there be? Men, women, children would come, on foot, camel, jeep; black, white, Arab; and by nightfall, the ancient steps would be full of the world.

The idea caught on. John and Yoko were for it and Paul, very much. Ringo said maybe it could work. John suggested we hire a small ocean liner so we could bring some of the audience with us, the English contingent. Yes, Paul said. They'd rehearse on the boat, and I'd film it for the documentary. Reservations were made for Mal and Neil to fly to Tunisia to check out the location, the hotels, and security problems. We were on our way to something fabulous and were, most of us, excited.

George had been silent during these discussions, moodily plucking on his guitar.

His position was a difficult one. He didn't want them to perform in public again; it had all gotten too crazy. I saw one of their final public appearances at a theater in London. The screaming was so loud, the balcony shaking, that they couldn't hear themselves play and had abandoned the show after a song or two. George just wanted to make an album and felt his position within the group wasn't as valued as his talent should demand. He'd been the youngest, fifteen, when Paul was sixteen and John seventeen, and, the story was, he'd carry the guitar cases as the other two strode ahead, discussing their great plans. And also, probably, he wasn't happy with the traditional album shake-out, artistically or financially. If there were twelve tracks, say, nine would probably be Len/Mac, another with Ringo, and two by George. And George knew he was soon to stake his claim to be his own man, a unique musician, passionate, tender, and ironic.

During the early days of what became *Let It Be,* the movie, Paul and George would squabble, John and Yoko would be in their own world, and Ringo would observe. By "observe," I mean no lack of regard for the position of one of the great rock 'n' roll drummers.

With a couple of notable exceptions, drummers are not usually committed songwriters and so are somewhat removed from the fractiousness and rivalry of the guitars and vocalists, which is usually where the songs come from. And also, of course, they sit behind the others on a rostrum, the perfect place from which to observe, and sometimes to provide the cooler counseling head. Charlie Watts of the Rolling Stones is the greatest exemplar of this. He has been the glue of the Rolling Stones for almost fifty years.

At Twickenham, The Beatles, Yoko, and I, often joined by our cameraman Tony Richmond, would have a proper lunch in the small dining room up a flight of stairs, adjoining a bar where some crew members and studio office workers would be sinking their couple of pints of beer before going off to their own lunch.

Macrobiotic for John and Yoko, a roast and chips for some of the others, and usually an omelet or fish for me. When one day I ordered a steak, John and Yoko, who had previously regarded me as something of a dietary ally, looked at the piece of meat on my plate, and then at me, as though I'd let them down, although I think I caught in John's eye a slight hint of meat envy.

The Beatles would talk about how uneasy they were about money. They'd made millions, but because of some dodgy deals or bad advice, or sums which were uncollected or had been siphoned off by foreign distributors, they felt financially things were out of control. They'd opened Apple, first as a bargain clothing store and then the company based in Savile Row, where inventors or dreamers or scammers would come in and say they needed money for this or that scheme and be financed and often not seen again. The Beatles felt they were hemorrhaging money. They knew they could continue to make it with their music but were trying to control the flow because, amongst other things, they all had large houses, grand Rolls-Royces and Mercedes, customized Minis (though Paul often traveled by underground), and a regular need for cash.

George was usually with us, joining in the conversation, affable and friendly and interested in the give-and-take, but on the day of the Tunisian discussion, he wasn't with us as the meal started. At the morning rehearsal, I could tell by his silence and withdrawal that something was simmering inside him, and so in my role as documentarian, I'd asked our soundman to bug the flower pot on the lunch table.

We'd finished the first course when George arrived to stand at the end of the table.

We looked at him as he stood silent for a moment.

"See you 'round the clubs," he said.

That was his good-bye. He left.

John, a person who reacted aggressively to provocation, immediately said, "Let's get in Eric. He's just as good and not such a headache."

Paul and Ringo would not be drawn in, and after lunch we went back to the studio where Paul, John, and Ringo improvised a ferocious riff, half an hour of anger and frustration expressed with guitars and drums. Yoko sat on the edge of the rostrum on the blue cushion which had been George's and howled into his mike.

(My bug had only picked up the sounds of cutlery banging on china plates, obscuring what the muffled voices had said.)

A few days of deep desultoriness followed but with phone calls and meetings between the three or four of them.

George said he'd come back if any plans for a TV special would be abandoned and that we'd leave Twickenham and go to their basement studio at Apple to continue work on the songs.

With this demand and for whatever other reasons, the negative outweighing the positives, that's what happened.

The studio had been built by Magic Alex, an inventor who'd ingratiated himself with The Beatles. The day before they were to arrive, I went into the studio with Glyn Johns, who was the engineer of the album, working with their longtime producer George Martin, and we found no one had invented any plugs for the electrics to go into. Overnight this was fixed.

And so we began again, with two cameras filming rehearsals: "The Long and Winding Road," "Get Back," versions one, two, or twelve, improvisations, conversations, songs which were from when they were teenagers listening to the radio, songs from Liverpool pubs. The mood did lighten, somewhat, at Apple, helped by the presence of Billy Preston, who joined in to play organ on the sessions.

But what would become of all of this, I wondered. I was learning from experience (the *RSRNRC* was unspooling because the Rolling Stones thought that on the day The Who were more dynamic) that if a project seemed to be losing momentum, it might be shelved, put in a closet, unseen; these great musicians and artists being subject to whim and lack of attention, or being seduced by the next thing which captured their imagination. I dreaded the idea that many of the fascinating things we'd filmed would never be seen and I knew we needed a conclusion to what had now become a documentary film.

After our first week at Apple, on a Saturday, we had lunch at the conference table. Nice girls who did the cooking would bring in a first course, to be followed by roast chicken, vegeta-

bles, and potatoes, with red and rosé wine, and something macrobiotic for John and Yoko.

"We need to have an ending for all this footage, somewhere
we're going. A conclusion," I said.

Yoko piped up.

"Are conclusions important?"

I'd run into my first trip wire.

I liked Yoko, admired the refinement of her beauty, her intelligence and questing artistic imagination, and her commitment to the union she and John were creating, and the magnetic
field she'd erected around them; but could not be unaware of a
sense of steely self-regard, probably necessary in the hard avant-
garde art world where she'd first made her reputation.

The way she looked at things was not always the way I did.
Her question had to be dealt with.

"I see what you're saying," I said to her. "In one way you're
right, conclusions aren't important, they're not, but in another
way, sometimes maybe they are."

I was happy with my baffling analysis of "conclusions."

"What if we call it something else? Just say it's the place to
stop this particular episode in your lives."

"Like what?" Paul asked.

I'd had an idea.

"Well, we didn't go to Tunisia and that's fine," I said, smiling
at George to signify no hard feelings (although they weren't
quite soft yet).

I remember feeling like Mickey Rooney in one of the Andy
Hardy movies: "Hey kids, this is a swell barn. We can put the
show on right here," when I said, "Why don't we do it on the
roof?"

"What on the roof?"

"A concert."

I put this forward believing that it could work but without a lot of confidence that they'd go for it. They were interested in their songs but I was interested in the film. To my surprise, they began to paw the idea, sniffing at it, knocking it from one to the other, to see if it was safe to take a bite.

After lunch, Paul and Mal, Tony and I, Ringo, a few others, went up on the roof and had a look around. I was seeing where the cameras would go. Paul said we should shore up the old roof from below to carry the weight of equipment and Billy Preston's organ, and he and I decided to try for Wednesday of the coming week. The Beatles would go on recording and I would get everything ready for the day.

On Wednesday, I had my eleven cameras and crew ready for the roof and street below. I'd had a two-way mirror constructed in the lobby to put a camera behind in case the police came in so they could be filmed without their knowing.

But there was heavy fog and we pushed to the next day. The plan was to begin around 12:30 to get the lunchtime crowds.

On Thursday, January 30, 1969, The Beatles, Yoko, and I gathered about noon in a small room off the wooden staircase leading to the roof and, to my dismay, I realized the enterprise was not secure.

George didn't want to do it, didn't see the point—what did it have to do with anything?

Ringo said, "And it's cold up there."

"Come on, lads," Paul said. "It'll be fun," enthusiasm covering the hard muscle of his determination. "Let's do *something.*"

But no one moved. The six of us stood there, stasis about to set in, momentum about to be fatally lost, ennui about to settle its cloud on our beings.

But one voice had not been heard from. Eyes under lids looked toward that person. Time froze.

"Fuck it," said John. "Let's do it."

And so The Beatles climbed the narrow staircase to the roof and into history.

The concert on the roof was the last time The Beatles ever played together to any kind of audience. It was their final performance, their good-bye, although none of us knew it.

And the wonderful thing was that they were happy, dispute and rancor forgotten. In the forty minutes we were up there, on that cold winter's day, they rocked and rolled and connected as they had in years gone by, friends again. It was beautiful to see.

When it was over, John stepped to the mike and said: "I'd like to say thank you on behalf of the group and ourselves, and I hope we passed the audition."

Twelve

Three months after we finished documenting The Beatles during this difficult time, they recharged themselves and went back into the studio to make the superlative *Abbey Road*. But, *Let It Be*, the movie, did not come out until the spring of 1970. By which time The Beatles had finally broken up.

I was in Hollywood by then. I'd been asked by MGM to make a movie based on a journal written by a groupie nicknamed Suzy Creamcheese, courtesy of Frank Zappa.

The rights to *The Adventures of Suzy Creamcheese* were owned by James William Guercio, one of the most enchantingly odd people I've ever met.

Only twenty-five, he'd already made a fortune as the producer of Blood, Sweat & Tears and Chicago, whom he also managed. Handsome, not tall, needing eyeglasses, liking cowboy boots, Republican by nature but Democratic by vote, he was kind, generous, funny, and, in those years of excess, didn't smoke, drug, or drink (although the last time I saw him he had one glass of good red wine and acknowledged he owned a sizable chunk of Colorado with his own recording studio). He had an eighteen-year-old girlfriend, Lucy, whom he later married.

He was polite and courteous at a time when these were not general attributes in the world of rock 'n' roll. He'd exchange a few words with a business associate on the phone, soft-spoken, but extremely definite and in control, for someone so young. He seemed to have an understanding of both music and money. I asked him how, with his good manners, he could navigate the murky and rough rock 'n' roll waters. He told me his family was originally from Cefalu.

"That's in Sicily." he said, then shrugged and smiled. "If you know what that means."

He'd optioned the journal written by the girl known as Suzy Creamcheese. In order to get the deal at MGM, he'd only shown them one page, what came to be known as "representative p. 94," thinking it would do the trick, which it did. Page 94 included six mentions of "blow-job," five of "cock," and three of Jim Morrison.

It was raining in Los Angeles when I arrived at Union Station. I'd traveled from the East by train, still not being an easy flier and still because I remembered sometimes being on these trains with my mother and Mary. On the trip, I'd been imagining the girl who'd written the journal and who was to pick me up. In my mind I'd cast her as a scrawny, washed-out blonde, based on some of the groupies I'd met in London.

So I was surprised when a tall, strong-featured, glossy dark-haired young woman approached me.

"I'm Pamela. You're Michael, right?"

"How'd you know?"

"Jimmy said I'd recognize you because all the other people on the platform would be over sixty."

She gave me a confident handshake, took one of my bags, and led me to her small car.

Pamela and I had a tuna melt at Ben Frank's on the Strip.

In an unembarrassed and easy manner, she talked about her book, two hundred pages about her middle-class youth in Southern California, her stern ferocious father, and her encounters with many of the rock stars of the time.

She said blow-jobs were the easy currency of rock 'n' roll dressing rooms because the girl could have a connection with the star, which was a thing to be desired, and, for the star, it was not time-intensive and he didn't have to take off his clothes. A blow-job before going onstage was something to be mixed with alcohol and drugs to send a variety of pleasant or disjointed sensations to the brain of the twenty-four-year-old fronting his band at the Whisky a Go Go.

"I'm known as velvet lips," she said with a laugh.

She dropped me at the Sunset Marquis.

I went to bed early that night, ten or so, train-lag probably, when there was a call from the lobby.

"I'm on my way up," said Pamela.

She put her bag on a chair, took off her boots, and got into bed beside me still wearing her jeans.

"Do you want to do anything?" she asked.

Loyal to the person I missed in London, but wanting to be polite, I said, "Thanks but I'm tired."

"That's okay," she said. And then, "Can I stay here? I get lonely sometimes."

She put her arms around me and went to sleep.

Over the next few days, Jimmy Guercio and I discussed how we saw the movie.

I had been struck by the way I'd imagined Suzy Creamcheese and by the reality and complication of the real girl, Pamela, and so we came up with the idea that a journalist from New York would arrive in Los Angeles to do a story and wanting to concentrate it on a girl people told him about as being very involved with all that was happening on the wild Sunset Strip, but she had disappeared. He'd only seen photos of her when she was young and that would allow him, in the episodes with the stars of rock, Jim Morrison, David Crosby, Phil Spector, to imagine her as a wasted young blonde but at the end, when he'd meet her, she'd be tall and dark, complex and strong, a different girl in every way. The movie would be an immersion in the sometimes glorious, often tawdry, culturally explosive world of California rock 'n' roll, and about how we create an idea of a person from what others say, and what the reality is. Jimmy and I were very pleased with our idea.

My agent, Bill Tennant, who was also representing the project for Jimmy, met us in an outer office at MGM where he'd arranged a meeting with the head of the studio, so we could discuss our movie about a groupie. Bill Tennant was a nattily suited man in his thirties, with close-cut hair and a firm jawline.

After only a brief wait, a good sign, the double doors to the inner office were thrown open by a small, trim, balding suntanned man about forty. He was dressed for tennis.

"James William, Michael Lindsay, come on in," said the head of the studio. "Call me Herb. Hi Bill."

The office, a corner site, was the size of a small gymnasium. A large desk was at the back of the room near a run of windows. On the desk was a telephone, a few scripts, and leaning against it a tennis racquet. The rest of the furniture in the room was an extremely curious mix of styles and periods.

Bill Tennant and I sat on a hard dark green velvet sofa, Empire period, with the back studded with little buttons, and Jimmy sat opposite on a bean bag. Herb pulled up a chair with a fur seat and animal horn arms and back.

"I bet you, Michael Lindsay and you, Bill, don't know what you're sitting on," Herb said. "Trust me, you won't."

Jimmy, Bill Tennant, and I looked at each other, shrugging our shoulders, playing along.

"Give up?" Herb asked.

We all gave up, eager to learn what exactly the game was.

"Greta Garbo's. From *Camille*. We're running all the old movie furniture through this office. We're auctioning off everything from God knows where that's ended up in our warehouses. Michael Lindsay and Bill, Greta Garbo sat on that sofa. And, you, James William, Doris Day once had her fanny on that bag."

Jimmy said, "Wow," thinking that would convey enough sense of general wonderment and also some fanny respect for the pretty Doris Day.

"What's yours, Herb?" Bill Tennant asked.

Herb turned to look at his tennis-shorted hip on the fur, took in the horn (antelope? bison?) on which his arm rested, and said, "No one's told me. It just came in this morning." He pressed a buzzer on a chinoiserie table next to him.

"Yes sir?" the female voice asked.

"Julie, talk to someone and find out what I'm sitting on."

"Yes sir."

Then the phone on the large desk rang, one of its little lights blinking. Herb got up.

I wondered if the furniture quiz we'd just participated in was a Hollywood metaphor: you weren't really sure what the game was, and only they knew the answer; but I hoped it wasn't.

"Sell it when it gets to fifty, that's what I told you," Herb said into the phone and then returned to sit again on his animal artifact, provenance currently unknown. He leaned toward me.

"So, Michael Lindsay, what's your idea for this movie?" His smile showed bright teeth.

I'd never done a pitch before but I'd thought about it and felt I had an interesting comparison to make, although I hadn't discussed it with Jimmy. As I opened my mouth to begin, Herb said, "Hey, Bill, what's that suit you're wearing? That's a nice one."

"Don Cherry," Bill said, naming a high-price Beverly Hills tailor. "I get all my suits there."

He fingered the modishly wide lapel of his pale blue suit.

Then Herb was back to me.

"Okay, Michael Lindsay, tell me. You've got this groupie who blows rock stars. How do you see the movie?"

Herb's prompt gave me a quick moment of biblical-scale doubt. But I was not nimble enough to be able to change what I'd planned to say, so I started.

"Harriette Wilson was a celebrated courtesan in Regency London. She wrote a book about her affairs with famous people, like Lord Byron. But she offered them the chance to buy their way out of the book. Interestingly, that's where the remark 'Publish and be damned' comes from. The Duke of Wellington said it.'"

I hoped Herb would see a connection between Lord Byron and Jim Morrison, and the Duke of Wellington with, say, Phil Spector.

I drew a breath to go on but could not be unaware of a sort of wary stillness in the room and a sudden rigidity in Bill Tennant beside me on Greta Garbo's sofa.

I continued. "The first chapter of her book begins, 'I shall not tell how or why I became, at the age of fifteen, the mistress of the Earl of Craven; whether it was the severity of my father or the indulgence of my own heart, I cannot say.' " And then I finished by saying, "So she was sort of like a groupie in Regency London."

Herb looked at me, then at Bill Tennant, then back at me.

"I don't understand. You want to shoot this in London?"

"No, Herb," Bill Tennant said. "He was just using a quote."

"What for?" Herb asked. "And who is Earl Craven? I haven't heard of him. Is he in a group?"

"The Earl of Craven," I said. "He was a rich man in the 1820s."

I thought this was an interesting piece of historical information.

Under the armpit of Bill Tennant's Don Cherry suit, a small dark sweat stain had begun to form.

"It's a comparison, Herb," Jimmy said smoothly, lightly, as though that had to be clear to everyone.

"Yes," I said, glad for Jimmy's aid and hoping to recover the ball, which seemed to have slipped out of my hands.

"I thought there was a connection between these two women. They both had strict fathers."

"So did I but I don't see what that has to do with anything," Herb said. "Do you have any other ideas?"

"Yes I do."

Harriette Wilson/Suzy Creamcheese may have cost us a few

yards but I felt confident that the terrific idea Jimmy and I had come up with would get us across the goal line.

As I was explaining about the writer from New York, I looked at Jimmy, who was nodding me on, and sideways at Bill Tennant, whom we had not told of our idea. He was sitting as though mummified and the sweat stain on his suit now a thin dark line down to his ribs.

I got to what Jimmy and I thought was our coup de théâtre, that at the end we'd see a different girl.

Herb spoke very slowly.

"A different girl from who?"

"The girl he's been looking for is blond and at the end he finds a girl with dark hair," I said.

"What, did she get a dye job? Why would she do that?"

Jimmy clarified.

"No, Herb, it's a different girl. We change girls."

The head of the studio sat back in his chair. The friends-together mood which had opened our meeting seemed to have changed. Jimmy caught my eye and gave a slight nod to Bill Tennant. The sweat stain had reached his hip.

Herb shook his head theatrically, as though trying to clear porridge from it.

"Look," he said, "we're making a movie about a girl, one girl the last time I looked. I've read representative page ninety-four. This girl's a tramp, and that's what we need to see, a girl who'll get her comeuppance. That's the movie we want to make. A movie with a great soundtrack which you can deliver, James William, that the kids will love."

"She's not a tramp," I heard myself say.

"Have you ever met her?" asked the head of the studio, something mean in it.

"I have, yes."

"Well, so have I. I saw her in a club and went up to her and said, 'I'm making your movie.'"

"Oh."

"And you know what, she just walked away from me like she wasn't interested."

His face was flushed and he summed up his encounter with: "And she's got a big ass."

The meeting was over. We all agreed to think about what we'd discussed and get together again the following week.

As the three of us waited in the corridor for the elevator to come, Bill Tennant looked at Jimmy and me and said, "I was a little worried at the beginning with the English stuff but, overall, I think that went pretty well."

I was still lying in bed at the Sunset Marquis at eleven on a Tuesday morning. I'd had coffee and was reading the *Los Angeles Times,* for a second time, to see if I could make it better, an article about *Let It Be* and me. The movie was to be released the following day at the small Vogue Theater on Hollywood Boulevard. I'd given an interview about it and was surprised, or concerned, that what had seemed clear to me when I'd said it had been reported without insight, with no recognition of irony or jokes. The Beatles were portrayed only as argumentative people, without extenuation, without subtlety. The article was accompanied by a photo of me. I'd been asked to sit on a bench and look out toward the traffic.

"Just think your thoughts," the photographer had said.

Thinking my thoughts had made me look pale and blank.

The telephone rang. I thought not to answer it in case it was one of the apparatchiks from the studio, with whom we'd had more dealings. Let the switchboard take a message. But maybe it was someone else. I picked up the phone.

"Hello."

"It's Orson," the deep rumble announced.

"Oh," I said.

It had been four years since the invitation to dinner with Marlene Dietrich.

"Hello," I said. "How are you?"

"I'm fine. You?"

"I'm all right."

"I saw the article in the *Times* this morning. About your movie."

"The photo wasn't any good."

"I thought it looked like you."

"A version."

"We all look like that in newspaper photos. An inaccurate version of ourselves. It doesn't look like you've changed much."

"I don't know if that's good or bad."

"Good probably. Are you happy with the movie?"

"Some of it."

"How so?"

"It's hard when your stars are your producers. And there were four of them."

"I know what that must be like."

"A lot I liked got cut out."

"It's torture, isn't it, when that happens. Like what?"

"I had to cut out half an hour of John and Yoko, really interesting stuff."

"Why?"

"We'd had a screening, they all were there, and the next day I got a call from Peter Brown to say it would probably be a good idea to cut the John and Yoko. I asked why. 'Let me put it this way,' he said, 'I've had three calls this morning to say it should come out.' "

"Did they think Yoko was tearing them apart?"

"They were torn apart anyway. Not by John and Yoko. Just by the fact that they'd become different people."

"That level of fame can be hard to deal with."

"I know." I said this in a way to show I recognized the connection between The Beatles and the extraordinary youth and fame that had been his. He'd made *Citizen Kane* when he was twenty-five.

From the original Citizen Kane *program, 1941.*

"But the footage was good," I said.

This was the longest conversation I'd ever had with him, just the two of us, no one else around.

"Well," he said, "I just wanted to wish you luck with it."

"Thank you. We'll see what happens."

Then there was a silence. Orson didn't speak for a moment, nor did I. The silence seemed loaded as though something was unresolved or should be said, as though a different subject should be brought up.

He was the elder. I wondered what he'd say next.

"Good luck," he said and he hung up.

I lay in bed glad of his interest and good wishes; yes, happy he'd called, it meant a lot, but also frustrated, as though we'd started on a web, just a few silken threads, each connected to the other, and now it was hanging there, incomplete.

I also recognized I felt in some way shy with him, not really being sure what the relationship was. I didn't imagine he might feel shy also, or some version of that.

A week or so later, I got a call from a secretary, saying Peter Bogdanovich was asking me to come to lunch at Columbia Pictures.

We sat opposite each other in the Executive dining room. We hadn't seen each other for seven or eight years.

Peter said, "I'm sorry things went wrong between us."

"How's Polly?"

"She's fine. She's working with me on this picture."

Peter was preparing to start *The Last Picture Show,* his wonderful breakthrough movie.

"Give her my love."

"Sure. You're working at Metro? How's it going?"

"We're not really seeing eye to eye."

"I've got wonderful producers."

"I'm glad."

"So, you've got a picture out with The Beatles. I'll try to catch it. I've never heard any of their music."

"What?" I thought to myself. I knew from our early friendship that Peter was a movie fanatic, as a teenager booking old films at the New Yorker Theater on the Upper West Side, coming out pallid after seeing three in a row. Movies were his art

form. But this was 1970 and to say that one hadn't heard a Beatles song was more than being out of touch with music but with
society at large. Maybe he was kidding.

"You haven't heard any of their songs?" I asked in a tone
meaning he could retract.

"Maybe on the radio once or twice, I'm not sure."

"Really?"

"Really."

He smiled his toothy smile, which glinted with a sense of
take it or leave it.

We finished our lunch, managing other subjects of conversation, but he and I knew that however polite we were and
would continue to be, what had been broken could not really be
mended.

Jimmy and I continued working on our script.

One evening I'd invited myself, Jimmy, and Jean Marsh,
who was visiting from London, for dinner with Charlie Lederer
at his house in Beverly Hills; Charlie, the man who'd given me
my first taste of beer when I was five. He'd written many famous
movies with his partner, Ben Hecht, and we wanted to talk to
him about our script and ask his advice. When I called my
mother to ask for his phone number, she said I might find him
changed, that there was a story he was taking heroin, having
been turned on by someone during the many rainy months he'd
spent in Tahiti when he was working on the remake of *Mutiny on
the Bounty,* starring Marlon Brando. She finished by saying, "But
I'm sure he'll be glad to see you again. He always liked you when
you were a little boy."

We sat in a semicircle nook off the living room. Charlie's
housekeeper opened a bottle of wine and served us a version of
Boeuf Stroganoff. Jimmy and I talked about our intentions with
the script and at first Charlie seemed to be listening, occasion-

ally chipping in, but the conversation became more one-sided, if not a little desperate, as Charlie seemed to be falling asleep, his head nodding toward the plate, dipping into the creamy sauce.

Then he roused himself and said, "I'll just excuse myself for a moment. Be right back."

Charlie pushed himself away from the table, rose slowly, and wandered out of the room.

Half an hour or more passed and Jimmy, Jean, and I sat there in silence staring at our empty plates.

I said, "I'll go look for him."

I stood in the corridor with floor-to-ceiling glass doors giving onto the lighted large garden with beds of flowers and a big swimming pool. No Charlie.

I heard a faint sound coming from a room down another corridor to my left, quavery distant singing.

I followed the sound. I went into a bedroom; it was more a tuneful mumbling than singing, really.

The bathroom door was open and that's where I found Charlie. He was naked, bent over the bathtub, a rubber strap on his left arm, a small syringe dangling, its needle in his vein.

It was then that I recognized the song.

> *"Happy days are here again.*
> *Oh, happy days are here again."*

Jimmy and I finished the script. We had a scene in which the New York writer went to a studio to pitch an idea for turning his story into a movie. We thought our meeting at MGM had been hilarious and would make a funny scene. Jimmy and I had pretty much transcribed verbatim our meeting with the head of the studio.

MGM rejected the script and decided they didn't want anything more to do with the project.

Evarts Ziegler, the head of Bill Tennant's agency, was nicknamed Zig. He was a charming, elegant, revered older agent. He'd invited me out for a drink to commiserate.

He played with the ice in his scotch and I drank my martini.

"A little piece of advice?" he offered.

"Sure, anything."

"It's probably not a good idea to go to a guy and say, 'I want a million dollars of your money to make a movie' and then, 'And if you go to page thirty-four, you'll see what an asshole you are.' "

Thirteen

In 1973, I'd been asked by London Weekend Television to produce—between directing TV dramas—a talk show for what was a lot of money to me at the time, £300 a week.

Russell Harty was an intelligent, funny, somewhat camp man from the North of England. He'd been a teacher and then found himself through various career changes as the host of his own weekly television show.

London Weekend wanted me to give the show a boost, by bringing on some of my rock 'n' roll friends. I booked The Who and David Bowie and made a slightly under-the-table deal for Russell to interview the usually unavailable Rudolf Nureyev.

We'd gone to pick him up at the Royal Ballet to have lunch and a chat about what he and Russell would talk about.

"We've booked a table at Inigo Jones," I said. "Is that okay?"

Nureyev was still sweating from his morning rehearsal.

"As long as I can have blood," the Tartar said. "I need blood."

He repeated the word, sounding like a Dracula in the hokiest B movie.

He ate a large rare steak for lunch and drank a glass of red wine. He was wearing a beautiful short jacket of smooth animal skin.

"What's your jacket?" I'd asked him.

"The skin of an unborn pony," he said, the Dracula accent again, with a smile to match.

Maybe it was, or maybe he said it to see if that would be an affront to what he thought was a more delicate European sensibility. He was known to be an unsettling, sometimes violent, provocateur.

I'd had a tangential connection with Nureyev a few years earlier.

Kit Lambert, the manager of The Who with Chris Stamp,

wanted to share an apartment with Jean and me, which was fine by us because he was often in America. I'd known Kit since my only year at Oxford, which was his last.

I'd gone to look at a lavish apartment in Bryanston Square. The owner, a homosexual gentleman, asked what Kit and I did.

"We're in show business, I suppose you could say."

"Show business? Um, I'm not sure."

"We're very reliable," I said.

"I'm sure you are. It's just that the last person I rented to was in show business. The dancer, Rudolf Nureyev?"

He inflected his voice up at the end, checking that I'd heard of the world-famous dancer. I nodded.

"He was perfectly charming to meet and I was glad to rent to him. At first."

"Something happened?"

"My cleaner told me what must have occurred, what she deduced from the, um, evidence."

"Evidence?" I questioned.

"He'd come back late at night and stand as far from the wall as he could and yet still be able to hit it with his, um, vomit. She could tell by the way the, um, substance was spread around. And that wall," he said, pointing, aggrieved, "was lacquered at great expense."

"I can assure you that neither Kit nor I would ever do that."

I thought it best not to reveal that my dear friend was a heavy drinker and regular drug user, and so we got the apartment.

It was through the Russell Harty show that I had my next connection with both Bogdanovich and Orson.

One Friday evening, a program assistant called and said, "Peter Bogdanovich is staying at Claridge's and Russell wondered if you knew him and if he'd be good for an interview?"

Peter had followed *The Last Picture Show* with *What's Up, Doc?* and *Paper Moon,* and each had been successful.

I didn't really want Peter on the program, but questioned my motives and so found myself dialing Claridge's. Peter was out and I left a detailed message which was diligently taken down by one of the women on the crack Claridge's switchboard.

I was out the next morning when Peter left a message saying he was leaving England in a day or so to see Charlie Chaplin in Switzerland for a documentary so he couldn't do the show, but would I come for breakfast at 9:30 on Monday. Room 324.

Shortly after 9:30 that morning, I knocked on 324. No answer. I knocked again.

"Who's there?" A cross voice came from the unmarked adjoining door.

"It's Michael."

"Oh, Christ. Hold on a minute."

I'd stayed at Claridge's and knew that sometimes the bathrooms were on the corridor, with the lavatory near the door.

"Take your time," I said. "Don't hurry."

I stood there, counted to 10, 20, 30, heard a hearty flush from an old-fashioned water closet, which was the kind of lavatory Claridge's had at the time, the overhead cistern, the chain with the porcelain knob at the end, and then a bar of hard soap to wash your hands with, and the thick soft towel to dry them.

100, 110, 120 and the door opened.

It was three years since we'd had lunch at Columbia Pictures. Peter looked much the same but burnished by his recent successes.

"I've ordered breakfast," he said. "I hope you like fruit."

"And coffee," I said as I went into the suite to see a large round room service table covered by a white cloth, a china coffee service, cups and jugs, strawberries from somewhere else in the world, orange and grapefruit slices, apples and pears, rolls and toast in a basket, some breakfast cereals.

"Fruit," Peter said, pointing at the display. "It's good for you. Good for jet lag."

"I've already had something, but coffee would be great."

We sat and as he poured a tousled blond girl came in from the bedroom; her shoulders seemed big in the long striped rugby shirt she was wearing.

"This is Cybill," Peter introduced.

Cybill Shepherd was pretty and sleepy, gave me a friendly smile, then looked at the table and made herself a bowl of cereal.

"We had a wonderful dinner with Orson last night," Peter said to me. He and Orson had become friends with Peter trying to help him with movie finance.

"Oh, is he in London?"

Peter continued. "He's had a terrific idea for what Cybill and I should do next."

"Oh?"

"*Daisy Miller,* you know, the Henry James? He said it's just the thing for us now, for Cybill."

He leaned over and gave her a kiss, as if to demonstrate his love for her, and also to show that things had changed. I'd read that he'd fallen for this girl, whom he'd discovered for *The Last Picture Show,* and had left Polly.

Cybill kissed him and returned to her cereal.

"How is he, Orson?" I asked.

"He's great. He said Daisy Miller is the part she was born to play, and for me to direct."

"That's terrific."

Peter spooned his fruit.

"So you're producing a talk show now? That's nice. The host is who?"

"Russell Harty."

"Haven't heard of him. But you know I'd do it as a favor to you, if I could. But I have to go to Switzerland to see Charlie."

He turned to Cybill again and asked, "We had a terrific dinner, didn't we?"

"Um," she nodded, her mouth full of crunchy flakes and milk and sugar.

"Orson's smoking these enormous cigars now, Montecristo A."

Peter rose and went to the desk.

"He gave me one."

He picked up the ten-inch souvenir from the night before and waved it.

"You'd like them. I wish I had one to give you."

"I have some at my tobacconist," I said.

The telephone rang.

"Maybe it's Charlie from Switzerland. We're going there tomorrow. I'm going to be interviewing Charlie."

He picked up the phone.

"Hello."

He looked at me and mouthed, "Orson."

"We had a really nice time last night. Cybill sends her love," Peter said to Orson, looking toward Cybill.

Cybill nodded in the affirmative as she surveyed the strawberries, and then spooned some into her cereal bowl.

"I've sent someone out for the book. I'll read it again this afternoon or on the plane to see Charlie."

He listened.

"Sure, I'll give Charlie your regards. Oh, guess who's here, having breakfast with us? Michael. Do you want to talk to him?"

I half rose to go to the phone as Peter listened to Orson's answer. But then Peter waved me back and motioned for me to sit down again.

Peter said, "Oh, okay, I'll tell him."

Then, "I'll talk to you when I've finished the book."

Peter hung up, looked at the phone for a moment, then at me. He shook his head slightly, as though some puzzling thought had intruded, then shrugged his shoulders, as though it didn't really concern him.

"Orson said, 'Tell him to call me, if he wants. He knows where I am.' "

I hadn't seen Orson since the brief meeting at Le Caprice ten years earlier. It was seven years since the invitation to dinner with Marlene Dietrich and three years since the odd inconclusive phone call in Hollywood. I didn't know he was in England until that morning.

Cybill shook some cereal on top of the strawberries and added some cream. Peter talked about his Charlie Chaplin documentary, and I finished my coffee and left, wishing him good luck with his endeavors.

Daisy Miller was a flop for Peter and Cybill, to be followed by another two movies for Peter which didn't do well. He and Cybill split up, and then Peter's life took a tragic turn. A young actress who was in a movie Peter was directing, and with whom he had fallen in love, was murdered by her estranged husband, who then committed suicide. The friend from my teenage years suffered terribly.

One night a year or so later, Jean Marsh and I had gone for dinner at Mr. Chow in London. We were seated upstairs and I looked around the room, and there in an opposite corner was Orson having dinner with two men.

"What the hell," I thought, and went over and said hello.

He seemed unusually delighted to see me and introduced his dinner companions as "people in advertising," as if to make sure they knew their place. The two men smiled in unison.

Orson was much bigger now and looked older than his fifty-nine years, graying beard and hair, dressed in black.

He looked toward Jean at the other table. They hadn't met yet, but she was having success starring in *Upstairs, Downstairs,* the series she'd co-created with her friend Eileen Atkins.

"I'd invite you and Miss Marsh to join us," Orson said, "but these gentlemen and I are discussing business, and I'm sure it would be as boring to you as it is to me."

The two men smiled as though Orson had said something else.

"I'm really glad to see you," he said. "You know, I was watching television a few weeks ago, and a drama came on and I had other things to do, but I kept watching it. It was so *well* directed. I watched it to the end to see who'd done it. And it was you. It was about a wedding party. That shot you did, all on one camera, which started with the old man coming out of the bathroom, checking his fly, and then the camera . . ."

He described in exact detail the five-minute single camera shot, and finished by saying, "It was wonderful."

He turned to the two ad men.

"Did you see that show?"

They said they hadn't.

"Well, you should have."

They said they were sorry.

He turned to me again and asked, "How are you?" as if the answer were of the utmost importance to him.

"I'm okay. You?"

"All right," he said, but patting his tummy as though there was too much of it.

I returned to our table and Jean and I had finished the first course when Orson rose heavily from his corner.

He shooed the admen downstairs. He was complimentary to Jean when I introduced them and seemed to want to stand there talking to us, his small teeth showing as he smiled.

I took a cigar out of my leather case and offered it to him.

He smiled as if remembering when things had been reversed.

"Not now, thanks. My doctor says I shouldn't for a while. Next time."

And then he carefully made his way down the spindly spiral staircase.

Fourteen

FEBRUARY 16, 2008
Every so often I reread what I've been writing and I recognize I haven't yet tried to really describe my mother.

I began last night and wrote six pages and when I looked at them this morning, I thought I'd gotten nowhere near her; that, in some queer way, she had managed, more than two years after her death, to elude me.

Although, having said that, a few episodes from her middle life might be useful in trying to know her better.

In the late 1960s, a time of national tension, my mother teamed up with a Franciscan brother, Jonathan Ringkamp, on a project which would bring benefit and a sort of hope to many. They collaborated on a multi-character colloquial updated version of *Everyman,* the fifteenth-century morality play. My mother and Brother Jonathan would go into the poorest, most disadvantaged communities in Manhattan, Queens, Brooklyn, and the Bronx, announce their presence, and say they wanted to put on the play in the streets and there would be a part for anyone who wished to join in. And, lured by their piper's tune, kids and adults who'd never seen or read a play became actors, even if only temporarily, joining the community my mother had introduced to me when I was fourteen. Imagination was engaged, thought stimulated, pleasure taken, lives changed. Some of the participants in what came to be known as the Everyman Street Theatre went on to professional careers.

For her Street Theatre, my mother received the Handel Medallion, New York City's highest cultural award.

Not long after, my mother went into therapy with Dr. Mary O'Neil Hawkins. Dr. Hawkins had known Freud and was a friend of his daughter, Dr. Anna Freud.

My mother had tried to persuade Jean, who was often in New York, to go to Dr. Hawkins as well.

Jean said there were aspects of her life she didn't wish to talk about, her secrets.

My mother said, "I have secrets too. You don't have to tell your therapist all your secrets. There are secrets you have to keep."

As a result of her therapy, my mother did revisit parts of her earlier life, which led her to wish to talk to and question me.

These conversations usually took place in the kitchen on my trips to New York from London. She'd make a special supper for herself if Boy was out. She'd had some angina attacks and thought a change of diet was in order. She's grill sardines and cashew nuts together and that would be her meal, the smell of which would linger through the next day in the apartment.

"I wake up early in the morning," she said, "and can't get back to sleep thinking of all the ways I let you down when you were a little boy."

"Don't worry, Ma. It was a long time ago and I've turned out all right, more or less."

"But still, it tortures me."

I went to her and kissed her on the brow. She was only five foot three.

"It's okay," I said.

She went on stirring the sardines and nuts.

"Still."

Now, years later and in therapy myself, I wish I'd questioned her: "What do you mean? How?" But my feeling at the time and through a lot of my life with her was, I thought, to protect her from anxiety or pain, any further pain.

Which is how I reacted again when she asked me a startling question.

Another evening. She again with her sardines, me at the sink with a glass of water. We'd been talking, then there was a pause. Something seemed to be on her mind.

"You're not a masochist, are you?"

"What?"

"I've just been worrying that you might be a masochist."

I felt a bit brain-stunned. What?

"What kind of masochist are you talking about? A physical one or a—?"

"A physical one."

"No, thank God. If anything, probably a bit the reverse."

"Oh, thank God."

Whether she was thanking God that I wasn't a masochist or a bit the reverse, I wasn't sure.

I said, "Why are you . . . What made you think of that?"

"Just the way Mary treated you when you were a little boy."

"I don't remember, hardly remember, how Mary treated me when I was a little boy. I always felt she loved me though."

"Oh she did. She did. She always said, of all the children she looked after, you were her favorite."

Now, again these years later, the question is an obvious one. How had Mary treated me when I was a little boy, and if there was a likelihood that this treatment might make me a masochist in my adult life, why did my mother not stop it? She'd tried, I suppose, that night when I was eight and she'd fired Mary but I needed Mary, the only constant in my life, too much, and didn't feel my mother was up to the job, since she'd never done it.

I brought the conversation with my mother to a close by saying, "So you don't have to worry about that anymore. I'm not a masochist."

"I'm so relieved," my mother said. She turned around and hugged me and then pulled back and looked at me. There were unshed tears in her eyes.

Jean Marsh had been staying with my mother and Boy in 1975 when she was appearing in Alan Bennett's *Habeas Corpus* on Broadway.

One night, after the show, she was in the elevator stopping on their fourteenth floor. As the door slid back, she saw my uncle Buzzie waiting. He nodded, gave her a tight smile, and stood back to let her exit, and then, stone-faced, stepped into the elevator.

Jean opened the door to the apartment to find in the living room my mother and Boy, both seeming agitated. They said their "good nights" and went into their bedroom.

The next morning, Boy having gone off to his office, my mother sat on the long white sofa, looking at Jean, who was sitting opposite with a cup of coffee, and started to cry.

After a few moments my mother told Jean about the previous evening. After dinner, my mother and the Scheftel brothers got into a discussion about finances and it had been revealed that my stepfather was having no luck with his business deals and consequently had run out of money and that Buzzie had put him on the office payroll in exchange for Boy undertaking some managerial duties, so the family was now totally dependent on Buzzie and this made my mother very fearful.

My mother felt that Buzzie didn't like her, had never really approved of her or the marriage. After all, she had no interest in fashion, as had his flirty mischievous first wife, Sally, who'd died, or his second, Yolande, who would complain how "exhausted" she felt after her fittings every year at the Paris collections. Nor was my mother a gossip, as were many of the women in his set.

As a result of his childhood rheumatic fever and some heart incidents (as they were euphemistically referred to) after his heart attack, Boy's health had always been a factor in their marriage.

So my mother had true fear that were Boy to die she would be at Buzzie's mercy, or lack of. Although occasionally given to laughing at a joke and enjoying golf, or handing me $5 at Christmas when I was a boy with a twinkle in his eye, he was a cold man. So this was the cause of the previous night's agitation and this morning's tears.

As a result of this financial fear, my mother at the age of sixty-two began to make contingent plans. She developed a one-woman show in which she told stories of being a girl in Ireland during the Troubles and sang songs of that period and the Second World War in an uncertain, shaky voice. But what was really on display was *her,* her character, her wit, her nerve, and a kind of endearing vulnerability. And then she began to save money in any way she could. No new clothes, and she wouldn't take a taxi if she could take a bus and not a bus if she could walk. As a result of her frugality and the small but definite success of her singing act for which she would travel to Mafia clubs in New Jersey or gay ones in Los Angeles, she was able to put a down payment on a little house on a bay on Long Island, and so she felt that, no matter what, she would always have a roof over her head.

And then, the world being the queer place it is, after he was seventy, something good of his own devising happened for Boy, having to do with money.

He had always been a dreamer, which was not a quality that helped him in the business world, for he was driven more by what interested him than in what was shrewd. He liked sports and started *Sports Illustrated* magazine, then sold the title to Henry Luce for not much money, but he did get a lifetime subscription. He liked politics and had a real belief in civic duty. He ran for Congress and lost, and later managed the mayoral campaign for a Liberal Party candidate, who also lost. He'd have an idea and then need to get others to invest, not having any money himself. He thought the air rights above Grand Central Terminal might be worth something and was an original partner in the Pan Am Building (but couldn't afford to stay in the deal); a safari park in New Jersey, a wax museum and roller disco in New

York followed and none did well. He felt he was always just one idea away from making money and age and ill health did not hold him back.

He had always loved horse racing and betting, but was frustrated when he couldn't get the results as soon as he wanted, and would have to wait for the late afternoon edition of the *New York Post*. So he came up with the idea, and persuaded the phone company to go along, of having a telephone number to call for the results of, say, the 2:30 at Aqueduct. He took a cut, the phone company a larger one, of each call and fortunately there were a lot of them. And then he branched out into other telephone lines, a therapist, a psychic, time and weather, and so for the first time in over forty years he was solvent and not in hock, and their last years together were unstressed about money and, after his death, there was enough for my mother to be able to continue to live at home and be looked after and Buzzie became diligent in taking a concern for his brother's widow and her welfare, perhaps because he didn't have to pay for it.

Fifteen

From the 1970s for about ten years, I had a good run. On British television, mostly for the BBC, I was working with the stars of the time on dramas written by equally stellar playwrights: Trevor Griffiths (who went on to write *Reds* with Warren Beatty), Simon Gray, and then Tom Stoppard's *Professional Foul,* his only play written for television. Several BAFTA nominations. Videos for the Rolling Stones, The Who, Elton John, Paul McCartney's Wings. A movie, *Nasty Habits,* which I was not happy with but with a cast of brilliant women, Glenda Jackson, Sandy Dennis, Melina Mercouri, and Geraldine Page, who became my dearest friend and confidante from then till the end of her too short life. Pauline Kael saw what I'd call "my" cut of *Nasty Habits* and gave it a terrific review in *The New Yorker.* Alas, that was not the cut which played in movie houses. And in the theater, John Webster's crazy Jacobean *The White Devil* at the Old Vic, also with Glenda Jackson (such an interesting working life: two Oscars and later a ministry in Tony Blair's first Labour government).

Then another play, *Whose Life Is It Anyway?*

The central character is a witty talented artist who suffers an injury which leaves him a quadriplegic and who wishes to legally be allowed to die. Tom Conti played the part.

Tom and I had come a long way since our first rehearsals in a room so cold we blocked scenes near the radiators, which then had to be adjusted when we got onstage. We started in a small theater on the outskirts of London and then, on the strength of rave reviews, transferred to the West End.

Scenting fresh meat, American movie stars came over to see it. Dustin Hoffman was interested in doing it on Broadway, as was the recently Oscar-winning Richard Dreyfuss (who later did the misconceived movie version).

Tom was courteous, as is his nature, when they came back-stage to see him, but privately he was irked that he mightn't be given the chance to do the play in New York. He rightly felt that, with the friendly acquiescence of the author, Brian Clark, he and I had made the play the success it was, shaping the scenes, sometimes rewriting, soliciting accurate legal opinions, and adding a lot of jokes—jokes in the opening scene so that the audience would first be put at ease and then could more steadily accept their role in the seriousness of the play. (In the theater, the last important part to be cast is the audience.)

Tom and I would sit in his dressing room at the Savoy Theatre before a performance, both of us feeling ownership of this piece but also trying to stay afloat in waters which were getting murky, churned up by the complications of movie stars, and the attendant prospect of more money for the producers.

I knew Tom to be a great actor (nominated for an Oscar for a movie he did after *Whose Life Is It Anyway?*, *Reuben, Reuben*) and, in this play anyway, to be able to control the audience like a matador the bull. I'd look into his intelligent magnanimous brown eyes and say, as if to advocate patience on both our parts, "It's a long way from here to there."

And it was. Dustin Hoffman invited me to breakfast at his hotel during his trip to London. It was Wimbledon fort-night, and Jimmy Connors came over to say hello to Dustin, who was an avid tennis player. I knew Tom to be a skillful one also, from our Sunday games. I've often felt good actors are like good tennis players, in that a hard shot from one player elicits an unexpected return from the other. It is a game of thrust and vol-ley, originality and surprise and endurance.

Jimmy Connors left, and Dustin poured some apple juice into

his bowl to moisten his wheat flakes and said, "You know I'm supposed to be difficult to work with. Does that bother you?"

"Not particularly. I've worked with The Beatles."

He then discussed some very interesting ideas he'd had about playing a quadriplegic and finished by saying, as if it were a gold star on the school board, "I'm a perfectionist."

I nodded in acknowledgment. I was, and am, skeptical of the idea of perfection, for in whose view does perfection lie? I also believe in chance, the unexpected, and, if you keep your wits about you, the benefits which could come. I also find beauty in the imperfect, the crooked tooth in the seductive smile.

Then Dustin said that if he were to do it in New York, he'd probably want to workshop it before he made up his mind.

I thought this was a delaying tactic and said the thing was just to plunge in and start rehearsing. After all, the play worked. And I feared that a workshop with a self-diagnosed perfectionist could be an open-ended ordeal. Dustin is a rightly rewarded wonderful actor, and his way has certainly worked for him. But I believe in trying to guide the hurly-burly of an artistic democracy and not in martial law, pleasure rather than tension.

I was in New York a month later, doing the "Miss You" videos with the Rolling Stones, on the weekend Dustin was supposed to make up his mind. As luck would have it, the Sunday *New York Times* ran an article by their theater critic who was in London, saying the one great performance he'd seen was Tom's in *Whose Life Is It Anyway?* And Dustin decided not to do it.

So when the play was successfully running on Broadway, and Tom called from New York and woke me up in the dawn to tell me he'd won the Tony, I was thrilled. I'd been nominated also but lost to Jack Hofsiss for *The Elephant Man*. But I was not much dismayed because I was distracted by what I was doing. I was in Malta getting ready to start shooting the television series *Brideshead Revisited*.

The producer of *Brideshead* was a funny, worldly, enthusiastic, mischievous, unshakable man named Derek Granger. He and I had been working on it for eight months, casting it and trying to come up with a serviceable script, as well as looking for Brideshead itself, the grand house of memory and seduction and remorse and dashed dreams. Derek and I visited many of the great houses of England, but once we saw Castle Howard in Yorkshire we knew we had it—a place of scale, with its fine proportionate exterior; something imposing but also with a sense in its interior of good times mingling with private tribulation and heartbreak.

A big house, or a room of plaster and paint, has its own peculiar history, the imprint of the gone others who'd existed there and, I suppose, the larger the place, the more the indentations.

Casting a play or a movie is like making a family, a group of men and women with whom you will spend a lot of time, often happily, sometimes not. It can be an intimate experience, in lots of ways, during which you will learn their strengths and weaknesses, and expose your own.

I'd seen Jeremy Irons in *Wild Oats,* a Royal Shakespeare production of a late-eighteenth-century comedy. He played a foppish young man with a lisp and was very funny (always a good thing), and I thought his elegant looks would make him a wonderful Sebastian.

We approached Kate Nelligan about playing Julia. She was the unquestioned young leading actress in London, beauty mixed with a ferocious ambitious talent.

But we couldn't find a Charles, the character through whose eyes we see the story. In the first scripts we had from John Mortimer, there was no voice-over and so Charles's presence was muted. Perhaps that's why when we offered it to Malcolm McDowell, he turned it down.

One Sunday evening, Kate and I were watching a BBC production of *The Voysey Inheritance,* in which Jeremy played the lead. Kate said she thought maybe he could play Charles, and, if so, it might help her make up her mind.

In the few meetings we'd already had with Jeremy to discuss Sebastian, Derek and I had been taken by his intelligence and emotional insight.

Also, by this time we had junked the Mortimer scripts, not that they weren't all right for what they were, just they'd gone in the wrong direction. Perhaps in an effort to make this beautiful complex novel more manageable for production, he'd turned it into a nice little telly drama.

One weekend I'd been going over the novel in an effort to solve our script problems and realized I was looking right at the solution. I called Derek.

"Remember when you first read it?" I said. "And turned the page to chapter seven and it starts, 'It is time to speak of Julia,' and you knew that what you've been anticipating was soon going to happen?"

I'd remembered that sentence and what followed from the first time I read the novel when I was seventeen, signaling as it does the start of the love affair between Charles and Julia.

"What are you thinking?" Derek asked, maybe wanting me to speak what had also occurred to him.

"We have to hear that line," I said.

"As a voice-over?"

"As a voice-over."

"And then?"

"And then, all of it. From the book. The book is the script. Without the voice-over, Charles just wanders around, 'observing,' with no ammunition.

"Does the convention worry you? The voice-over. Do you think it's old-fashioned?"

"I don't think we have a choice."

I loved working with Derek. I'd suggest, he'd question. He'd suggest, I'd question, and we usually seemed to arrive at something that was good, and I greatly enjoyed his company.

And so we went back to the novel, using it for dialogue and the voice-over as the spine. Derek, in conjunction with a bright young man named Martin Thompson, started to work it through all the episodes, while I was meeting actors and out looking at locations.

Derek and I were wondering how best to approach Jeremy about switching parts. We thought we'd play it by ear.

Granada Television, the producing company, although it was based in Manchester in the North of England, and had studios there, owned a large gray building in Golden Square for their London offices.

On a late-winter's afternoon, Jeremy arrived wearing a long, banana-colored, double-breasted velour overcoat. He was excited by his recent purchase.

"It's beautiful, isn't it? It's from the 1920s, the man said. Feel the material, how soft it is."

Derek and I admired his new coat and exchanged a look. For all the world, Jeremy looked like Sebastian, elegant and of the period, and also seemed to be acting like him. Only the teddy bear was missing. Maybe our task would not be as easy as we hoped. He took off the coat, revealing a handsome tweed suit underneath, and accepted our offer of a cup of tea.

"Well, how are things going, the casting?" Jeremy asked, eager to catch up.

"The casting. That's a good question," I said, having been offered the opening. "Look, um, Derek and I have been thinking."

"That's always a good thing," said Jeremy, teasing.

"Charles," Derek said, jumping right in.

"Charles? How do you mean?"

"For you."

"Oh."

Jeremy was silent for a moment and then said, "I'm very happy with Sebastian. I've been thinking about him a lot."

I wondered if he'd bought the new coat to wear as part of his costume.

Jeremy took a sip of tea.

Jeremy was, and is, a smart actor and realized that Sebastian, with his glamour and sadness, his golden youth coming to a sodden end, was a gift. (Look at what he later did in his Oscar-winning performance as oddball did-he-or-didn't-he-poison-his-wife Claus von Bülow.)

Our card was on the table, put down with little warning. Jeremy mentally considered his hand and knew it to be a good one. Was there to be any other enticement?

"I think I'd like to stick with Sebastian," he said.

"Ah-ha," I said. "There's something we haven't told you yet."

"Which is what?"

"The voice-over. Charles's voice-over," said Derek. "We're putting it all back in. So we'll see it all through his eyes. Your eyes."

"That's an interesting idea," Jeremy said. "Do you think it'll work? All those words, all that 'thinking'?"

"If you're saying it, why wouldn't it?" I asked.

I'd said what I believed to be true.

After a few days, having reread the novel but with no real scripts in place yet, Jeremy agreed to play Charles, but not without some reservations. He knew he was giving up something he could play on his head for something which would not really be in place until photography was over, even though we'd do test voice-over tracks as we were shooting.

Derek had already talked to Laurence Olivier about playing Lord Marchmain, but there were all the young parts to cast. To make our family.

I'd worked with Simon Jones on Shaw's *The Millionairess* at the Haymarket and knew he could play Bridey, the elder son of Lord Marchmain, and make his obtuseness infuriating, touching, and funny.

Phoebe Nicholls had played the young nurse in *Whose Life Is It Anyway?* and Jane Asher, a sympathetic doctor. Phoebe played Cordelia, and Jane, Celia, Charles's cool abandoned wife.

John Grillo, also a playwright, had been a sinister doctor in *The White Devil* and created the unforgettably buttery Mr. Samgrass.

I'd always wanted to meet the multitalented Simon Callow (still now an actor, but also a theater, film, and opera director and much read biographer and memoirist). Derek and I had a very entertaining afternoon talking to him about the part of the sharp, witty, homosexual Anthony Blanche. I almost changed my mind, hearing Simon's ideas. But a few years before, I'd seen Nickolas Grace playing Biondello in *The Taming of the Shrew* to Alan Bates's Petruchio, and had been entranced by him.

Kate Nelligan decided not to play Julia. Derek and I met Charlotte Rampling. She was fetching, a small perfect head under a lot of hair on a lean body, but she turned it down, thinking perhaps that an eight-month commitment in England mightn't be good for her new marriage to a handsome young French composer.

So, no Julia and now, no Sebastian, and we were shortly to begin three weeks of rehearsals and costume fittings before we had to start shooting.

And I was commuting by Concorde every week or so for three days at a time, to get the New York production of *Whose Life Is It Anyway?* ready to start previews. Tom Conti ran the rehearsals when I wasn't there.

Surprisingly, there weren't a lot of actors for us to choose from for Sebastian. Not many had the right upper-class accent, or were willing to adopt it.

This was a time when younger English actors were both professionally and socially wanting to play working-class characters, of which there were many good ones. England was entering the divisive years of Prime Minister Margaret Thatcher. She had come into office looking to bust the power of the trade unions.

In England, the class system was a vicious distortion of an equitable social order; where a large section of the populace was meant to know their place, tip their caps to the M'lords, suffer privation when they tried to unionize, face danger and illness, not to mention low wages, in the mines, and were unable to move above their station if they had the wrong accent. (Though the accent issue had begun to change with rock 'n' roll, when regional accents, or rougher urban ones, forced their way into society and became, in a perverse way, one to emulate: you'd find boys from Eton, in their holiday time, talking with working-class accents.)

But although the accent pool was shallow, the few actors swimming in it were talented.

Derek and I had whittled the choice down to two for Sebastian and wanted to give ourselves the weekend to think it over. I had to fly to New York for the first preview of the play.

On the fabulous British Airways three-and-a-half-hour Concorde flight to New York, where the caviar was served by stewards in white gloves and the champagne poured by pretty and intelligent women who would later bring around Havana cigars (and Jamaican on the way back because of the Cuban embargo), I had a thought which, when I discussed it with Derek when I landed, effectively reduced our candidates to one.

What I thought was that the actor we were leaning toward for the part had a face similar in construction to Jeremy's, thin with a pointed chin, and I felt that to cut from one to the other would not help us to differentiate between the two, and that in a two-shot they'd look more like brothers than men from different worlds.

Anthony Andrews had been lobbying hard for the part. He'd

done theater and some featured parts in television and then scored his own TV series, *Danger UXB,* in which he played a World War II bomb disposal expert. He insisted that Derek and I watch his best episode, in which his character has a nervous breakdown. And he was very good. In person, he had an easy confidence, as if to say why should good things not come his way.

And although he was slim, his face was round. Derek saw my point, and we had our Sebastian. And lucky we were too.

One day we had a casting free-for-all. It was just after lunch, and Derek and I were about to begin several hours of talking to actors when an anxious assistant came into the room.

"We've got a problem," he said.

Problems were a daily, if not hourly, occurrence.

"What?" asked Derek.

"Well, you know we've block-booked a flight to Malta for all the characters we need there and, since we don't know who's playing what . . ." Here the assistant looked at us.

If a sense of professional anxiety can be combined with a languid demeanor, he had it down pat. He wanted us to be sure to know where the responsibility lay for making his life more difficult.

He continued, " . . . we've booked seats in the names of Mr. Brown, Mr. Smith, Mr. Green."

"So?" from Derek, with a slightly acerbic tone.

"Well, we've just had a call from the airline to say that they need the real names *today,* otherwise they'll release all the seats. And so there won't be anyone in Malta to say the lines."

Another look here: "And whose fault will that be?"

"Got it," said Derek. "Now go and do something useful."

Luckily, Charles Keating, who found wit in the boorish Rex Mottram; Jonathan Coy, who played Kurt; and Nicholas Le Prevost, who played the French doctor in the sanitarium; and three other talented actors came in that day, and like choice items on a menu, they were all chosen, and delicious they turned out to be.

Jeremy and Anthony and I would take an early train in London for the four-hour journey to Manchester.

On the train, the three of us would have a full English breakfast and then Jeremy would light his pipe and I my cigar, and he and Anthony would each have a miniature of whiskey to fortify themselves to deal with the rigors of starting to rehearse and be measured for costumes for a not fully cast massive production which did not yet have a finished script.

The first sequences we were going to shoot were the ones set in Morocco where Charles goes to tell an alcoholic Sebastian that his mother, Lady Marchmain, is dying, and for that we were using Malta and the nearby small island of Gozo.

Derek and I and some of the production team flew to Malta together, with the actors and crew to arrive a few days later.

On our first night there, Derek and I had dinner with Doreen Jones, the head of casting for Granada, who had gone on ahead. And also an attractive blond woman of my age who lived in Malta who was going to work on local aspects of the production.

As the conversation moved around, I could tell our guest had a trace of an Australian accent.

"Did you grow up there?" I asked.

"No. In Ireland mainly. My father worked there. In the embassy."

"I spent a lot of time in Ireland too," I said.

"Where?"

"In Dublin and sometimes at Brittas."

Brittas Bay was a holiday spot an hour or so from Dublin.

"Brittas? I spent time there too."

"Did you have lots of picnics in the rain? I did."

"Of course," she said, laughing. "And played tennis in the rain, as well."

"So did I. What's your name?" The dinner introduction had been indistinct.

She told me.

If our dinner had been a scene in a 1940s movie, the screen would have blurred and rippled, and at that point, time would have gone back twenty-five years, to see me as a shy thirteen-year-old playing tennis on a churned-up clay court near my uncle David's rented summerhouse, with my cousins Nicholas and Caroline, sometimes joined, not nearly as often as I wished, by a coltish freckled brown-haired Australian girl, whose father worked in the embassy. Her parents thought she should be dressed properly when she played, and so she'd be wearing a short-sleeved white Aertex shirt over a flat chest with small shy protuberances and a white cotton skirt (which, probably, the summer before would have reached nearer her bony knees). Her tidy little hazelnut bottom barely distended the material as she reached for a ball.

We'd play doubles, she with one cousin and I with another. She wielded her heavy wooden racquet with skill. I'd watch as her eyes squinted to sight the ball as it came toward her and then she'd whack it with a girl's firm stroke, with an audible exhalation, as though she took pleasure in the effort.

Once, I returned an uncharacteristically hard shot which she missed and the ball hit her below the pubic bone. She grunted.

"Are you okay?" I called in alarm from the other side of the net.

She looked at me for a moment, as though my question had been impertinent. A haughty tomboy. And then she said, "Let's put it this way, it's lucky I'm not a boy down there."

Her reply was provocative to my early-teenage ears, acknowledging as it did the different way she was made to the way I was made. And then, with an inner start, I wondered if she'd grown any hair on the part of her body the ball had hit, or was she still a child, as I was.

One late afternoon, after tennis, the four of us went for a walk in the dunes. Unusually, the day had been warm. With a skill I had not practiced before, I managed to separate the girl and myself from my cousins. I saw them disappear over a sandy hump, and I swung in another direction and she followed. With all that I was feeling, I found it hard to talk. And what I was feeling, at thirteen, I couldn't have put a name on exactly, but I knew it was to do with my being male and her female. And to her, off the tennis court, there was a reserve, not unfriendly, just private as though she had a secret and would not, for some time anyway, decide in whom to confide. So we walked without speaking and then sat on top of one of the dunes and looked down to the shaley beach and the seaweed-colored water beyond.

Her fingers raked the sand. I was preparing to speak and hoped it would be interesting. A breeze had come up and I noticed little goose bumps on her freckled arm above the elbow.

"What would you like to do when you grow up?" I asked, looking out to the sea.

She didn't answer right away but scooped up some sand and held it in a tight fist. She looked at it as she spoke,

"Have adventures, I think. I'm not really sure, but probably have adventures. Travel, not get stuck," she said in her funny flat accent. "You?"

"I don't know," I said, and then, wanting to seem more grown-up in her eyes, I added, "But have adventures too. Not get stuck."

She nodded as though what I'd said had something profound in it. She opened her fist a little, and the sand flowed back from whence it came. We sat together a while longer in benignly charged silence.

D inner was over, and Derek, Doreen, and I went back to our hotel and she to where she lived.

We had dinner together the next two nights. There wouldn't be much time after the others arrived. We laughed about our tennis days.

On the second night we went back to the hotel, and to bed. At a certain point, she rolled over onto her tummy, arched her back, folded her knees under, and put her head down. The hazelnuts had been replaced by soft honeydews.

She reached behind and, around my erection, she put her hand—the same one which had held the sand a quarter of a century before—and said, "You're built like a stallion."

To flatter probably, and not literally true, of course, which was probably a good thing in view of what she said next.

"Please, would you bugger me? I always think it's so nice and intimate."

Her husband was Maltese. They had a little boy and were separated. He wouldn't let her take their child off the island, not even for two weeks to see the boy's grandparents in Australia. Her husband's family knew important people in the government, she told me, and so his wishes were what she had to deal with. She didn't say it exactly, she tried for a lightness of tone, but I knew things were not easy for her.

The actors and crew arrived the next day. As requested, Jeremy had had his naturally fairish hair dyed brown. We'd asked Anthony to dye his dark hair blond. He was wearing a tweed cap, giving an odd squire-ish look to someone who favored white jeans.

"Cool cap, Tone," I said.

"We have a problem," he said.

"Oh?"

"I sat out in the garden at home on Sunday. It was such a nice day."

"So?"

"It wasn't a good idea."

With some chagrin, he took off his cap. His hair had turned an interesting shade of green.

S till we had no Julia, and the part was to begin shooting after our two weeks on Malta and Gozo. Derek and I had been impressed by the work we'd seen of Diana Quick, but her agent didn't know exactly where she was, only that she was somewhere in South America with her then boyfriend, Albert Finney. After a few days the agent called us to say that Diana and Albert were going up the Amazon, and he didn't know how to reach her, but he'd try. (Remember, these were the days before communication by cell phone or e-mail.)

I don't know how we got the script there. I pictured it flying from England to Brazil, where it would then be brought as far by jeep as possible, then given to a runner who would try to find the dugout boat making its languorous way along the largest river in the world.

M alta went very well, with Jeremy and Anthony, who were dropped into the middle of the story, already understanding their characters and able to fight for their points of view; and even though their theatrical backgrounds were different, they became firm friends.

I took a small car that doubled as a taxi to see her the afternoon before that evening's flight back to London.

As the cab made its slow way up the inclined main road of Valletta old town, honking people out of our path, I was looking out the window and saw going the other way, down the cobbles, carrying some belongings, a beautiful dwarf, with the prettiest face on top of her cruelly stunted body, and not simply pretty, but with sultriness and sexiness and great sensitivity. I turned in my seat to follow her as she continued, with her compromised walk, till she was out of sight.

I fervently hoped she'd be recognized and admired and that she would find a good life for herself amongst the rough men of Malta.

The cab stopped outside a white-walled house.

Inside the big room it was cool, with a few pieces of once nice furniture, grown fatigued by overuse and the jumping of a small boy. The sagging sofa on which she sat was covered with an old shawl. She asked if I could stay, or come back when filming was over. I said I was sorry, but it was probably not something that would happen. I liked her but which her?—the pretty woman on the island or the freckled teenager in the dunes, with her goose bumps and dreams, whose wish was to not get stuck.

Back in England, filming went on its usual grinding way, on sets in Manchester or in real locations redressed by Peter Phillips and his ace art department, or Castle Howard, the great domed beautiful edifice we used for Brideshead.

But there was something dark on the horizon.

There was talk of a strike by the ACTT, the largest union representing cinema and television technicians, in this case against all the independent television stations. From the time we got back from Malta, there'd be summoned union meetings of the Granada shop. Sometimes, if we were somewhere else, the crew would have to stop work at two or three in the afternoon, in order to be back in Manchester for the five o'clock meeting. Sometimes there'd be a work-to-rule, which meant we couldn't start until a certain time and would have a hard finish exactly eight hours later, with no overtime.

My admiration for what it is actors do is usually pretty high. Everyone has a part to play in making a movie, but it is the actor who has to go over the top of the trench with a knife in his (or her) teeth.

On one of the work-to-rule days, Jeremy had, with Anthony, played a hungover undergraduate being sprung from the cells in the morning, and then that afternoon he was a world-weary painter soon to leave his wife. The schedule is not usually made with much thought given to the actors; it is more to do with how much can be accomplished in proximitous sets, or how much work you can get out of a certain piece of expensive equipment. How Jeremy went perfectly from youth to disillusionment with only a lunch break in between and the addition of a mustache, I've never forgotten.

But even more heroic that afternoon was Nick Grace, who had one of his most important scenes to play.

Actors have varying degrees of talent and skill, but what they must have is nerve and pluck. Whether in the theater or movies, an actor is often faced with things unanticipated, which can affect what he's trying to do, which is his best.

The scene takes place in a dingy gay bar where Charles and Anthony Blanche, old university friends, have repaired after the gallery opening for Charles's paintings, which had been two years in the making.

We had already shot Jeremy's angles and had yet to turn around and light Nick's angle. It was nearly 4:30 and we had to stop at five, no overtime, and were due at another location the next morning. Nick had a few single lines and then the vital speech which shows his love for Charles and also his disappointment in the paintings, something bitter for both men.

We were coming up to 4:45 and I went to find Nick.

"You know what's going on," I said, a statement more than a question.

"No overtime. Yes I know."

"I need two angles on you, a mid-shot and a close-up. And I don't think we can do more than one take on each angle, and we haven't started yet," I said, looking at my watch.

"Don't worry," said Nick. "I've got it."

"I hate that you're put in this position."

"I'd rather be here, at this moment, than anywhere," Nick said.

Four fifty-two the camera is ready. The crew is concentrated and Nick is popular. It is wonderful to be on a set and to feel everyone in lockstep. The camera assistant is ready with the close-up lens. We do the mid-shot. I ask how long it ran. The script girl says four minutes. Close-up lens on. The union rep is ready to pull the plug at five. I say to Jeremy and Nick, I don't need the first couple of lines, I'll use the mid-shot, and to pick it up halfway through.

"Right," they both say.

"Roll it."

With an acute sense of criticism and regret, Anthony Blanche reminds Charles he'd always warned him about charm.

"Charm is the great English blight. It does not exist outside these damp islands. It spots and kills anything it touches. It kills love; it kills art; I greatly fear, my dear Charles, it has killed you."

Nick nailed it on the dot and the lights went out. Grace in one take.

April had given way to May, then June and July, and then early August. The grievances of the ACTT against all the employers of the Independent Television Network had calcified the arteries of communication. We were still shooting as much as we could, traveling to various locations in the North of England, and then to Oxford, to shoot at Christ Church (my old college) and in the streets and bookstores.

On Saturday, August 11, I was in the hotel's coffee shop having breakfast with our indefatigable costume designer, Jane Robinson, when Derek appeared.

"We've been shut down. The whole network is on strike."

"What'll we do?" I asked.

"I don't know."

I took the train that afternoon to London, and before dinner that evening with a girlfriend I went for a walk around Campden Hill Square, where I lived. That day's late-summer sunset had odd disturbing colors in it, some purple, like a bad bruise.

I was in bed but not asleep at 2 A.M. when the phone rang. It was my sister from New York.

"Our mother's got cancer."

"Where?"

"Breast."

"What's going to happen?"

"She's going to have an operation on Tuesday."

"Shall I come over?"

"Up to you."

The next day I called my stepfather and mother. They both seemed unconnected to what was going on and didn't seem to think it necessary for me to come over. Maybe they were on tranquilizers, but they seemed to feel that whatever was going to happen was of no great importance.

Four years before, I'd directed Trevor Griffiths's intentionally provocative TV play, *Through the Night,* which was about a working-class woman having a mastectomy under the assembly-line obliviousness of the British National Health and how she learned to ask questions and fight for herself. It caused a sensation and opened a debate about the quality of care in the Health Service.

During the course of working on the play, I'd learned something about breast cancer and how, at that time anyway, until a mastectomy is under way, there's no real way to calculate how far it's spread, to the lymph glands, for example.

I had dinner that night with the girlfriend, who was one of the prettiest, most clearheaded, unusually sophisticated, and funny, if hot-tempered, women I've ever met. (I'd be glad to say her name but know she wouldn't wish it. She's very private, and, of the few women I've been very close to, she is the only one I don't speak to or, rather, she doesn't to me; it makes me sad to this day.) She and her siblings had been brought up by a resourceful loving mother, pretty much on her own.

I told her of my conversation with my family and how maybe there was no point in my going.

"What are you talking about? She's your mother."

She said this as though that were the only thing which mattered, although she knew we'd be separated.

The strike was on, I couldn't work, and so I went to New York the next day. After all, she was my mother.

Sixteen

I visited my mother in the hospital the afternoon before the operation. Her anesthetist arrived shortly after and, knowing that job to be of utmost importance, I'd elicited from him that he was a theater buff, and offered him tickets to *Whose Life Is It Anyway?* with the idea that he'd pay extra attention to her on the morrow. My mother, aged sixty-five, looked pretty and seemed to be in a tranquil mood. She told me that the night before the diagnosis she'd had a dream and, in the dream, a well-known society woman of her age had appeared. I knew the woman to be flighty and neglectful of her daughter, who'd been a friend of my teenage years. My mother said the presence of this woman in her dream made her know she had cancer.

The next morning, my stepfather and I were at Sloan-Kettering, New York's leading cancer hospital, at 8:30. That was a misguided arrival on our part. We had been told the operation would begin at 8:30 and be over in a couple of hours. But from what I knew about hospitals, 8:30 can mean the time the operation starts, or when the gurney is left in the hall, with the patient somewhat sedated, while hospital people deal with scheduling screwups and so the operation might not start till nine or ten and go on for two or three hours.

The main sitting area at Sloan-Kettering was large, which was probably a good thing, because the anxiety of waiting family members had further walls and ceilings to bounce off. There was an escalator, like in a department store, coming up from the ground floor. You signed in at a long desk, staffed by four or six women, so they'd know who to summon when things turned out whatever way they did.

My stepfather had brought the morning newspapers and I

some weekly newsmagazines. We sat together, chair arm to chair arm, with the occasional reference to something we'd read.

Bald cancerous children were being escorted, like dignitaries from another planet, over the orange shag carpet from one oncology room to another.

A loudspeaker would periodically blurt, "Will the family of Hester Levine (or William Collins) please pick up the nearest courtesy telephone."

This was a refined form of torture, when the head of the family of the afflicted would pick up a phone against the wall, shielded by a half length of hard plastic on either side, to be told the operation had gone well, or that the family should go to Dr. So-and-So's office (which was not so good).

About one in the afternoon, after my stepfather and I had spent the last two hours in silence, the announcing voice said, "Will the Scheftel family pick up the nearest courtesy phone?"

My stepfather folded his newspaper, stood, righted himself, buttoned his jacket, and went to the phone. I accompanied him.

Picking up the phone, he said, "For Mr. Scheftel?" As though for a business call, as though he did this every day.

He listened to the muted voice on the other end, and then looked at me. "Your mother's all right."

And then back to the phone, and then again to me, "They think they got it all. She's asleep."

He hung up. We went out into the street.

"I'll go to the office," he said.

"I'll go for a walk I think," I said.

"All right. Let's talk later. Thank you for coming with me."

"That's what I'm here for," I said, feeling as though I were playing a part, but realizing that was the truth.

We parted, tested together, members of a family.

My mother came home, with her left arm having had some lymph nodes removed.

And I went to Los Angeles to talk to Mary Tyler Moore, who was going to replace Tom in *Whose Life Is It Anyway?* with the part rewritten for a woman.

But all the time I was on the phone to England to see what was happening with the strike.

Nothing, it turned out. The union issues were thorny and complex.

And there was another problem.

Before I'd started *Brideshead,* I'd agreed to do a movie for George Barrie's Brut Productions, the company which had produced *Nasty Habits* three years before.

Brut was a cologne marketed by Fabergé, George's fragrance company. He liked the name and used it for the movie company he'd started. He'd produced *A Touch of Class* for which Glenda Jackson won her second Oscar, and he'd been nominated for co-writing the Best Song. George was a small, hardheaded, dapper man, not without charm, who was a heavy drinker.

When I'd go for a meeting with George, there'd be several vials of scent in a rack on his desk, and he'd uncap one and offer it for a smell.

"What do you think of this one," he'd say. "It's jasmine."

I'd sniff.

And then he'd offer another vial.

"What do you think if it's combined with this?"

And then he'd get down to talking about the movie, and then we'd go to the Friars Club, where he'd drink several scotches, and I'd have to circumvent the alcohol, and look for his lucid moments to discuss how I saw the movie.

Brideshead Revisited was supposed to cover the four seasons, and if we'd been able to stick to the original schedule, without a strike, I'd have been free to do the picture for George, called *Kingfisher,* which was about a group of young Russian Jews who hijack an airplane to escape persecution. "One man's freedom fighter is another man's terrorist." The script was adapted by John Hopkins, a subtle left-wing writer, from a book and he was artfully able to recognize all the contradictions of such a subject. And I knew how to do the movie.

Early on, I'd told Derek about this project, and he'd agreed to let me do it. The editing of *Brideshead,* I could supervise in person, via Concorde, or, at a distance, with tapes. He and I knew the editing would take a long time anyway.

So I'd signed a pay-or-play contract with Brut to do the picture in the spring of 1980, with the idea that *Brideshead* would be finished with principal photography by the end of 1979.

At the time, no one thought the ACTT strike would really happen, or that it would go on for months.

Derek and Jeremy and I talked all the time. Jeremy needed a break to do *The French Lieutenant's Woman* with Meryl Streep, and I asked Derek if we could go back to *Brideshead* in the summer, so I could do the movie and then continue with *Brideshead.*

"I don't know," he said. "I don't know if I can hold it together that long. Granada might pull the plug. But who knows how long the strike will go on. Everything's possible."

In New York, I'd begun a romance with a tall beautiful woman I've made reference to earlier, who was somewhat older than I. I was eager to do the movie and receive my first big paycheck. And to complete *Brideshead.*

And then, overnight, the strike ended. And I was stuck. Brut wouldn't release me, as they were planning to be shooting by the early spring.

"This is awful. Can't you do anything?" Derek implored.

"I'm not sure. I don't think so."

I went back to England for a week to attend a grisly little cocktail party in the basement of Granada TV's London headquarters, the same place that Jeremy had come in wearing his velour overcoat ten months before. It was to celebrate the end of the strike and the resumption of photography on *Brideshead Revisited.* I had been replaced by another director.

Several of the actors were there and I realized that they thought I'd abandoned them. No one had told them of my professional conflict, and I felt it too late to elucidate. We exchanged stilted remarks with each other; they, now, my fractured family.

Laurence Olivier was at the cocktail party, dressed casually in a sport coat and tie. He was no longer the dazzling creature of his youth and middle age. He was slightly flushed in the face, whether from whiskey or from fighting a set of debilitating illnesses, I did not know. He came over to me.

"Can't you get out of your damned movie? Derek told me."

"I don't think so," I said in a way to mean I couldn't.

"I was so looking forward to working with you. I had such a good time with your mother on *Wuthering Heights.* She was the best thing in the picture."

"You were both good."

"And it's not only that. I saw the *Electra* you did with Eileen (Atkins). I never thought anyone could do the Greeks on television. But you did. Isn't there anything you can do?"

My heart was clenching inside me as I said, "I don't think so."

He looked at me. Although his eyes were watery with age, they still glistened. After a moment, "Well then. Good luck with it," he said and returned to his companions.

I went to Castle Howard to meet the director who was my replacement, Charles Sturridge, and I thought to show everyone I supported (however reluctantly) what had happened and that I still cared for them. But our great argumentative camera operator, Mike Lemmon, would barely shake my hand. It was as though we all had been as a family who had set out to travel a great distance and then they thought I had gotten off at the first big town.

I got on the train to go back to London and my heart, which had clenched at the cocktail party, was now broken.

As Mary Tyler Moore was settling into the hospital bed at stage center of the Royale Theatre, I was working on the script for *Kingfisher,* with John Hopkins and Bob Lawrence, who was going to produce it. He was also a very gifted editor and had helped me to recut *Nasty Habits* after it had fallen into different hands, before it was recut again.

The first sign that something was wrong was that the casting for the movie was pushed back; but don't worry, George Barrie said, we'll start soon.

I was offered a job to direct a revival of *Look Back in Anger,* in the theater with Malcolm McDowell. But Brut wouldn't release me because we would soon be going into preproduction.

Dates were set, then erased, and then set again.

It was only later that I learned what was happening. There were some problems inside Brut which constrained George Barrie's ability to use it for financing his films. He felt he could raise the money independently and he was proud and unused to being in the position of a supplicant, but he was and he couldn't.

I wasn't allowed by the terms of the contract to work for the six months it took for the project to unravel. I got paid. *Brideshead Revisited* went on without me.

During this time, Mick Jagger had asked me to the studio one night to hear a new single, "Emotional Rescue." I liked it but not with the enthusiasm I'd felt for previous (and later) songs.

But it seemed implicit that when the Rolling Stones got around to making a video, I'd do it, as I had with them since "Jumpin' Jack Flash" to "Angie." "It's Only Rock 'n' Roll (But I

Like It)" and "Miss You" (and later, "Start Me Up" and "Waiting on a Friend"). It would be a quick job and I could do it without Brut knowing (or caring).

I hadn't heard from Mick for a few weeks when I rang Jane Rose, who ran their office.

"What's going on with 'Emotional Rescue'? Anything?" I asked.

"Sure. They're shooting a video today. David Mallett's directing it. I thought you didn't like it."

Not being able to work and being rebuffed by my old friends, I felt in a rare surge of self-pity and fell into a depression.

The vista which had seemed so broad and clear and promising the year before had been reduced to a stony, barren field.

I rented a small house in Quogue for August and went there with Jean Marsh, who, no matter where we were in our relationship, has always been a constant in my life.

Thanks to her and her good humor and the steadiness of her character, and her good meals, plus swimming and running, the feeling of being marooned in a depression started to lift.

I'd always wanted to write but, being so busy with directing, I never had the time. And now I did. In the month on Long Island, I wrote the first draft of *The Object of Beauty* which I directed with John Malkovich and Andie MacDowell ten years later. Grueling, how long it can take but, if you believe in what you've got, worth it. Or, putting it another way, don't give up, as Humphrey Bogart said.

In 1982, I directed *Agnes of God* on Broadway, with the combustible beauty Elizabeth Ashley, my heroine Geraldine Page, who was nominated for a Tony, and the singular Amanda Plummer, who won the Tony.

When my stony, barren field had started to bloom again.
Me, Keith, and Mick. The mysterious eminence behind Mick
is our friend Lorne Michaels, whose company had produced
the video shoot. The song was "Neighbors," 1981.

That same season my mother directed *Mass Appeal* on Broadway. She and the playwright Bill C. Davis had nurtured it through rewrites and an off-Broadway production.

I was on vacation in Mexico with a new girlfriend, and we went to the only public telephone we could find, which was on a wall outside a dentist's office, for me to call my agent at William Morris in New York. The Tony nominations had been announced that day, and I was expecting one for me. After all, I'd received one for *Whose Life Is it Anyway?*, and *Agnes of God* was playing to excited audiences and settling in to what would be a run of a year and a half.

"Nope. Sorry," Johnnie Planco said before I'd even asked the question. He was straightforward with tenderness underneath.

"Well, who was nominated?" I asked somewhat querulously.

He named the directors of three plays. I knew there were four in the category.

"Okay, and who's the fourth? Some jerk, I suppose."

He paused then said, "No, not a jerk. Your mother."

Interlude

The Belgian, the nightclub girl, the wife of a family friend, an art student, an actress, a dental assistant, a television producer, a PA, an actress, another actress, a magazine editor, a stage manager, my cousin's ex-wife, an actress, an actress, a novelist, an actress, a costume designer, a movie producer, a singer, a mother of two, a screenwriter, a painter, an interior decorator, someone I met at a dinner party, a television star, a fey imp, an actress, a television producer, a businesswoman, another screenwriter, an actress, a commercials producer, an actress, a hotel receptionist, a lawyer, a television producer, an heiress, a PA. And then, an actress-photographer, with sui generis taste and imagination, complicated and funny.

Except for those I've already mentioned or alluded to or will, these have been my lovers.

And I think there would have been a few others if something hadn't come up at the last moment.

The tall blond striking German girl, later to be part of the Velvet Underground, had sung tunelessly on *Ready Steady Go!* She called late one evening asking me to come over for a drink. I was sitting in her small Chelsea apartment at one in the morning, staring at her startlingly beautiful face, having what we both thought was a conversation which might lead somewhere when she began to talk in a gloomy way about death and bodies in the street in Berlin near war's end, her big hands interlocked, and I was struck by how thick her fingernails were with horny ends forked down over her fingertips, and wondered if they, the nails, were a sign of her being, in some way, unwell, or was it to do with wartime malnutrition? Something about them disturbed me.

There was a tantalizing quality to do with the contrast

between the nails and her exquisite face but not tantalizing enough.

A few weeks before, I'd been dallying with a pretty blonde I'd picked up in the local chemist's where she was dispensing prescriptions, and we were discussing going to bed in the next few minutes when, for why I don't know, I said to myself if she was wearing blue knickers, I wouldn't go ahead. I toyed with the top of her jeans, undoing the belt buckle, opening the top button, to see the waistband of her blue cotton underpants. Though perhaps it was really an unease I was feeling because this encounter was in a small house I shared, most of the time, with someone else who might, who knows, have turned up.

Some years later in New York, I had walked home a very successful model soon to be a somewhat less successful actress, someone I'd come to like very much and I felt we could really hit it off. It was two in the morning and we were standing under the canopy of her apartment building on 58th Street. She asked me in for a drink and just before I was to take the step she said, "I hope you don't mind dogs. I've got a big sloppy one."

I had not yet learned to love dogs as I do now, the result, perhaps, of a childhood biting, and I didn't see how a big sloppy dog would fit into my plans, so I pulled back and for a long time regretted it, but ten days later I was to meet Nona Summers, who became very important to me. She was the girlfriend with me in Mexico.

Nona was beautiful, slim, and unruly, had long Titian red hair and was married to a successful English art dealer and had a small daughter, Tara.

She spoke six languages fluently and picked up others, Arabic, Japanese, on a need-to-know basis. She was funny and a whiz at Ping-Pong and gin rummy.

She helped me with my fear of flying. She had none herself, being able to sleep through five hours of thunderstorms at

35,000 feet on our way back to London from a trip we'd taken to Thailand. And then it was a delightful experience we had on a flight from Los Angeles to New York where I was able to recover what had been lost all those years ago over the Rockies.

She was high-flying herself. In her London house, she and her husband would give large parties, which might end with Jack Nicholson and a few others including the remnant pretty girl or two, still wide awake at five in the morning discussing philosophy, religion, or some such, or Art Garfunkel singing, or the police arriving to deal with noise protests from the neighbors — drink, drugs, sexual trysts, nights going into the dawn, the excess of the Roaring Eighties.

Reports of these goings-on reached my stepfather, whose nature was conservative, and he became alarmed at my connection to Nona, which was deep. My mother hewed to my stepfather's opinion and the disapproval my family felt drove a temporary wedge between us. If Nona and I were in New York, I sometimes wouldn't call them, not wishing to be subject to their evident dismay but I believed in her essential goodness.

And I loved her and her easy carelessness, which was so different to my native caution and I was even, against my nature, admiring of how she got herself out of pickles. For example, Nona was booked on the 9:30 Concorde flight to London and had only left, after hurried last-minute packing, our hotel in New York at nine. She arrived at Kennedy Airport at 9:25 and realized she'd forgotten her passport. She showed security control a picture of herself in *Women's Wear Daily* and had been allowed on the plane. (This was before the time of exploding shoes and flammable underwear.)

After twelve years, we broke up but are still friends.

I picked up a prostitute on the Sunset Strip and brought her back to the Chateau Marmont, where I lived for fifteen years, then in its most ramshackle days. Once in the room, I felt I'd made a mistake, so I offered her a drink and we just talked, her dark face handsome and her eyes clear under her glossy black wig. We talked about how she always tried to insist on condoms but sometimes was forced to have sex without them. Before I walked her back across the street, I'd offered her some money for her visit, but she refused, asking only for a book of matches, saying she'd like to keep them as a souvenir of being in this old hotel and show them to the other girls on the Strip.

Some on my list of lovers, I had strong feelings for, a version of love but not, perhaps, the true metal, and I was glad when what I felt was just a kind of strong affection. Because only a very few people have I loved deeply enough that I could bear my sense of their vulnerability without it stopping my erotic drive.

I have always thought that eros, at its core, is a ruthless brute with scant interest in tenderness, unless tenderness helps it get its way. I am not talking of sadism nor ignoring the niceness of an affectionate intimacy but just about the heedlessness of the drive, and only from the point of view of a particular male.

Which brings me to another point. I have always felt at home with gay men (and women).

From my earliest days in the theater, as a teenager in the 1950s, I, having faced my own versions of adversity, felt an emotional kinship with, and admiration for, men and women who dealt with something harsher. In the world of arts—theater, dance, painting, fashion—it was, at that time anyway, perhaps somewhat easier, at least in the big cities—New York, Chicago, San Francisco, Los Angeles. But what of the others: on the subway, in quotidian jobs, salespeople, or working in a bank or a factory job; what dangers and humiliations would they face, and what degree of courage would they need just to get through the day?

But I have never had desires in that direction, for two reasons I think. The first is that I like soft skin, and the idea of snuggling against a bristly cheek or kissing a hirsute body is the opposite of a provocation for me. The other is that one of the things which has always occupied me was a deep curiosity about women, their bodies and minds. I have no curiosity about men's bodies, being a man myself, but was always interested in a woman's body under her clothes, how she was made, and, further, how she thought, and often it is through sexual intimacy that someone might reveal herself, a kind of truth and, following on that, stories and revelations which you would not otherwise have known of. This sense was not a prurient one and the secrets are always safe with me, but I was glad to be a possessor of them. I think I have a lot of female in me and perhaps that's why I like women so much, or perhaps there were so many females around, big and small, when I was a little boy on the beach. And then, in terms of how things work, except for the penis, there is not any way a male body can be loved that a female one cannot. Although it doesn't totally work the other way.

I had an affair with a pretty actress. We'd been to bed a few times, and everything had gone pleasantly, excitably enough, but I felt maybe there was some sort of mismatch, or reticence on her part.

Lying there, I began to ask her some questions. She at first answered evasively and then said, "I'm really a lesbian. I like women."

"That's fine," I began with a tone of smug masculine tolerance which I hoped would convey understanding as well as some sort of superiority. I continued, "But when you think about it, there's nothing a woman can do for you that a man can't."

She considered this for a moment, put her hand behind her head, and then said, "That's not really true."

"It isn't?"

"Not really."

"How so?"

She gave a little laugh and said, "You see, the thing is I like licking cunts."

Seventeen

It began with occasional forgettings. Or she'd say something as if for the first time when she'd already said it. Boy, Susie, and I would talk about my mother in a wary furtive manner at first, as though if we just danced around the subject, if we treated it lightly amongst ourselves, it would, itself, be light.

"She's usually so bright and intelligent. Maybe it's just a little old age," my stepfather said.

"I hope that's it," said my sister, by then a clinical psychologist and married to a public defender, Rick Finkelstein.

I was elected to talk to her, to see if she was aware of these lapses of, what?, concentration.

My mother and I went for a walk one day and as we stood on a Park Avenue corner, waiting for the light to change, I was conscious of how much bigger I was than she, my six feet next to her small self bundled into a coat, and of how much I wanted to protect her.

I began, "Ma, I'd been wondering. Sometimes, you know, you seem to lose the thread of a conversation. Just every so often. Or maybe repeat something you've just said. Not a lot, just every so often. I was wondering, do you know when it's happening?"

She was as still and silent as a stone. I felt if I reached toward her she might flinch, if a stone could flinch. Then she answered.

"Yes, I do. I know. And when it happens I feel like an icy hand is grabbing at my heart."

The light changed and, after a moment, I took her arm and we crossed the street and went on to talk of other matters in a perfectly normal way, but I was troubled; we both were in our different ways.

She was hired to play in a television movie and then fired for not being able to remember her lines. She was seventy-eight. I called her.

"They kept changing the script," she said. "I could've remembered it if they hadn't kept changing the script."

The thing about her hideous disease, for that's what we were recognizing it was, is that lucidity and intelligence can, at first and for a while, coexist with forgetfulness and muddle. But odd behavior would occur.

A couple of years after the conversation in the street, I thought I'd drop in on my mother and stepfather after dinner. I was in the neighborhood and Nona was in England.

I had a key to their apartment and just thought to check on them.

There was a crisis.

My stepfather, because of his chronic heart disease, sometimes became short of breath, which, on this evening, was what was happening. He'd already called Dr. Bienstock, who lived nearby in the East 70s, and was kind and sympathetic enough to be available for a late night house call.

Breathing with difficulty, but trying not to alarm my mother, my stepfather gasped, "I need air."

My mother, in her nightdress, went to the window and opened it, and cupped her hands, looking to do what was needed, and reached outside to gather up some nighttime New York air, and came toward Boy lying in bed, her hands in front of her, as though bearing an offering, and said, "Here is air for you, my darling," and wafted toward him, with a breath, what her hands contained.

Fortunately, Dr. Bienstock arrived at that moment and hooked Boy up to a portable oxygen tank and sat with him as he started to breathe more regularly. Thereafter, an oxygen tank was part of the bedroom furniture.

Eighteen

L ike so many of my connections with Orson, the last one was at a remove.

Carrie Fisher had taken over for Amanda Plummer in *Agnes of God,* and she was good in the occasional performances her vocal problems allowed her to do. A year or so later, back in California, she gave a party to which I went with my girlfriend, Nona. Lots of people were there, including Henry Jaglom, a rich director, who was a regular lunch partner of Orson's, who had been making money as a spokesman for Paul Masson wines. I'd known Henry somewhat over the years. We found ourselves talking about Orson.

"He loves *Brideshead Revisited,*" Henry said, his characteristic floppy hat on his head. "He keeps looking at it. He tries to figure out which scenes are yours."

"They're all over the place," I said, not really wanting to rehash the painful story. "I'm glad he likes it."

"You should give him a call."

B ut I didn't, because that wasn't how it had been set up. The meeting at Mr. Chow had been, what, ten years earlier? I never called him, although I could have, but never felt there was an invitation, but maybe I didn't need one.

A nd then it was 1985. At the Public Theater, Joe Papp producing, I'd directed the first production of Larry Kramer's theatrical hand grenade *The Normal Heart,* which took on the early days of the AIDS crisis. *The Normal Heart* caused a sensation and became the longest running play in the history of the

During rehearsals for The Normal Heart
at the Public Theater, 1985.

Public Theater. The doing of *The Normal Heart* would be a small book in itself.

On October 10 of that year, I was in New York editing a video I'd shot in Nashville with one of the Mandrell sisters. There was a small television set playing in the corner and a news show came on. The newscaster said, "Orson Welles dead today, at the age of seventy." There was a somber shot of a black wagon pulled up outside his house. My editor, a friend, who knew I'd known him, looked at me.

"Seventy was too young for him to die," I said, not wanting to say more. I did know there was something sad about the way it had all gone. How could I say it, if I looked for pith not pleth, to someone, however sensitive, who'd only known of him as a movie giant from forty years before? The sadness was not to do with the past but with the unachieved future. His great bold multicolored glorious banner had become more tattered, battered, and threadbare as the years went by; but still he'd stood there, his fist on the staff, stout of girth, full of dreams, wise but not jaded, the inheritor of his past, and the tempestuous child of his unique imagination; and now "dead at seventy." How could I explain my feelings about this man I'd met?

My stepfather died in 1994, still acute of mind but his body, or more accurately, his heart failed him.

The last time I saw him was when I dropped in on them a day before Lisa and I were to travel back to California.

Lisa, who was my new girlfriend, had made a great difference to my life with him.

Boy, who always had an eye for a pretty girl, found Lisa, blue-eyed, dark-haired, tall and slim, a calming influence on me and, therefore, something similar for him.

When I met Lisa, almost from the first, I felt I'd arrived at a destination I didn't know existed, somewhere safe, sunny and replenishing.

That day in the apartment, things were not right. Boy, who always attempted to put a good face on things, was in a very agitated state.

"I don't know why, but I feel very nervous, very uneasy," he said.

He was wearing a pajama top and boxer shorts and, tied around his waist, one of the small Irish rugs from their trips there.

My mother, also agitated, suggested remedies.

"Take a pill. Have a vodka."

He did drink a vodka, his usual before-dinner tipple, but it was only four in the afternoon and he was not really a drinker. I excused myself and went into another room, closed the door, and called Dr. Steiner, his venerable cardiologist. I explained what was going on.

"Is there anything else we should be doing? Is it his heart?" Dr. Steiner said, "At a certain point, if you have a weak heart, there's only so much we can do."

"Only so much?"

"I know what I'm saying may not be comforting, but we've done all we can for him and it may be enough for a while. But there's only so much."

I knew what Dr. Steiner was saying was that my stepfather was being kept alive by the medical equivalent of Scotch tape and glue.

Dr. Steiner finished by saying, "Don't let him go out if it's too cold."

I went back into the other room and said, "I've spoken to Dr. Steiner and he said this is only temporary. It'll pass. Keep wrapped up, keep warm."

I kissed my mother and smiled what I wished to be a reassuring smile to my stepfather. We never kissed, and I thought a handshake would have a doomy kind of formality to it, so my smile would have to convey my heartfelt wishes.

For him, who'd taken me on, and had been as a father, who'd done his best.

That night Lisa and I had dinner with my sister and Rick. Their pretty, intelligent daughter Sophie (whose hair was the same color as my mother's as a girl) had had her supper and was in another room, and their sparkling son, Jesse, was in his crib. So we could talk.

We remembered some funny and good times we'd had with the mother Susie and I shared and the father that was hers. We recalled with tenderness a story my stepfather had told us, which was: in the early 1940s, before he'd met our mother, he'd gone one afternoon with a pal to the movies and seen one she was in, and as they went out into the street my stepfather had said to his friend, "I'm going to marry her one day."

It was now 1994, and we realized the memories were precious and that we'd remember their luster, made brighter by the darkness coming around them.

The next day Lisa and I went to California and that weekend went to Desert Hot Springs. On the Sunday, I was asleep in the early morning and was woken by a movement in our room, as though in a shoe box being shaken by a giant. Lisa was at the sliding doors, having just woken and gotten up.

"It's an earthquake."

And it was a big one, in Northridge.

Lisa called her daughter, Jane, who was that night with her father, Bill Moseley, in Los Angeles, and they were okay. I called Jean Marsh in London and then my mother and stepfather in New York to say there'd been an earthquake and that we were all right.

My stepfather, who'd answered the phone, said, "Thanks for letting us know."

"How are you?" I asked. "Feeling a bit better?"

"I'm all right."

"I'm glad," I said.

Three days later, I was in an editing room cutting a TV movie I'd made for CBS, or rather, trying not to be recut by dolts and idiots, when I got a message, forwarded from my hotel, to call Ann at my stepfather's office.

"Ann, it's Michael. What's up?"

"Your sister told me to call you."

"Oh?"

"There's a problem with Mr. Scheftel."

"Oh?"

"He was having lunch . . . and something happened . . . and he passed away."

It had been a very cold day that January 20 in New York and my mother had wanted to take a bus on her own to have lunch with my sister. My stepfather wasn't sure, with what was going on in my mother's mind, if she could manage this on her own, and had insisted he put her in a taxi, to be met on arrival by my sister. They'd rowed. My mother barely acquiesced.

"You'll be the death of me, if this goes on," my stepfather had shouted at her and then went off on a crisp walk to meet his brother for lunch at Taxi, a bistro near their office.

They ordered a cocktail at the bar and were looking at the menu when my stepfather, my dear Boy, who wasn't sure if I loved him, dropped dead.

I flew to New York that night and went to the Frank E. Campbell Funeral Home the next morning to meet my family and discuss the price of caskets. Two days later was the funeral.

Did I wish to see the body, I was asked on the day of the funeral.

"Yes."

My stepfather was in a casket and didn't look like himself at all. I wondered if whoever had done the florid portraits on the wall of the owners of the funeral home had also done the embalming. Neither the portraits nor my stepfather looked like any version of a human being I could recognize, and all seemed to be wearing makeup.

His brother chose not to see the body.

I think he realized that to see the cosmeticized figure, with a little lip gloss, would not shake his last image of his brother on the floor.

Later, at the cemetery, the service over, cars at the ready, we others waited as Buzzie stood, head bowed, at his brother's grave for a full five minutes before he straightened himself, turned, and went directly to his car. They loved each other for over eighty years. Maybe Buzzie wasn't so cold.

After my stepfather died, I routed travel as much as possible through New York to see my mother. Lisa and I and her beautiful young daughter, Jane, who would spend a week with her father and then a week with us, lived most of the time in Los Angeles.

Nineteen

In those years, my mother went through stages of anger and lashing out at people she'd known for a long time. Sometimes, wishing for things to seem just as they'd seemed before, for her and others, in her mind anyway, but with the protective sheath having already sheared away from her wings, she'd unlock the front door at midnight and with, sometimes, a coat over her nightdress, would say to the elevator operator, with a winning smile, some of her old charm intact, a memory of charm, "I'm just going out for a walk."

She'd go through the building's late night empty lobby and out into the street and walk to the corner and turn left and continue along the pavement. She'd walk past the coffee shop, owned by friendly Geogiou, but he would have closed up for the night, the lights out, and she'd stand there, not knowing where she was, to do with local geography, or in her brain.

By that time, the elevator man had called up to Frances Goff, who stayed with my mother and who hadn't heard the click of the door, perhaps she'd fallen into a much needed sleep, and then she'd be out in the street, a coat over her nightdress.

"Geraldine," Frances would say in her soft Irish accent, a comforting cadence to my mother, as if a voice from her youth.

"You should come home now. It's cold outside."

And Frances, a loyal, kind woman, would take my mother back to the apartment and put her to bed; and then throw the bolts on the front door, and get back into her own bed and lie awake there, listening to my mother's breathing go to snores, so Frances would know my mother wouldn't try to escape again that night.

Escape from the apartment and trying to escape from the darkening thunderclouds which were gathering more substance to strike again at her brain's neurons.

In the mid-time of my mother's dementia, before she was all gone, I felt like she was the dealer in a card game, in which she should only have been a player, grateful for whatever cards came her way. But no, she dealt a game with no rules. I wouldn't know if we were playing poker, canasta, or snap, and the cards would change value at a whim, and the stakes raised or decreased in the same manner.

In her life, she had tried never to lose, nor did she want to now, and she didn't ever want to leave the table.

Her mind was going, but not her nature. She had an inclination to amuse and, maybe, depending on the circumstances, to deceive. And, sometimes, I think her ferocious emptying mind was communing with the anarchic spirit of her Irish compatriot, the bleakly hilarious Sam Beckett.

After being with her (alone, or with Lisa), I'd go back to our hotel and make notes in my diary, so I wouldn't forget.

APRIL

Ma looking at the almost empty plate of what might have been a nice supper, jabbed at the plate with her fork, and said, "I want another fuck."

Then she looked at me and we laughed, she knowing she hadn't come up with the right word but also aware that it had sounded like a joke, which was always preferable.

SEPTEMBER

Ann, from South Africa, was one of the helpers my mother liked, along with Frances, and an early companion, Michael O'Neal. Ann told me Ma had been up, full of vim, from midnight till 3 A.M. the night before, her coat on, ringing the doorbells of her neighbors on the fourteenth floor, to ask if they'd like to go out to dinner with her.

OCTOBER

"Who are these people who are always in the apartment?"
she'd asked Michael O'Neal. Michael said Frances and Ann
and then a new woman who went jogging a lot in her time
off, another caretaker.

"Who I hate," said Ma.

Then she paused and said, "I just added that in case it
might be helpful."

OCTOBER 24, 1995

A conversation with so much in it and what do I take away
from it?

First she'd been talking about when I was a boy, and how
important it had been in her view that I'd had a "proper
upbringing," good schools, so that in case people ever found
out "anything" about me, they couldn't, she said, looking at
me, "kick you around." She seemed clear on this point.

I knew she was talking about something that was specific (as specific as it could be) to her. What was this "anything"? Bastardy? Was that why people could have kicked
me around? Not if I'd had a "proper upbringing," she'd
thought.

Thinking I'd deciphered something, I asked her the
question I'd never asked directly before.

"Who's my father? Orson or Eddy?"

"Why, Orson Welles of course. You even look like him."

So, the Ace was down. Finally I thought. I was aware I
breathed a great exhalation of relief. There it was. After
years of struggling in cloud, I felt I was standing on the
peak with the air clear around me. In some way it was
probably too late but at last I was there.

My mother was silent for a moment. Then she said,
"Edward Lindsay-Hogg is the father of Michael Lindsay-
Hogg."

What? Who'd shuffled this deck?

"And not Orson Welles?"

"No. Although he or she could have been."

Then another silence, as my mother moved the cards around again. She looked at me and asked, "And who are you? Are you my cousin?"

"No. I'm your son, Michael."

"And who's your father?" she asked.

"That's what we were just talking about."

"There's one thing I do know," she said.

"What?" I asked, wondering which card she'd play, the Ace again or another Joker.

"Who *my* father is," my mother said.

"And who is that?" I asked, curious to find out who she'd claim.

"You. You are my father."

As time went on, my mother declined. Within eighteen months she was no longer able to recognize or understand who was with her.

I always talked to her as though she could understand me. I'd tell her about what I'd been doing and mention people we knew together.

"I was talking to Noel Pearson the other day. Remember Noel, who produced *My Left Foot* and my movie *Frankie Starlight*?"

She couldn't communicate but I wasn't in her brain and so couldn't know if there was any cognition there. Could she understand and not tell me? I never thought not to talk to her as one adult to another, just in case.

These times with my mother were a combination of boring, with our one-sided conversation, and anxious-making. How much worse would it get and how much longer would it go on?

The only perverse benefit from what was happening was that

I felt my mother was dying incrementally, month by month, year by year, and so when the time came it would not be such a blow.

I kissed her on the head and went out into the street to hail a cab to go back to the hotel to Lisa, my girlfriend, who is now my wife.

In the taxi, I started to cry.

"Damn it. Damn it to Hell," I thought to myself.

"I never got her. Not when I was a little boy, she was always earning the rent, and Mary was as if a mother; not when she'd married my stepfather; and then I was in England working for a long time, and she didn't fly till she was much older, and so it would only be every couple of years; and now that Boy is dead, I could have had her. We could have gone to the theater, or for a walk, or out for a meal together, and I could finally be with her, the two of us only. And now I'll never have her, to myself, alone."

Twenty

Near the end of 1998, my stepmother, Kathleen, died in Ibiza. She and Edward Lindsay-Hogg had been married for over forty years. She was a sweet woman with a prettiness slightly marred by too many years in the sun, giving what were soft contours an overlay of crocodile creases.

I'd seen them the year previously in Ireland when Lisa and I had dinner with them and my cousins, Caroline and Maggie. My father got merrily drunk, smoked a cigar, and had to be helped into a taxi. He was eighty-seven at the time and Kathleen somewhat older.

Caroline called to tell me of Kathleen's death. I dialed the number of the telephone in their small apartment, its balcony over a pizza parlor. There was no answer.

My father had gone to stay the night with friends. I spoke to him the next afternoon, his time. I was in Los Angeles and he in Ibiza, a nine-hour difference. He sounded sedated.

"She said she felt tired and was just going to lie down for a while. After an hour I went to look in on her. She was dead. I called the ambulance."

His voice was slurring a little, but then he shouted: "They took her away in a plastic bag!"

"I'm so sorry," I said.

His mother in the stream was an elegant countrified death, I suppose, compared to this one, seventy or so years later, with his wife, sacked up in plastic, being brought lumpily down the stairs on the shoulders of the weary municipal men, called out near midnight. A bit of me was outraged that he'd found himself in a place, at this time, at his age, with no armor, so that his wife could be transported thus to the morgue, not even in a canvas zip-up, but in significance, more like garbage. The outrage was because I wasn't surprised, and then I found myself outraged by my outrage. Where was my sympathy?

The next day in our phone call, he asked me if I could come over for the funeral, which was to be the following day. I said I couldn't, that the sixteen hours of travel from Los Angeles to Madrid to Barcelona to Ibiza wouldn't get me there in time, and, besides, I said I was working. That wasn't quite true, in that I wasn't getting up in the dawn to go to a location, but I was preparing to direct a TV movie and a play, and I knew a few days wouldn't do it—that once there, it would be for weeks.

What was more true was that there was an absence of something in my heart. It was as though my relationship with him had always been at the wrong end of a telescope, and as the years had progressed, he had become no more prominent. When I was a little boy, and after, when maybe I could have really used him and the essential gentleness of his nature, I rarely saw him.

My mother had told me they'd agreed that when I was twelve, I'd be given to him to go to school in England, but when I reached that age, she said, I was too unhappy to be handed over.

"Where would I have gone to school, if I'd gone?" I asked her, later. "Eton?"

"No, your father hated it there and said he'd never send a son of his there. It was too brutal."

I liked that he thought that way but was never sure if the fault lay with my unhappiness at the age of twelve or if, rather, he was not in any shape to undertake this responsibility. I suspect my mother and Boy were concerned about his drinking and fecklessness and didn't want to hand over their fat little charge. So, instead, I went to Choate, which was brutal and dangerous in its own way.

So the high point of my relationship with my father, in an emotional sense, occurred when I was seven and he'd taken my hand as we crossed O'Connell Street on our way to the cinema. And that moment was never bettered, or equaled.

If I felt guilty about not going, I just put it into the mental drawer which was stuffed with a variety of emotional chits and IOUs, or feelings I didn't know what to do with.

I called him often over the next several weeks and also spoke to the few friends of his whom I'd met on my infrequent trips to Ibiza. The friends told me he was starting to behave oddly, being curt and unpleasant to the women they'd sent in to tidy up the flat, until the women, first one, then another, wouldn't come anymore. There was nothing for it, the friends said, but for him to go into a nursing home in Ireland. He'd never learned more than rudimentary Spanish in his decades there. He'd let Kathleen speak for him. He also gave an impression of not really liking Spain or its people. He couldn't stay in the dirtying apartment, and so his friends helped organize his papers and put the property on the market.

Then came the surprise over his financial position.

It seemed that over the years the friends had come to the conclusion that he was comparatively hard up, and he did nothing to discourage this by his behavior. The Irish wife of one of his friends told me that on more than one occasion, if Kathleen had come back from the bakery with a fresh loaf which had cost two pesetas, he'd sent her back to get yesterday's for one peseta. Consequently, at Christmastime, they would give gifts of provisions and wine, house staples rather than a scarf. But trying to organize his affairs prior to his departure, they found bank statements which told them he had more money than some of them. And that made them angry, feeling they had been gulled. I don't think that was his intention, but I don't know. I'm sure he preferred the wine to any scarf they'd have picked out. In his last ten years or so he had become more frugal, saying that he wanted to be careful so that he would have something to leave me. I never paid much attention to this. I made my own money, was sometimes flush, sometimes not at all, but always told him I wished him to be comfortable and not feel he had to enter his purchases and expenses in a little diary.

His friends tried to prevail on me to come over and do my bit in sorting out his life. I didn't go, feeling that whatever emotional mess had occurred between a small group of insular retired expatriate householders was their concern and not mine.

My cousin Caroline found a nursing home near Dublin, and my father took up residence there in the spring of 1999.

After thirty years on the Balearic island, had his wife not died, or had his temper not frayed, or had he been able to speak Spanish, he might have been able to stay on in the apartment, and there would have been no need for his well-intentioned friends to try to organize his things, and popular, well-mannered, amusing, sometimes-having-a-drop-too-much Eddy Lindsay-Hogg would not have had to leave the island with ill will and opprobrium dinning around him.

I spoke to him regularly at the nursing home, and he seemed to be settling in. My cousins Maggie and Caroline brought him a cake for his eighty-ninth birthday in May, and I would be seeing him when Lisa and I went to Ireland later in the summer.

Then things started to go downhill. He seemed to be getting confused in our telephone conversations and saying people were acting against him, were disturbing him with construction work outside his room, were trying to steal his money and that I was one of them.

"You're not my son," he shouted.

I spoke to the matron, which was how the person in charge was referred to, who said he was possibly reacting to a change in his pills and that, yes, there was some work being done outside his room on some days. I asked her to have it stopped at least until he'd adjusted to his new medicines.

Then his lawyer called me and said with well-aimed brusqueness, "You'd better get over here if you want to see your father alive again."

Lisa said whatever was really preventing me from going was not the issue anymore and that the time was now; so two days later we arrived on the new direct Los Angeles to Dublin Aer Lingus flight, and I went straight to the nursing home.

I rang the bell and waited. As the door opened, my glance was aimed at where, more or less, I expected the opening person to be.

"Hello."

The very old lady who'd spoken barely came up to the doorknob. Her dress was black with half sleeves, her hair bright white, and her face was soft but with deep lines.

"And who would you be?" she asked in a lilting Irish voice.

There was something unexpectedly girlish, almost flirtatious in her manner, a skill I sensed she'd been honing for eighty years or more. Tiny, she stood in the doorway, as though playing a game. Her portal would not be breached if I didn't somehow acknowledge by the way I gave my answer that I saw her as female and not just old. Aged as she was, there was something attractive about her so it wasn't difficult. I said my name. She smiled and stepped back, allowing me inside.

"Ah yes, Sir Edward's son. He's here, but not here," she said, waving her skeleton arm toward the common room behind her, where sat men and women of late age in various stages of falling apart.

"Come with me," said my new friend, scuttling through the first room and then another.

Some were shakily bringing teacup to mouth. A few were shouting in hard-of-hearing conversation. Another man, sitting on his own, was shouting to no one.

"I'm Gladys. We've had quite a day. Maureen, who's ninety-three, tried to escape, saying she had to find her mother."

She laughed at how dotty people can be.

Others were asleep, others staring at nothing, or at their pasts, some with small dribbles on their chin. They all seemed clean enough.

My guide pointed toward a slim young girl with a dark fringe wearing a green-trousered outfit from a medical haberdasher.

"Joan will fix you up," she said, giving me a pat on the arm. "I'm off for tea."

I approached Joan and asked where Sir Edward was.

"Downstairs, along the corridor, and first on the left when you make the turn."

She was quite pretty and I wondered if she couldn't find a nicer place to work.

I pushed open the door to my father's room and came in a body's width, so as not to startle him. His bed was on the right against a wall. There was daylight coming in from glass doors which gave on to a little stone courtyard. Most of the stones were up and broken, there were mounds of earth, and a forlorn little digging contraption sat idle and unattended.

I couldn't tell if he was dozing or if it was just that his eyes were closed.

"It's Michael," I said softly, looking toward my father.

After a moment, he opened his eyes and adjusted his focus to see where I was, and smiled.

People used to say he had a beautiful smile, and here I saw it, or was reminded of it, his teeth were out; the way he'd smile when he wasn't just being polite, when there was reason to be relieved, or to rejoice.

"Michael," he said as a statement, although his voice was already starting to be far away.

"Yes, I'm here."

I went to the bed. His hands were folded on top of the sheet and I took one and held it, long fingers, the skin dry and blue-veined, the old bones as thin as a small bird's.

I hadn't wanted to be here before but glad I was now, knowing that our story would not be much longer. He looked at me.

I'd forgotten what nice brown eyes he had. His eyes were full and liquid, whether from old age or tears, I wasn't sure. Then he shut them and seemed to be asleep again. I stroked his hand with my other one and then put his hand back with the other on the sheet and pulled up a chair and sat beside him.

He woke once, looked at me, smiled his smile, slept again. I sat there for an hour or so. Then I quietly got up and said, "I'll see you tomorrow."

He signaled he'd heard me with a slight movement of his eyelids.

The matron's office was uninhabited. I waited. After a few minutes, a small middle-aged woman, proud of her bust, prominent and supported by a white bra under her see-through blouse, with hair dyed a flat blond, came in. I introduced myself. She was carrying some vestment-like regalia, which she folded and put over a chair.

"Poor Mr. McCafferty. May he rest in peace. The priest arrived before the end, thanks be to God. Not much traffic."

This recent piece of good fortune appeared to have put her in a similar mood. She smiled at me and asked if I'd like a cup of tea.

"No thanks. How's my father?"

"He's very old, you know."

"I know."

"He was nervous so we gave him a little more Valium."

"Is that good for him?"

"For his nerves. Yes."

I knew in places such as this, patients could be drugged so as not to be nuisances, but he was eighty-nine and what else could be done?

"I'll be here tomorrow."

"Ah, good. I'm sure he likes to see you."

"I hope so."

I came the next day and sat beside him while he slept. On a round table in the middle of the room were many small leather books. I picked one up to see it was a diary, with every three months being a separate insert. His handwriting was thin and slightly tilted to the right, but with leftward tails on the *g*'s and *y*'s. I remembered it from the occasional letters he'd written me when I was young. There was a studied elegance to it, as though to make what was expressed similarly elegant.

"Bus to Palma. Dinner. £3. Pretty evening. Kathleen quiet."

"A wasted day" and then, following, "Another wasted day."

Then: "Another night like that, the wine. Row. My fault." And after that, the next entry: "Quiet day."

The diary entries followed that pattern. An excursion, or dinner or to someone's house, too much to drink. Remorse, a quiet day after.

Another jotting was a reflection following a description. He'd cut his hand and lost a little blood, and that had made him muse: "I think of the loss of life in that war and wish now (but not then) I'd taken part in it."

I stiffened, finding something ridiculous in the connection, a self-indulgent inflation of his wound and the bloodshed and loss of World War II. Though I wasn't judging the issues of duty or courage or fitness. I hadn't been in the army either.

I'd gone up for the American draft when I was twenty-two, when I was having my breakdown all those years ago in Ireland. Inspired by President Kennedy's inaugural address, I'd decided to go in if they would take me.

I got a couple of days off from my Irish TV job and had reported to a U.S. military base in Ruislip near London.

I'd done some paperwork in the morning, had a rather discreet physical ("Everything all right below the belt?" the doctor had asked), a hamburger and good cherry pie lunch in the commissary, and then, after a little mix-up with a nurse at the Dental Health Clinic, was rerouted to the Mental Health Clinic, to be interviewed by Dr. Levine. I described my fear of dying in the night and my pervasive anxiety.

"Don't you think that eighteen months in the army of the United States of America might cure you of those feelings?" the plump young military doctor had asked.

"I wish I thought that could be so, but I don't think it would work out that way."

Dr. Levine made a little note on his pad.

I think my flat feet were not in my favor but what might have really queered it was that on the morning's questionnaire: name, date of birth, education, sports, etc., I'd ticked any boxes which seemed appropriate, and then gone over to page 3, which began:

"Your last period was (check one): normal, excessive or scanty."

This gave me pause. I considered the options and checked "scanty," as being closest to the fact. And then when I'd gone on to the next question: "Are you now or have you ever been pregnant?," and I realized I'd strayed onto the women's section; the indelible pencil had done its work.

Two months later, I got the buff envelope with my draft qualification and page one told me I was classified 1-Y. 1-A meant you were in, and I guessed that 1-Y was a version of that. I turned the page over. 1-Y declared: "Only to be used in case of extreme National emergency."

On the next day, he seemed restless, moving in bed, throwing the sheets off. He was wearing a nightshirt which had ridden up, and the pad around his lower parts had become unclasped and I saw his genitals for the first and only time in my life. And my thought was, they looked like mine. Not a lot of pubic hair, and the balls and cock like mine, if I'd been lying in a warm bed.

He became more uneasy.

"I want to piss. I want to shit."

I'd never know what words he used to describe these functions, so distant had we been all our lives.

I knew I couldn't move him on my own so I went to find a helper.

Joan, the pretty girl with the dark fringe, was in the corridor.

"I think my father wants to go to the bathroom. And it'll take two people."

"He just went a short time ago. He's forgotten," she said, not unkindly.

"Are you sure?"

"Marie and I helped him. I'm sure."

"All right," I said, then asked, "Why do you work here?"

She looked at me, as if to gauge where my curiosity came from, and then felt she could say, "I was brought up by my grandparents. They were old. It doesn't bother me. And besides . . ." Rather than looking away, she looked at me, "I have a little girl. I bring her up on my own."

"How old?"

"Eighteen months." And she finished by saying, "It's a job," with a sense that she knew many worse.

I went back into the room and he was asleep again.

On a bureau with a stand-up mirror was a hairbrush and comb and a small box, blue leather with a brown square in the center, with a gold filigree decoration, probably Spanish. In it was a small tie clip, a couple of gold-plated collar studs, a rosary. And four small photographs. One was passport size, sepia with age, of Kathleen, her hair in a fashionable style from the late 1930s, when she'd been married to an Irish journalist, one of two previous husbands who'd leave her a widow. Then a strip of three, similarly sized, taken in a photo booth. I was seventeen, fat, hair neatly parted, with a fixed glowering stare, wearing a raincoat.

I close the box and go beside his bed and take a couple of pieces of Kleenex from the container. I stand at the bureau, and with a piece of tissue lift some strands of hair from the brush and comb, wrap them in the other piece of Kleenex, fold carefully, and put the soft item in my pocket.

I sat beside my father for another little while. I thought he had died when his breathing seemed to stop and he was still, but then he took a breath and his chest lifted.

I came the next day. I had been told his doctor would be coming that afternoon. An hour or so later than expected, the doctor was deferenced into the room by the Matron of the Uplift.

The doctor was tall, my height, with short gray hair, shy but wary eyes, and an aggressive chin, wearing a tweed jacket. A giant virgin I thought, in her skirt and laced shoes.

Although my father was in a deep sleep, we spoke softly.

"How's he doing?" I asked.

"As well as can be expected. He's very old," she said.

"Yes, I know."

"We're giving him plenty of Valium, to keep him calm."

If she'd said, "to keep him quiet," I wouldn't have been surprised.

"Is that a good idea? Can't too much Valium go around the corner, as it were, and make him feel weird, disoriented?"

New York, 1957.

"We're not giving him too much Valium."

The aggressive chin was not for nothing.

"And," she continued, "it's to stop him feeling anxious."

"He's dying," I said. "Do you think that's why he's feeling anxious?"

"From having talked to him, I'd have said he was always anxious. But you're his son, you should know."

She looked at me, to see what I might or might not know of my father, then asked, "When did you get over?"

"Four days ago."

When I'd arrived was not her concern. My arrival was not to do with her doctoring.

"Tell me, doctor, how much time . . ." I hung the question.

I was thinking of my daily visits, but more than that; if possible, if it would be of any use to him, I wanted to be there when he died, to hold his hand. He might know, but since I thought it would probably happen in his Valium sleep, he might not.

"You can't tell, but I'd think a few weeks, or a month."

"Not today?"

"No. Not today. I'll look in again next week. And we'll keep an eye on the Valium."

Her utterance was accompanied by a sympathetic smile: "I know what you're going through," and an eye glint: "I can handle the pills, bub."

I left not long after the doctor.

My father died that evening.

The next morning, Lisa and I and my cousin Caroline went to the nursing home to meet the undertaker.

The door had been opened again by tiny Gladys, who said, "I'm sorry for your loss. But these things happen."

I wondered if she had hit ninety herself yet. Probably.

The undertaker said he'd like me to choose a suit for my father to be buried, or cremated, in and would we like to go down now and pay our respects, and choose the suit.

Caroline and Lisa and I went downstairs and along the corridor, and pushed open the not fully closed door.

My father was lying in the bed, his hands crossed, as they had been a few days before, on top of the sheet, but now a small wooden cross, a thing of perfect symmetry, was underneath them, and behind his head and over his shoulders was a satin vestment scarf. (I wondered if these items were the same as had accompanied Mr. McCafferty on his last journey. Were they new, or recycled?)

His skin was waxy. Caroline bowed her head for a moment and then left Lisa and me. Lisa cried, then wiped her lovely hand across her eyes, and she and I went to his wardrobe. We chose the pale green tweed suit from his London tailor, Stovel & Mason, and laid it on the hanger at the foot of his bed. He'd looked handsome in it. Then Lisa left the room.

So there we were. Since the taxi, meeting the undertaker, walking down the wooden staircase to the dark corridor leading to his room, I'd been thinking of a kiss. A kiss good-bye. Would I? A sign of filial regard? A sign of affection from one human to another? We used to kiss on greeting, after time (years) apart. I usually found I was kissing the top of his jacket, he being a bit taller, sometimes his shaved cheek. I liked my kisses to him, and his on my cheek. I'd never kissed any other male family member, not my stepfather, nor his ferocious terrier brother; and kissing had seemed to me a good thing, a step forward, in relations between men. The French, who get many things right, kiss each other all the time, men and women, not once but twice. And their children too. It's a sweet sight to see a French father kiss his little boy on the cheek, the flesh, before a separation, a day at school, say.

I stood there. No one would know of this last moment unless I tell of it. I went from the foot of the bed to the side but not closer to him yet. I could stay as long as I wanted, the time would be given me by the marshaling forces of lifters, bed strippers, dressers, cosmeticians, measurers.

I stepped to beside him and thought, at first, to put two fingers of my right hand to my lips, make a soft kiss, and place them on his forehead. But then I reconsidered. It didn't seem courageous enough, or to say enough, whatever it was I wanted to say with a kiss. So I leaned forward and put my lips on his forehead, keeping them there till they, and I, recovered from the frisson, the short shock of the temperature of his brow, not cold yet but more than cool, as though I'd kissed the belly of a reptile. After a pause, I withdrew my lips and myself, went to the door, looked back at him, he never again to move of his own volition, the wooden cross beneath his elegant hands, and left the room, shutting the door behind me.

A few months later, I sent the hair I'd taken to a DNA place in Baltimore. A few months after that, they replied they couldn't pull any DNA. The strands would have had to come directly from the hair follicle.

My mother would be next, but not for several years.

Twenty-One

In July 2004, in one of my regular calls to Jean Marsh in England, I was in Los Angeles and Jean told me that her best friend, Eileen Atkins, had recently had lunch with Simon Callow. Simon, actor, director, writer, total homme de théâtre, was working on the second volume of his biography of Orson Welles. They had discussed me, Jean said.

"Oh? Why?"

"It was about you and Orson."

"What about me and Orson?"

"Simon told Eileen that one of the people he'd interviewed for the book was an eighty-eight-year-old woman who lives in New York. Eileen couldn't remember her name. Simon said she'd been a friend of your mother's and that this woman thought you were Orson's son."

"Why?"

"It seems it was a conversation she'd had with your mother. You should call Simon. I'll get his number from Eileen."

Simon was away working and so it was almost a month before we spoke.

I remembered from when I'd met him during the casting for *Brideshead Revisited* how approachable and intelligent and funny he was, and he hadn't changed. After a quick catch-up with each other, I asked, "This eighty-eight-year-old woman who'd known my mother, does she have all her marbles?"

"Sharp as a tack, my dear fellow. She still does a cabaret act, singing and what-not."

"What's her name?"

"Paula Laurence."

Wait a minute. My memory tumblers clanged into place.

Wasn't Paula Laurence the woman my mother said she didn't like, who'd given the cocktail party over forty years ago for Virginia Welles Lederer Pringle, who later that evening my mother had labeled a "pathological liar."

I said I'd like to speak to her. Simon gave me her number and said he'd call her first to tell her I'd be calling. I then continued, "This has all gone on such a long time. I tried to get some DNA from Eddy Lindsay-Hogg but it didn't work. I've thought of calling Chrissie Welles, to see if I could get some from her."

"I'd talk to Paula first," said Simon.

"What do you mean?"

"I'd talk to Paula if I were you."

Two days later, on August 26, I telephoned Paula Laurence. What follows are diary notes I took immediately after our call:

Paula Laurence—

Says she has total recall and she does seem very sharp.

Remembered me as a little boy, and then meeting me again when I was in my late teens and early twenties.

It was in Santa Monica in 1946 or 1947 that the conversation took place, she said. My mother, Paula and Virginia Welles Lederer were sitting out on the deck of Paula's rented house, having tea and painting their toe nails, and the talk got around to men and then to which of their lovers had been the "best." And Ma said Orson. Virginia hadn't known, Paula said, and Ma said, "It's time you did." What Virginia had known was that Orson was relentlessly unfaithful, and acknowledged an affair or two of her own.

To do with lovers, Ma said it was a toss-up between Orson and Henry Miller.

I asked Paula about Raymond Hakim, the name from

that evening with wine in Dublin. Paula said maybe and then that Ma had an "endless list of men." Ma was a "fascinator" and could "put spells on people." Re: Virginia being untruthful, especially re: my mother saying, Virginia said to Charlie Lederer, that Geraldine said he was gay. Paula said my mother did say to people that Charlie was gay because, Paula thinks, Charlie had rebuffed an approach from her.

She'd said Ma had more secrets from Boy than anyone, and he couldn't have taken it if I were a bastard. She said Ma married Boy because of me, for the money, and Paula knew there hadn't really been any, but that he'd been the best of those who were available to her, having burned bridges and wanting to get out of Hollywood.

She said Orson and Ma were always close and always loved each other in some way.

"Like you and Jean," she finished.

Her husband had produced *Caligula* off-Broadway with Jean's ex before me, Kenneth Haigh, who created the part of Jimmy Porter in *Look Back in Anger,* and she said Jean, as a young woman, was "beautiful beyond belief" and a "traffic stopper." And is a wonderful woman. I agreed, of course.

Paula said she always thought I was OW's child because of the shape of my face, my weight struggles when I was young, and because, she said, as a little boy, I walked like him, forth-right strides on the earth, and also because of all the surrounding stuff, and what Ma had said.

We hung up. I sat at my desk and considered our conversation. I was sure Paula was in full command of her faculties. She'd had a sense of time that had passed and irony, and was quick to appreciate, or make, a joke. Whether there was something mischievous or malicious in her nature I couldn't tell; if there was any sense of rancor in her story toward my mother or Virginia or my stepfather, I had no way of knowing; I could only write down what she'd said and the tone in which it was said. I made the notes in my diary and realized that I was looking at old images under the new lens of our conversation and that memories seemed to be jumping into sharper focus.

And my mind went back to a taxi ride, I, stoutly sandwiched between my mother and stepfather, on the way to Paula's little cocktail party for Virginia Welles Lederer Pringle, where I'd seen my childhood pal, Chrissie Welles. The yellow cab had stopped at a red light, and my mother made a point of reiterating what she'd said before we'd left the apartment: Why were we going?, she didn't like Paula, "something unreliable" about her, she'd said, and looked across me to my stepfather, who said he didn't really like Paula either. Whether his opinion was solicited by my mother's steely glance, or was his own, I didn't know.

When we entered the party, to a group of twenty or so, drinking martinis and highballs, Paula Laurence, an elegant woman with a definite nose, seemed particularly welcoming and friendly.

And then why, after we'd returned home, had my mother, a drink or two inside her, spent some minutes reminding Boy of what she might have told him before, and aiming to convince me, that Virginia, our neighbor who'd been nice to me when I was a little boy at the beach, was a "pathological liar"?

Could these two women have been innocent; one of being "unreliable" and the other of being untruthful?

Could it be that my mother in her vivid protective imagination saw herself one day as being in the dock accused of only she knew how many serious crimes—crimes against relationships, against love, crimes against honesty—and felt it vital that the jury (my stepfather) regard the evidence of at least two of the witnesses who might be called to testify for the prosecution as being suspect, subtle work having gone into the knee-capping of their characters?

Fascinated I was by these thoughts, and found it remarkable

how time and new information can shift the way you look at events, and at people.

Icalled Simon again and told him of my conversation with Paula and, because the information was so at variance to what my mother had told me, took a risk and asked him if Paula in any way could be lying. His attitude was incredulous, not offended, thank goodness.

"Why on earth would she do that? No, she's not a liar nor do I think she'd waste her time inventing a scene which didn't happen. What for?"

I then asked if he thought I could get in touch with Beatrice Welles, who'd been a little girl on the *Chimes at Midnight* train to Belfast. He said he thought it was unlikely. He described her as a beautiful female Orson, but also as unsettled, often moving, nomadic (like her father).

"No one among the Orsonics has been happy," he said.

A curse to be escaped, I thought.

In the summer of 2005, I directed *The Lark* with Amanda Plummer at the Stratford Festival Theatre in Canada, an hour and a half outside Toronto. On the afternoon of Sunday, July 17, Lisa, her college-bound daughter, adorable Jane, and I were lying on the big bed, watching the Food Channel, Jane wishing to be a good cook, like her mother, and I, with a novel in my hand, also watching the Food Channel. I had a rehearsal that evening. The phone rang. It was my sister calling from Maine, where she and Rick had just arrived to put their son into camp. My sister said that Joe, the helper on duty with my mother that day in New York, had called to say she was running a high fever and should we get a doctor in to give her antibiotics.

Our mother had a "Do Not Resuscitate" notice above her bed. This was a reluctant decision on the part of my sister and me.

When not in bed, my mother was belted into a recliner so she couldn't fall out, her pabulum meals were spooned for her, and her eyes, when not closed, rolled in their sockets, unfocused and wandering. She was ninety-one. In the bedroom, the king-sized bed she had slept in with Boy had been stripped and pushed to the margins of the room, to near the windows, which gave a nice view onto Central Park but were now covered by shutters. My mother slept in what was really a large crib, with a barred partition which could be lowered, so she could be put in and taken out with a hoist.

My sister and I thought that if our mother had a medical crisis, we should let it run its course and not interfere, that her life was no life. But on this day, our resolve weakened, we did not want her to be in pain or to have a fever flaming over the already scorched earth of her mind. So we decided to call a doctor.

Then Rick's cell phone rang, our mother was having trouble breathing. Susie said, "I'll call you back. I'll get a doctor."

But she didn't hang up, she was talking to Rick, who was talking to Joe in New York, and then my sister said, "She's dead."

She started to cry and said, "It's just the two of us left. We'll have to stay close."

A couple of hours later, after I'd made a lot of phone calls, to Jean, and to family in Ireland and England, Jane and I were walking to the YMCA gym, where we were both going to exercise. I said to her, "I don't want you to think because I haven't cried that I didn't love my mother. I did."

I stopped for a moment and then said, "I've been saying goodbye a little every year."

Jane, always intelligent, nodded, understanding what I was trying to say.

I felt I owed it to my mother to explain to Jane why I hadn't cried, and because Jane had a mother also, my wife, Lisa.

I went to the theater that evening, to rehearse on the big stage, and before we started, backstage in the wings, I told only Amanda and our smart motherly stage manager, Ann Stuart, someone I could talk to, I having lost a mother.

Paula Laurence sent me a kind note of condolence, written in large-charactered firm legible handwriting.

I called her when Lisa and I were in New York after *The Lark* opened, asking if we could meet her that weekend. Her machine fielded my call.

She called back when I was out and spoke to Lisa. They had a nice chat but Paula said she was "otherwise engaged" that weekend and was working Monday and Tuesday, but "don't stop trying."

Lisa and I went to France that Tuesday and so we didn't meet.

Paula Laurence died later that year.

Twenty-Two

After my mother died, I found letters, telegrams, some photos stuffed in old manila envelopes. And a diary.

Some of the letters were from 1942–1943 to my mother, from Vladimir Sokoloff telling about how happy he and his wife, Lisa, were that my nurse Mary and I were staying with them, how much they and everyone, including Al the milkman, loved me and how funny I was. I always did feel loved by Sokoloff. And then another letter telling my mother that I'd been ill and they had been very concerned about me, and then another, when Mary and I had gone to see my mother in New York how happy she must be to see me, even if I was looking a little pale.

And then a lot from Henry Miller, probably from 1944. I can't be sure if they were lovers in the carnal sense, but love of some kind seemed to be flowing between them.

Letter dated January 30, 1944. Henry Miller had written a long typed letter to a colleague criticizing a book he'd written and forwarded a copy to my mother probably because of the way it ended:

> And now here is where Geraldine comes in. When Geraldine talks, and her talk is pure wild Irish, there is joy and sense in it. And food! And drink! And perfume! . . . She may ask for a jonquil to wear between her toes, or she may switch to beer and pretend to like it, but whatever she says, still talking the human language, she makes divine sense.

Undated letter to my mother, typed:

I hope you are reading everything of mine, down to comma and semi-colons, as I am reading you, your dots and dashes, your last minute flurries and capririccios. You have a sort of "arpeggio" style which I find exciting. I always think of you talking to me, there at the threshold of the kitchen, your legs spread wide apart, your elbows on your knees, your face alight. Varda [an artist] is right—you are the Muse. And an oracle too.

Another typed letter written on "Sunday night," after he'd seen my mother in the movie *Wilson*:

It's strange and disturbing, because at that moment I fell in love with you, and that was almost like falling in love with an anonymous host. Falling in love with a being who could never belong to any one person, but only to the world. I was smitten and I was desolate at the same time. And now I feel it's alright to say I love you because that's what everybody is going to say and my voice is just another added to the litany.

A four-page handwritten letter, undated, ends:

Have a good sleep. Go forth in the bleak dawn with the light and airy tread of the antelope. Cover your white skin in chamois. And don't leave perfumed kerchiefs or scarfs behind you—they're very disturbing. Leave only your perfume behind you.

Your seven year old fan—
Henry Miller

Another letter typewritten:

Trying to describe you to Lynda [someone he was renting a shack from] I said: Geraldine is a fairy vixen who will probably remain eternally young. She can be meaner than hell, can rub you out with three words, if she wants to, and then be adorable, angelic. She has character and her beauty lies in her character. Coming off the lot (in full war paint) she rivals any of them for glamour. But her true glamour is in her Irish soul. When she turns on that battery she's invincible. The colour of her hair? I don't remember. Red, I think, or russet. Height medium, figure trim, gait elastic. But you must hear her talk! When you hear her talk you won't remember what she looks like. She can resemble anything she chooses to be . . . but when she opens her throat . . .

One letter I found was from her to him, typed, probably by my mother's assistant, Mary-Ellen Quinn, and has the appearance of being the carbon copy. It is dated March 20, 1944, and begins "Dearest Henry":

The life of the "great artist" is very complicated at present. I don't know whether you read the newspapers, so perhaps you did not see that my great friend, advisor, and protector in time of insolvency died last week. His name was Myron Selznick and he was one of the few genuinely eccentric characters the movies have thrown up. He drank himself to death. He was only 45. I hate seeing the laws of cause and effect being fulfilled in their inexorable manner. It alarms me in the same way as a policeman does. And I was always hoping that little Myron would buck these laws, find the file in the loaf of bread, and be able to escape from cirrhosis of the liver, thrombosis and all the ghoulish jailers who were chasing him. I used to quarrel with him a great deal, but luckily when I saw him the night before he collapsed, we had one of those moments of rapport (and don't let the use of this word mislead you into unleashing any more French on me. Because it is about the only word I know.) which occur so seldom in a friendship. I really loved him for a moment and he loved me. I don't know why I'm telling you so much about a man you did not know, in a profession which everybody more or less despises, except that he is on my mind and I must talk about him before I go on to other things. In a business way his death has made my life less easy, because his advice was always completely courageous and sound. At present I'm trying to make up my mind whether I should go to New York in August to play in Rose Franken's new piece, and I have no one really wise enough to guide me. Myron's office in which Gloria Safier works is trying to secure that I shall be in the movie which will be made after the play has completed its run, and if we cannot get these rights, I think I had better not do it. Because I'm just now at the point where I may do very well in the movies after such a long sweat, and we are all afraid that if I should suddenly disappear for six months or so I will have to begin all over again.

With any luck I'm going to have a house on the beach for the summer. It is very beautiful, with an open porch off the living room from which one may look down into, and even fall into, the sea at high tide. It is very expensive but Gloria will stay there and pay some of the rent. She asked me nervously if I should insist on talking business to her all the time if she stayed there, to which I rightly replied that I do not consider talking about *my* career business, but rather a very very interesting discussion on art and philosophy.

This was our house in Santa Monica.

From Henry Miller to my mother, a postscript in a handwritten letter:

One evening, when a car is available to haul me a few miles, I'll give you a ring long distance. Your voice rings in my ears. I do adore you—forgive me.

Another, handwritten, letter ends:

. . . You will know that wherever I go, whatever I become, I shall be sending you messages always. And this is the last message for tonight . . . signing off . . . "Sweet dreams, dear Geraldine, and may your deepest desires be realized!"

And then the diary.

It was written in a blue leather book, the thickness of a small novel, that Edward Lindsay-Hogg had given her on December 7, 1942. She had been twenty-nine the previous November and would stop it before her next birthday. She wrote at intervals, with only the occasional date, and more pages were blank than those which had writing.

She seemed to have written in all moods, and sometimes when she'd been drinking. The handwriting would change from neat and orderly, to slanting on a large diagonal right-sided scrawl, depending. There are poems and a couple of pages of all-right drawings. She'd been an art student in her teens.

Some of the diary I find sad, to do with a sense of doom and failure in this young woman. Some of it reveals fierce conflicts in her heart to do with my father and her inner self.

And then she ceased writing her diary, why I don't know, sometime in 1943 when she was still enduring the slights at Warner Bros. Perhaps life took over and she was too busy, or distracted, or, perhaps, like some pages which she'd torn out, she did not wish to, really, reveal herself; that to put down her thoughts and secrets was unsafe, and she could be called to account for it. Did she think someone would read her diary, and that's why she'd torn out pages? Did she write some of her entries to be read?

Some of the writing is very self-aware and some beautiful, I think, especially to do with her memory of her eccentric great-aunt, Georgie, whom she'd loved, and been loved by, as a young girl. Her grandmother's sister could not be as other people and had a sort of heedless bravery to her conduct.

I think my mother always held individuality and bravery as traits above others, and that she always wanted to be brave herself, but perhaps sometimes couldn't manage it.

When I hold her diary, I feel I hold something precious and intimate in my hand, something like a part of her, delicate and cognizant, as my mother puts down her thoughts when she was only twenty-nine.

Today is the anniversary of America's entrance into the Second World War. Eddy and I are living in New York. Michael and Mary are in Hollywood. I miss Michael terribly and worry about him. Eddy must miss him far more as he may have to return to Ireland soon and not see the baby for a long time perhaps. It pains me (us, I am sure) to think of him so far away.

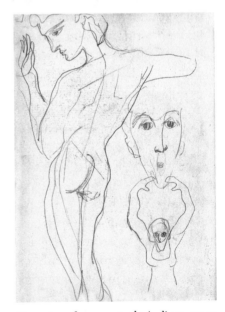

This is the last mention of me in the diary. I don't know why they were three thousand miles away from me. I do know that when Mary and I did go to New York some months later, my father was not there.

Drawings from my mother's diary, 1943

DECEMBER 12, 1942

I saw Myron Selznick today. He was sober. Said he had not been drinking. Said he had not been drinking for 4 months. I know this is not true, for it was less than 3 months ago that he was sick in the dining room of our house in Camden Drive, Hollywood. All the same, I have always observed even in myself, perhaps I should say also in myself, that people always exaggerate the times they spend away from liquor.

A little after this entry she wrote about a play she wasn't sure she wanted to do, to be directed by Max Reinhardt, the king of European theater in the 1920s, who'd lived in a castle in Salzburg, and then had left when the malignity of the Nazi regime could not be ignored.

After a dinner with Max Reinhardt, my mother wrote:

The bother of this decision made me miserable and I got very drunk, annoyingly so. Jack Houseman called. I told him I was unhappy and he replied you must make a life of your own. I do not understand what he meant by that. I feel I have done so. At least in the eyes of others I have done so. I do not believe anyone can ever say of themselves I have made a life of my own. It is a purely subjective statement. Every human being must feel they have failed miserably. If they do not it only means they received something in this life which they were not specifically searching for, i.e. radium when one was searching for gold.

Then a page was torn out.

One of the next entries begins with an extravagant description of EL-H's lean physical beauty, and then she wonders why, with his intelligence, he is not able to really achieve anything. Is it to do with a fundamental lack of confidence? And then she goes on:

I have read of and even seen women who might be in some way as exquisite as he is, although I doubt it, only a tree or a child or some fresh new gesture of nature could equal him. And so loving and unselfish. He drew a bad one in me. I am always meaning to be as good to him as he is to me. I can't seem to manage it. His unselfishness springs from an easy and ever freshened source, like his lovely looks, while mine is full of effort, self-conscious and often I am afraid with ironic or malicious overtones.

And then:

I lie beside him, pale plump green eyed half baked, stewing in my own bile, black as black bog water, bitter as old gall

Later was a poem:

> *As I do figures of eight*
> *Across the firmament*
> *Twirling*
> *And whirling*
> *Into the abyss*
> *With a comet for a sail*
> *Or like a tin can*
> *Tied to a dog's tail*
> *I look at my little*
> *Ed*
> *Safe in bed*
> *Warm, well fed*
> *Hagridden, half dead.*
> *He looks at his darling*
> *His icy starling.*
> *Now race through the dark*

My lovely spark
Your skates skid and jar
In the winterbound garden
Of my heart
And I awake
Frozen with fears
Skate now on the tiny lakes
Of my tears.

And then, two pages torn out, and the next page was continuing a thought:

. . . them. I mean the men that I have loved (not the men who have loved me). A strange thing—when I first set out on my career as an actor I was only anxious to be understood as an intellect. Now as I grow older, I wish to make plain to an audience the happinesses and the terrors of the passions. In those sicknesses of humanity, it seems to me one touches the heart of every human being, be he idiot or genius and/or saint. I think I never understood anything until I experienced these feelings.

What had been in these destroyed pages? Were they confessions she could trust to no eyes other than her own?

Then she contrasts love and hate:

These are indeed akin in that they are both uncontrollable diseases of the character, and for one or both of them, a person will forego their home, their husband, their children or their career. They seize hold of the body as violently as malaria or the plague and from the moment of the catching the disease one cannot be held accountable for one's actions, even to oneself, the most strict of critics.

Another poem:

AGED 29 YEARS

White bird
Black Sky
Black souled
Am I
O bird of my childhood
Fly across that lost wildwood

About her great-aunt Georgie:

I have come a long way, have I not, from the nights I used to walk the dark tree lined roads in Greystones with my dear most dear Georgina Arabella Roper. And the treetops made archways over the bumpy mud roads, and the sea sighed like a tranquil giant or roared and pounded on the cold dark dangerous shore, and so the train (Arklow to Dublin) passed through the night unheard on its one gauge track against the murmurs and moanings of the sea. We both walked slowly up and down and round about the roads both talking in dreams. She of what had past. Myself of what I hoped would come. She of how one morning she awoke to find birds, flocks of birds, perching on her bed-stead, squatting on the brass rails at the head and foot of the bed, four white birds quietly sitting on each of the four brass balls which decorated the four corners of the bed of this beautiful young creature. While she lay there, as at home with the birds as they were with her, her mother came into the room to say "8:30 Georgie, time to get up." She saw the birds grouped around this drowsy black haired blessed one, and she cries: "Georgie, if this ever happens again, I will send you to the lunatic asylum." How funny, how heartbreaking. I think it broke Georgie's heart. I did not hear from her if the birds ever came to her room thereafter, but I do remember that she could live three or more weeks in the mountains, eating berries, sleeping in the shelter of rocks and gorse bushes. When she would return from one of these vigils, she would be brown and burnt and leathery skinned as a gypsy at a fairground.

She and her sister, my maternal grandmother, Adelaide Roper Richards, loved each other. She understood Georgie and took her into her house to live after Georgie had given her inheritance (from her mother) to a woman selling newspapers, a crying woman, down on the Quays in Dublin one rainy miserable night. Georgie loved me too. It makes me happy to be able to write that down. She loved us all really. Except perhaps my father who frightened her.

My brother used to be a little embarrassed by her but he was always polite, although a little off-hand and aloof in the hopes that this mode of response would keep her within the bounds of his notion of proprieties. He couldn't say it did. One night he was at the Gaiety Theatre with several of his friends from college. The Trinity College racing set. The Binocular Boys. All very grave, very grown up, too poised to express any enjoyment at the end of the play if it were enjoyable, and they were slowly walking out looking neither to right nor left, drawling to each other where they should spend the rest of the evening, admired by all, when suddenly to his extreme distaste, David finds one of his hands seized and kissed by a wild looking old lady with long black locks hung on each side of her face and down her back, and no shoes on her feet. It was Aunt Georgie. She took her hair down when she enjoyed the drama, her shoes she had given to a beggar on her way to the theatre, the kiss on the hand was to do with love.

Ah Georgie, your memory I hope will never fade from my mind, and if I laugh at many things you did and said, it is to laugh never with mockery or patronage, but lovingly and joyfully.

And a poem near the end, before the empty pages, when my father had gone, or was going.

> *Why should I*
> *Be fond of me*
> *Since I share the*
> *Faults of we*
> *Why my interest in*
> *The fuss*
> *Of killing me*
> *And saving us.*

So what was this marriage to Eddy Lindsay-Hogg, the husband she told me she'd written to as though nothing was wrong, although it looks as if much was, for three years of separation when she'd, amongst other things, met another man she wished to marry?

And when Edward Lindsay-Hogg left America to spend the rest of the war in Ireland, had he been oblivious to my mother's feelings of insecurity and misery. Or, knowing he was going to leave, did she bottle up her feelings and only occasionally confide them to her diary?

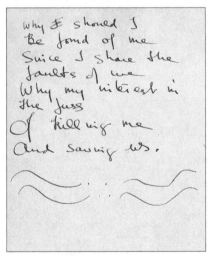

Why should I / Be fond of me / Since I share the faults of we / Why my interest in the fuss? / Of killing me / And saving us.

So what was true and what wasn't?

M y mother used to wake in the dawn suddenly, she'd tell me, with a revelation about something or other, and she was usually right. For instance, when I was studying the English poets for my Oxford exam, she woke at 5 A.M. and said to herself, and later that morning to me, "Wordsworth," and, sure enough, a week later, the only mandatory question on the exam was about Wordsworth.

O n March 14, 2007, while I was in the early stages of writing all this, I awoke, snap, fully conscious at 5 A.M. with my revelation, which is:

I think my mother was like a small company which, because things are not ship-shape, keeps two sets of books, one for the auditors, and then there's another one.

The auditors in this case would be Edward Lindsay-Hogg and Stuart Scheftel, and the books she showed them would have been done in neat script, the margins with straight edges, and the sums would all add up and the figures would all come out on the plus side.

The other book would be messier, hard to follow, with ink splotches and items entered, then crossed out, confusing.

I think Edward Lindsay-Hogg was my father.

And the reason there were the rumors about Orson, always around, never verified but constant, was because that's what my mother wanted. She was a bright woman and why would she want that?

I think they probably did have an affair, he twenty-three or twenty-four, she eighteen months older, both in shaky marriages, both very attractive, both at the beginning of careers which started fast, then stalled, his arc being of epic proportions.

And so, however the story got started, maybe gossip at first, and juicy gossip it was, or because others thought it, she embraced it, but subtly, for she was clever. Her denials were contradicted on her part by glancing hints, innuendo, maybe giving some clues to some people in Hollywood, which would keep the story going, and hard no's to others. It gave her cachet, and she, in spite of her beauty and wit and intelligence and passion, felt she needed it in order to exist in the hard brutal world of movies where she lived and worked. To have this child who, for whatever reason, looked more like Orson Welles than any other male, would perhaps get her extra favors, at least in the artistic *quartier* where she wished to live.

But when she (and Mary and I) moved to New York for her to begin her second marriage, she would have had to reinvent herself to play the Park Avenue wife of the successful businessman. It was not a role she was cut out to play, and he, at the time, was not successful and so there were bound to be stresses and, on her part, a reworking of the past. Out with raffishness, in with respectability; although she would adopt the curious habit of bringing up the subject to acquaintances or friends or interviewers, only in order to strenuously deny it.

When I was rehearsing a play in New York a few years ago, I was working on a scene with Mark Ruffalo and Illeana Douglas. During a short break, Mark made some reference to Martin Scorsese and Illeana said, "Oh, Marty and I lived together for four years."

Mark looked at her.

"Oh," he said. He had not known of this. Nor had others in the room.

We went back to rehearsing, and you could see because of her close connection to one of the most gifted directors of the past half century that, for a while anyway, there was something to Illeana other than her talent.

This improvised design of my mother's was a deception which would have occurred out of fear, fear of being displaced, removed, being broke, unable to hold her own or to look after me. The fact that it led to more than half a century of an ongoing story, with twists, and feints and clues, and probably compromised whatever relationship I might have had with my father, although he was culpable in his way, was not something she could have foretold when she fell into it. She was going day to day in Hollywood where the rewards were great, in a way, but she knew the wardrobe department held the greasy suits of failed comedians and the ball gowns had sweat stains under the arms, to be erased with chalk for the next wearer; where beauty became sodden with too many nights in fashionable boîtes, or wrecked by trysts with careless lovers, of high or low degree, and where, for both sexes, beauty was a commodity, on-screen and off, to be courted, coveted, envied, desired and then, as the lines from the mouth descended, patronized, ignored, mocked; as the laugh lines lit out by the crafty cameramen became wrinkles; the body once trim, filling out; the breasts, once objects of lust for the mammary-fixated, pulled by gravity.

The highlit world was only temporary and made prominent by the dark behind it; the Dark soon to throw its cloak over those in the foreground and hustle them into the wings where they would be thrown on the ground and, knee in chest, dispatched. Such, at the time anyway, was what was in store for the golden boys and girls, not that when they were twenty or twenty-five or thirty or so would they have seen it that way, but that is what it was.

It seems for a long time I was looking for a father: there was the absent one, the fantasy one, and the one I did not recognize in time, who took on the responsibilities and shouldered the burdens of being a father, who loved me and I him, in my confused way, although we never fully understood each other; and so, in a way, that quest has been a sad one. And to do with my beautiful, which is how I remember her, mother? I didn't ask enough questions for fear of upsetting her, although I'm not sure of what answers I'd have been given, their accuracy. I loved her and think I now understand her better, and that's a good thing. And, by inviting me to that rehearsal when I was fourteen, she gave birth to me a second time, for which I will always be thankful.

Twenty-Three

I thought it was over, that I was done with it, not any more alert for clues, or looking for footprints under the magnifying glass.

My own life: directing, writing, painting, marriage to Lisa and being a loving and dedicated stepfather to Jane, had taken over the emotional ground. I'd moved on.

I now know that the previous and, I thought, final chapter with my speculations, informed by what I had collected, sifted through, and at last finding a precious nugget, or so I thought, is only fool's gold.

I am undone because the light that shone onto my porous dinged pan was held by my mother, and she did not really want me to see its contents; so she constantly moved the light, sometimes onto me it was, sometimes up to a sky where it would not register, or toward the ground, or, briefly, onto herself and then off to the side again.

I could never have imagined, and by what an unexpected history of connections, the way I'd learn how I'd missed the dark circle in the center of the board.

My Mother

Chanel No. 5 was her perfume. I recently went into the Chanel boutique in Beverly Hills and asked for a spray of it. So I'd remember my mother. The smell of her. And with this version of a madeleine cake, my mind went back to the years of my youth and teens with her.

Her hair was red, nothing orange about it, more a lustrous auburn with licks of flame. Her eyes were hazel green. She was five foot three with slim legs and nice hands, as practical as pretty. She smoked Chesterfields, three or four puffs, and then she'd put it out. Usually on a diet. And then she'd light another, a few puffs and stubbed out. (She stopped when my stepfather had the Irish heart attack.)

Painted from the back by Henry Miller, in a picture he called, because of a wandering staircase on the right, "The Contradictory Staircase," she had rounded full hips. And full breasts. Earl Wilson, the *New York Post* gossip columnist, wrote sometime in the 1950s what at the time would have been considered a compliment, "Geraldine Fitzgerald may not be stuck up be she'll always be stuck out." My stepfather was a nightly reader of his column.

(I remembered this quote when my mother had her mastectomy. And the second, two years later because, she said, she felt unbalanced.)

She was a seductress whose magic would work on whomever she chose to show it to.

She knew she could whisk a Kleenex into a silk scarf, and she liked to beguile, needed to probably, and to draw in, to include, to make allies, I'd call them, as much as friends. The Siamese twin of her charm was a sense of empathy, so that the recipient would feel noticed, understood, and in so being, valued also, cared about. For the most part, I'd say, this talent, for that is what charm is, and a dangerous one in irresponsible hands, was for the common good. And her own good too, for whoever was under its spell was, in some way, disarmed, rendered incapable, as if from the bite of a dulcet spider. Better sweetness than venom, although that was an option.

She was funny, nice funny or un-nice funny. Sometimes a person who had lobbed an aimless, or thoughtless, conversational potato at her would have thrown back at him a firecracker.

And that was part of her too, something dangerous, something ferocious. It could be a firecracker, or sometimes with greater (to her mind) provocation she would retaliate with small arms or heavy artillery. And this would be as unwelcome as it was unwelcoming. There would be a coldness, anger underneath with sometimes the hostility exposed, but more often a seeming absence of feeling, of empathy—excluding—yesterday's warmth today's ashes. It could go on for a short period, minutes or hours, or as in Paula Laurence's case, half a lifetime. And when the coldness met up with the shiv that was her wit and both were joined by the looking-for-trouble thug, vodka and water (a mixture I likened to drinking Sterno), it was as though the world could no longer be recovered.

I think at that time, the mid-1950s to early 1960s, she drank, as many do, because she was unhappy. She was not getting as much acting work as she'd have liked, her role as Park Avenue wife of a (not) rich businessman was proving an uneasy fit; a teenage son and a young daughter and she with perhaps not instinctive mothering gifts. And what had happened to the life of the "great artist," as she teasingly referred to herself?

What had happened to all her dreams?

But she was always my champion. She stored remarks I'd made as a child and reminded me of them whenever she thought I should be encouraged to think of myself not as fat, bullied, and squashed but, in some way, as better than that.

We'd been discussing God. I was seven, and I'd asked her, "Can God do *anything*?"

My tutor in God-matters was Mary Gillen, who was at work day and night and twice on Sundays training me in devotion. My mother was, she often told me, an atheist, but she acquiesced in the conversation, so as not to upset my somewhat fragile status quo.

So she reluctantly said, "Yes, God can do anything."

She told me I paused for a moment, considering God's omnipotence, and then asked, looking for confirmation of His great power and might, "Can He eat a sweater?"

And then the next year, in their bedroom, before my stepfather had come back from his office, the two of us alone together, I'd asked, "Can you prove to me that I'm a child and not an old man dreaming of my past?"

There was a dinner party in our apartment when I was in my teens and struggling with fatness, a word so distasteful I could not speak it till I was older. We were standing by the sideboard that held the dishes on offer and to which I had just helped myself.

I said to her, "Girls will never like me. My weight."

She looked me straight in the eye and said, "I promise you, girls will like you. I'll bet you five dollars." She smiled and said, "Do you want to take the bet?"

Five dollars was a lot to me. I looked at her and saw her confidence in my amorous future and said, "No. I believe you. It'll be okay. I suppose."

A couple of years later we were in Ireland, and I'd accompanied her to a dinner in someone's house where there was a pretty girl I was too shy to talk to. I was still corpulent. (When she'd take me, in my earlier teens, to an adult bargain shop for clothes, I'd be measured, taped around upper and lower body, and the salesman would call out to another, "What do we have in Executive sizes? See if we have a 'Company President.' ")

That evening at the dinner party I asked her how Orson did with women, this after *King Lear,* to do with his weight.

She said, "If Orson was in this room, no matter what size he was, he could go home with any woman, including the little brunette you're looking at. You should go and talk to her."

To me, when I was young, my mother was the epitome of beauty, something electric and on fire about her, although I knew the sparks could ignite and burn, but with a sympathy which was only for me.

And I suppose I felt, or included, in my feelings for her, something of the erotic.

When I was sixteen and at home on the day off from Stratford, and my mother and stepfather and sister were in Ireland, I was wandering around the empty apartment and went into my mother and stepfather's bedroom. I stood by the bureau where she kept her underwear. I felt the same frisson of tension and apprehension which would come over me before I'd shoplift small items from exclusive stores. I opened the drawer which contained what she'd left behind and took out and fingered black and white silk panties, full bras.

And then, in the bedroom, there was a large chest, cedar-lined, in which my godfather, Gene Markey, had kept cigars before he gave the chest to my mother. I opened it and saw letters, manila envelopes, and an onion paper copy, only a carbon from the original, a draft of *Quiet Days in Clichy,* Henry Miller's bombshell of fucking and sucking in Paris, with a paper-clipped note attached: "Darling Geraldine, I'd like you to have this. HM."

I was still a virgin at sixteen, wishing for that not to be the case, but didn't know when I would breach that dam (or dame). Not for two years. And so I was on fire myself, looking for anything to do with sex, for information, for titillation, for several orgasms a day. I worried if I had only so much sperm inside me and if I'd deplete the source. And if some of my feelings centered on my mother, so be it, I thought, without guilt. I never thought it was Oedipal, just that she was female. And she loved me.

Gloria

I first met Gloria Vanderbilt in 1956 when Sidney Lumet asked my mother, stepfather, and me for dinner, saying he wanted us to meet someone. He and my mother had become good friends since *The Doctor's Dilemma*. A small Italian restaurant at a cozy table, Sidney and Gloria opposite my mother and me, Boy at the end next to Sidney. I immediately was captured by Gloria, as many have been from the time she was in her teens. Tall, with a delicate face of perfect proportion, with shiny dark hair, a full mouth with a slight overbite, and her eyes, an exotic accent to them, not Oriental exactly but something of that. The story they told was even more compelling: an intelligence, a sensitivity, resilience having triumphed over old hurts, looking for the funny in the serious and serious in the funny, and, more than that, a sense of honesty both given and asked for.

Sidney reached under the table and took her hand and said, "We've asked you here, Geraldine, Boy, and Michael, because you're dear friends. I wanted you to meet Gloria because we're going to get married."

Exclamations of happiness, champagne ordered, then spaghetti and red wine.

Over the next few years, I'd go to Sidney and Gloria's grandly large apartment on Gracie Square, while I was still at school or home from Oxford and once from my job in Ireland.

A few dinner parties, cocktail parties, all filled to bursting with the talented and bright of the time.

When I was twenty, I was staying with my mother at the Chateau Marmont in Hollywood and was looking for a job and was fatter. At an interview on that trip, the first question the potential employer asked was, "How much do you weigh, kid?"

Age twenty.

Gloria, who had been acting in a TV play, had come, at the end of her day's work, for supper. With the struggles I was going through, I was glad to be in the company of someone who seemed only feminine, with all the strengths of such a nature, and again I was entranced by her direct and unencrusted manner.

My mother and Gloria became great friends from their first meeting, and early on, as Gloria was pursuing her acting career, she would discuss with my mother parts she would be playing. Sometimes, before Oxford, when I'd come home from whatever New York school was presently educating me, I'd find the two of them in our living room, the tea finished, talking in quiet and intimate tones. About acting I supposed. They formed an enduring friendship until my mother's dementia could no longer understand friendship, although Gloria would continue to visit her.

For my twenty-first birthday, my parents said they'd give me a small party and take me out for dinner before. Was there anyone I'd like to join us? I knew Sidney was away working, and I asked if they thought Gloria would like to come. The four of us went to the Colony Restaurant, Boy in his dinner jacket for the occasion and I encased in mine. I was hitting the scales at 240 pounds at the time. Gloria gave me a beautiful pair of Jean Schlumberger gold shell cuff links.

Then I went to work in Europe for the next twenty years. Gloria and Sidney divorced, and sometime after she married Wyatt Cooper, and we lost touch.

I was in New York while the *Brideshead Revisited* strike was going on. Wyatt Cooper had died. Gloria learned from my mother that I was in town, and she asked me to a small dinner in her new apartment. Oona O'Neill Chaplin, married to Charlie at the age of eighteen, was there. She and Gloria had been friends since their teens, and it was fascinating to see the two of them, friends forever, now both widows, talking, listening for nuance, making jokes, with such a wealth of happy and sad history between them. I thought that night what a wonderful thing it must be to have a friend from your teens with a past series of experiences inhabiting the present.

There was another dinner at Gloria's a week or so later, and, after, she and I went to see Bobby Short at the Carlyle.

In the street outside, I, thinking I'd be going back to my hotel, but having other feelings, leaned into the back seat of her car to kiss her good night. I put my arm out toward the back seat to balance, to steady the kiss.

She put her hand on my wrist and yanked. I tumbled into the seat beside her. She was stronger than her slender frame would indicate.

Back in her apartment, leaving her in the living room, I went into the bathroom for a moment, understanding that the long history of our relationship was about to have another chapter.

I came back into the living room. She went toward her bedroom, asking me to join her in a few minutes.

I was excited but also apprehensive.

I went over to the bar on a side table and undid the cap of a bottle of Absolut vodka.

I hoped that so much past—from the time I was sixteen and she thirty-two—would make what was to occur seem like a natural progression, a pleasure long denied, and not, in some way, an unwelcome impediment.

I lifted the bottle to my lips and saw on the rim a circle of red lipstick and knew she had felt the same.

We spent a lot of time together, some in that apartment but not so much, because across a hall was where her two intelligent young sons, Carter and Anderson Cooper, lived. There was another little nest in the West 50s where she had a studio, the rooms decorated and crowded with objects which showed, to do with design and proportion, a bold, imaginative, flawless taste, scented by the mysterious seraglio perfume she wore.

Gloria had to travel sometimes to do with a new venture, a successful and lucrative blue jean business, and I missed her. All that I'd guessed about her since I'd first met her proved true as I knew her in this different way: funny, alert, candid, clear-eyed, mischievous; with experiences—ups, downs, and sideways—which would inform our time together in interesting and unexpected ways. And I include in this her intelligent and shrewd opinions and observations about people and things; a timeless beauty with a bratty lower lip.

I've never forgotten a Zen-like remark she made to me: "There are rooms you haven't been in yet, where your life will change forever."

But then I had to go back to England and then to Los Angeles for work, she working also, and this step we'd taken was tripped by the sharp wire of separation. Sad, we both were, feeling something had not been given its full life. Our time together, the memory of its imprint, has never left me.

A lthough we spoke on the phone occasionally over the years, and wrote, I did not see her again till after my stepfather's memorial service when she came to the wake get-together in my mother's apartment. I was so glad to talk to her again. Some of my drawings were in the apartment, and she said they reminded her of Paul Klee. No greater compliment could I have wished, Klee one of my heroes, especially from an artist and painter herself, and someone so fine in discernment.

We were, by then, on different paths, and we had no communication till she, in 2009, sent me her novel, *Obsession,* a fascinating examination of duality or, perhaps, singularity between two women and a man they had in common, with a strong erotic content. Reading the novel, I sensed that, perhaps, there was use made, in subtle and shifted ways, of some of the time we'd spent together.

I wrote her and said how much I liked it and sent her a drawing I'd done. I asked her if she'd like to read this memoir I'd been writing.

She read it and wrote back her feelings about it, which pleased me very much.

I then recalled how close Gloria and my mother had been and wrote again to ask her, did she know anything more about my mother's story; that, in my conclusion about Eddy Lindsay-Hogg, I was really only guessing, and what did she think?

She replied in her bold clear handwriting—"Perhaps G[eraldine] didn't know . . . I hesitate to say more."

I was sure from her reply that she did know more and that, perhaps, there were secrets that they had told each other, both being women who might have had complications in their lives.

So I wrote again and asked, directly, if she thought the conclusion I'd reached was the correct one.

She wrote back, dated July 24, 2009:

When G told you that she "never had an affair with Orson," it was because your "father" was still alive, and she wanted to protect you in those years when you were coping with growing up. She did tell me that Orson was your father. I hesitated to say more when you first asked me as I wanted to remain loyal to her wishes. But the important thing now is to once and for all find peace. And I know this is what she would want for you.

Your memoir is truly remarkable and it makes me happy at long last that I am able to tell you what she told me.

XG

I replied on July 27:

D. G. [D for Darling]—Your letter of July 24 was to say the least a bolt, a jolt, a real head snapper, and I thank you with all my heart for writing it.

But, oh my goodness, after all this time it is hard for me to adjust to, especially since I'd maneuvered myself into another conclusion.

I then went on to ask her some specific questions about the conversation and where it had occurred. And finished by writing:

I know my mother always loved you and would have trusted your nature, your sensibility, your own extraordinary life experiences—trusted you enough to unburden (is that the right word?) herself to. And I am also sure that whatever you have done with this information she would have respected. I know that.

In my adult life, I think Ma's real worry was more to do with Boy than Eddy. Paula said Boy couldn't have "taken" it, if I'd been illegitimate—to do with how he'd cast my mother's character in his mind. He was a very decent man but had a judgemental side. I do not.

She *might* have told me after Boy's death. But maybe (see pages 215–16) she tried. She took the step, faltered and stepped back. Her good intention foiled—a moment of clarity, then fear, then the befuddlement coming on again.

In telling me, you have been, as always, the dearest and most honest friend I could imagine.

Love as always,
M

She replied:

D. M.—Ever since I sent July 24 letter have been *agonizing* that I did the right thing? Yours of 27 a *great* relief to receive. G. told me at 10 Gracie Square sitting in the library. I have never told anyone of our conversation (until now telling you), and I never will.

She feared mostly what you might think of her and also knew that Boy would not take it well.

Remember the young age you were at the time/also the attitude of many at the time. She said she couldn't risk how knowing might change your opinion of her. Then as the years passed and you were grown up it is my feeling—it was too late. As we get older it can take a terrible toll to open a secret door—shattering the balance of a peace hard won.

She spoke in quiet tones, relieved to confide in one she

trusted. She was *not* regretful and told me she and O had been passionately in love and involved (one never regrets that) and that it continued on through the years . . .

Love, always,

G

I wrote her again, asking a couple of more questions, one being: did Orson know, the other about my mother and Boy.

Darling Michael—

Yes—Orson did know. (No wonder he wanted Marlene to meet you!)

G married Boy because she respected him and loved him, and he could give her despite all a security that you can't find in Hollywood. He came from a distinguished family, a stable family, and <u>judgemental</u> as she knew him to be could be <u>depended</u> on, which Orson certainly could not. She did <u>fear</u> Boy's rigid judgement of so many things, and, of course, most of all herself. This was catching her in a terrible dilemma. Remember too that the 40s and 50s were very different than what is acceptable and understood in 2009. She knew most of all that she could always <u>depend</u> on him to be a responsible stepfather to you. <u>And</u> take care of her.

All my love,
Gloria

Coda

Where does all this leave me, Michael? They're all dead, and there are no more days for us to spend together.

I now know my mother had a serious romance with Orson, although she always denied it to me and to most others, and it probably continued.

Recently, I found a telegram he sent to her in 1941 when I was a baby and she was still married to Edward Lindsay-Hogg. In it he explained that, because of work, he couldn't make a lunch date with her and ended by saying, "I have so many wonderful things to tell you about yourself. You might think me extravagant unless you know I'd time to cool off. I never will about you. Orson."

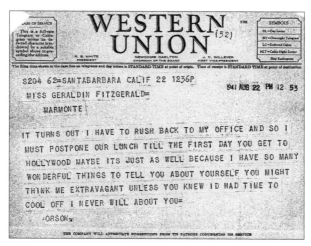

Telegram from Orson, 1941.

Thanks, or not, to Mary Gillen, I still say prayers at night. I don't know who or what the God I pray to may be. But, at least, before I go to bed, it gives me a chance to think with the utmost fondness of those who are, or were, important to me.

Now consider what might be the relation between the living and the dead.

After my dear friend Geraldine Page died, I felt for some years that there was an aspect of her which was still in my life, wishing to encourage me in some way, or trying to deflect my aptitude for making decisions which were not in my best interest.

If there is an afterlife in any way, even the wildest conception, the most fanciful belief or far-fetched explanation of the existence of the soul, what do they owe us or, more importantly, what do we owe them?

Is my mother's spirit relieved that, although her frailty and self-interest and deception are exposed, she is, also, more understood and, with understanding, absolved?

And Boy Scheftel—I hope his decency, and his failings, and his honorable nature have been made clear in these pages.

But Edward Lindsay-Hogg, I fret for him. He was proud to be a, my, father.

Born in Edwardian England, his selective view of things is clear to see, when on my birth certificate, where the father's profession was asked for, he wrote: "Gentleman."

He was not competitive in life in any way, nor did he value that. Perhaps he envied it but he could not enter the arena. It was as foreign to him as horses and alcohol and an acceptance of the weaknesses of others was not.

With this story, I fret for his shade more than that of the others.

But I cannot help what happened.

"God bless Mummy, Boy, and Daddy." Edward Lindsay-Hogg does still play the part of Daddy. Too much time and too much history.

Santa Monica, 1944.

Orson once said to me the greatest sin was betrayal. In a sad way he knew whereof he spoke. The great betrayal in his life was his own, the misuse of his stupendous gifts.

Lies are a betrayal. But more than that. Early on, Lisa and I were talking about fibs, say, versus big lies, and she said what the liar really should be held accountable for is the creation of a false reality for the lied-to, who might have gone this way and not that or made that choice and not this, were it not for the deceit practiced upon him, or her.

In writing this book, I have come to learn of many lies and deceptions.

There is something I wrote to Gloria Vanderbilt which is perhaps worth mentioning, as it sums up much of what I feel about human behavior.

"I think now as I did in my teens. People do what they do, for whatever reasons. They wish to do what is right, but sometimes can't or don't manage it."

And if there's any doubt, you know, it doesn't really matter. That search is over, for in the end, I see, I recognize this— that the choices, good, bad, failed, successful, have been mine, so, in a sense, I have become my own father.

Acknowledgments

First, I'd like to thank Rebecca Zoshak, who since early 2008 has typed every draft and revision on revision of this memoir. What has been more important than her practical skills is her intelligence. I'd sometimes ask her, does this sound better than that, does it make more sense to say it with that word versus another, and her advice was always considered and spot-on.

The following have read beginning, middle, and/or late drafts and were all acute and generous in their comments:

Julian Sands and Evgenia Citkowitz

Marc Kristal

Wayne Lawson

Marcelle Tosi

Dr. Katrina Wood

Jonathan Becker

Jean Marsh

My brother-in-law, Rick Finkelstein, for his help and advice on related issues.

I owe a deep debt of gratitude to Gloria Vanderbilt for her kindness in allowing me to use her letters and for her uncompromising candor and support.

Special thanks goes to my clever, funny, and fiercely protective editor and champion, Victoria Wilson, at Alfred A. Knopf. She critiqued and tweaked and guided me in my final choices.

I also admire the casual good taste of her clothes, that taste being the outward show of a similar-styled mind.

Also thanks to Carmen Johnson, Vicky's smart right hand at AAK, who helped me navigate the sometimes choppy waters of copyright and clearances, and who has shown endless patience with my preferred method of communication, the telephone call rather than e-mail. She has been a great help.

And also to Callie Wright, whom I'd met on a project at *Vanity Fair* and who became my demon fact-checker and extra eye.

Without my literary agent, Judith Ehrlich, there would be no book. About six years ago, she first suggested I write a memoir. I said I didn't want to and continued to say it for two years. I knew there were memories but didn't want to open the box, not knowing how the pieces would go together, what pattern I'd make, and concerned that some might be broken and hard to repair. In late 2007, Judith invited me for a drink at the University Club, to persist again in her gentle, stubborn manner.

"There are probably things you could write that might be of interest to people," Judith said. "And, maybe, you'll find out, learn things about yourself, as you write it."

I did. Thank you, Judith, for your persistence on this one, and your advice and loyalty over the years.

And finally, or firstly, my wife, Lisa, who read all drafts and gave me praise and criticism, each coming from a mind I know to be both perceptive and honest.

Sometimes, I felt it was as though I had an old crumpled map in my hand with just a dot to show the starting place and no markers to direct me to a place on the other side of the island, and I wasn't even sure what I was looking for. But Lisa urged me on, telling me she knew I'd find the route, and, whatever I found, the trip would be worth it.

It has taken four years and I couldn't have done it without her.